NARRATIVE BONDS

THEORY AND INTERPRETATION OF NARRATIVE
James Phelan, Katra Byram, and Faye Halpern, Series Editors

NARRATIVE BONDS

Multiple Narrators in the Victorian Novel

~

ALEXANDRA VALINT

THE OHIO STATE UNIVERSITY PRESS

COLUMBUS

Library of Congress Cataloging-in-Publication Data
Names: Valint, Alexandra, author.
Title: Narrative bonds : multiple narrators in the Victorian novel / Alexandra Valint.
Other titles: Theory and interpretation of narrative series.
Description: Columbus : The Ohio State University Press, [2021] | Series: Theory and interpretation of narrative | Includes bibliographical references and index. | Summary: "Integrating narrative theory, gothic theory, and disability studies with analyses of works by Charles Dickens, Robert Louis Stevenson, Wilkie Collins, Emily Brontë, and Bram Stoker, this study illustrates the significance and impact of the multi-narrator structure in Victorian novels"—Provided by publisher.
Identifiers: LCCN 2020031960 | ISBN 9780814214633 (cloth) | ISBN 0814214630 (cloth) | ISBN 9780814280911 (ebook) | ISBN 0814280919 (ebook)
Subjects: LCSH: English fiction—19th century—History and criticism. | Multiple person narrative. | Narration (Rhetoric)
Classification: LCC PR871 .V35 2021 | DDC 823/.80923—dc23
LC record available at https://lccn.loc.gov/2020031960

Cover design by Andrew Brozyna
Text design by Juliet Williams
Type set in Adobe Minion Pro

CONTENTS

ACKNOWLEDGMENTS

I am lucky to have had such wonderful teachers, mentors, and colleagues. Karen Chase at the University of Virginia made me feel that I could become a Victorianist. Her belief in me enabled me to believe in myself. The incomparable trio of Jonathan Arac, Troy Boone, and Marah Gubar at the University of Pittsburgh challenged and championed me. There are no better models of how to mentor and teach than them. They continue to guide me, and I am grateful for them lighting the way. At the University of Southern Mississippi, my colleagues in English—too innumerable to list—have encouraged and advocated for me; particular thanks to Craig Carey, Luis Iglesias, Jameela Lares, and Eric Tribunella for the hallway chats, candy bars, and honest advice. My USM students have brought me joy and laughter; they have taught me through our enlightening discussions. I am also grateful for funding from Pitt and USM that facilitated archival research and sustained writing time: at Pitt, the Lillian B. Lawler Predoctoral Fellowship and Barbara Nietzsche Tobias Fellowship; at USM, the Aubrey Keith Lucas and Ella Ginn Lucas Endowment for Faculty Excellence.

I offer special thanks to several USM colleagues and friends. Emily Stanback introduced me to disability studies; chapter 4 of this book would simply not exist without her guidance and encouragement. Morgan Frank and I have consumed too many cake balls and Snappy Turtles to count, and I am grateful for her stalwart support. Allison Abra has helped me through every step of this project and has adventured with me across the South and Europe—thank goodness we met on that golf cart!

At every stage of my career, classmates and friends have been buoys, cheerleaders, and lights. My Pittsburgh coterie were fellow explorers of the city's eateries, art, and sites: Jonathan Auxier, Mary Auxier, Sarah Hammock, Robin Hoffman, Kerry Mockler, Loring Pfeiffer, Celanie Polanick, Rebecca Wigginton, and Alicia Williamson. My fellow Wahoos—Eileen Conaway, Kate Harpin, Kelly Ramsey—continue to encourage me from afar, and my yearly meetings with my oldest friends—Heidi Castro, Rene Conable, Kelly McLarnon, and Evie Mpras—rejuvenate and ground me. Jill Abney, Courtney Luckhardt, Andrew Ross, Rachel Spear, and Laura Stengrim made Hattiesburg feel like home, from painting nights to Oscar parties to Writing Wednesdays. Two coffee shops—Tazza D'Oro in Pittsburgh and T-Bones in Hattiesburg—provided havens of good music and good desserts. As I write these acknowledgments, T-Bones's disco ball sheds its revolving sparkle-shafts across my table.

Everyone at The Ohio State University Press has treated my project with care. Ana Maria Jimenez-Moreno has been unfailingly responsive. I appreciate Katra Byram, James Phelan, Peter Rabinowitz, and the anonymous reviewer for providing such insightful, specific, and useful feedback.

An earlier version of chapter 3 was published in *English Literature in Transition, 1880–1920* 58.1 (2015): 3–29. I am grateful for the journal's permission to reprint this piece.

To my friends in the Victorian, children's literature, and narrative theory communities, particularly Tim Carens, Victoria Ford Smith, Nicole Lobdell, and everyone who has participated in the North American Victorian Studies Association Theatre Caucus productions, thank you for your friendship, counsel, and camaraderie at conferences and beyond.

I thank my parents (Nancy, Paul, Raymond) for providing a childhood of books and theatre and encouraging artistic and intellectual creation. My brilliant sisters, Raychel and Brittany, are steadfast allies whose creative spirit and output inspire me. Robert has been an anchor—a source of unflagging support, silliness, and happiness.

~

Unity and Reliability in the Victorian Multinarrator Novel

I N MARGARET OLIPHANT'S *A Beleaguered City,* published in 1880, an invisible legion of a town's dead invades the French town of Semur. The visiting spirits forcibly oust the living inhabitants from their homes to the area outside the city walls to teach them the "true signification of life" (Oliphant 25). Martin Dupin, Semur's "bourgeois" mayor and the first narrator (3), enlists four other town residents as "eye-witnesses" to help him tell the story of this strange and ghostly coup (103): the local "dreamer" Paul Lecamus (13); the erstwhile "noble" Félix de Bois-Sombre (75); Dupin's devout wife Agnès; and Dupin's widowed mother. The five narrators possess clashing political views, spiritual beliefs, and class identifications; additionally, several of the narrators don't like one another.[1] And yet, Dupin manages to collate these "different accounts of the mystery" from this heterogeneous selection of the town into "one coherent and trustworthy chronicle" (10). Out of multiplicity and diversity can come unity because none of the five narrators present a fact that invalidates or contradicts facts presented by other narrators. The characters' interpretations of those facts predictably differ, but the facts themselves

---

1. Robert and Vineta Colby illustrate how the narrators take different sides in the debates of "church versus state, science versus religion, theism versus agnosticism, idealism versus materialism" (297). Trela remarks that Oliphant's work often exhibits "a level of experimentation with form" (17), and Rubik identifies *A Beleaguered City* as "the most intricate and complicated" of Oliphant's works "in terms of narrative technique" (285).

align. When the narratives overlap in time and plot, as they frequently do, they give remarkably similar descriptions of fantastic events, crystalizing the storyworld rather than splintering it. In *A Beleaguered City* and other Victorian multinarrator novels, the multinarrator structure offers the fantasy that characters who hold different worldviews can still see the world in the same way; furthermore, *A Beleaguered City*'s structure mirrors the plot: Dupin's act of joining together the individual narrations parallels how the supernatural crisis unites the once-splintered town. *Narrative Bonds* not only highlights how frequently Victorian authors used this structure but also demonstrates how this structure is always part and parcel of the story: the novels' themes and the characters' interpersonal relations are manifest in the collaborative multinarrator structure.

A *Beleaguered City*, and the Victorian multinarrator novel more broadly, meditate on the advantages, costs, and very nature of collaboration between persons—in both the plot and the narrative structure. This book's title, therefore, gestures to the positive and negative connotations of "bonds": narrative collaboration can lead to intimacy, harmony, and victory, but it can also involve coercion, anxiety, and threats to the self. The Victorians both desired and feared collaboration. On the one hand, the multinarrator novel evinces optimism that narrators who differ in gender, age, class, race, or (dis)ability can still agree on the facts; the narrators all remain reliable, to use James Phelan's terminology, on the axis of reporting (50). And collaboration—in both structure and story—proves useful and effective in almost all of these multinarrator novels. As it does in *A Beleaguered City*, it binds lovers, strengthens families, overcomes threats, and solves mysteries. And, as I discuss in chapter 1, this focus on collaboration in plot and structure differentiates the Victorian multinarrator novel from similar iterations in the eighteenth and early twentieth centuries.

The form, on the other hand, exposes collaboration's possible effects on the individual; just as a group can become a thoughtless mob, narrative collaboration can threaten the autonomy and identity of individual narrators. In Oliphant's novel, the ghostly visitants push out the town's inhabitants, all of whom are possessed by "a sense that [they] must go" (Oliphant 29). Although the collaborative narrative seeks to document and comprehend this mysterious expulsion, it also contains a compulsory element. Lecamus, on the verge of death after his draining experience with the spirits in the town, struggles to compose his account before he dies. He insists, "I must make haste, I must write" (86), echoing Dupin's sense that he "must" leave his home (29). Dupin's mother considers writing her narrative "a great difficulty" that she only completes to please her powerful son (88). While critics often assume that narrating is a desirable power and privilege, some narrators in these novels deem it an obligation, a "difficulty." Miss Clack, from Wilkie Collins's *The Moonstone*, encapsulates such a perspective, as I explain in chapter 4; she bemoans, "I am condemned to narrate" (208).

In *A Beleaguered City*, Dupin decides to organize the official town record in this manner to bond the town in the aftermath of the spectral invasion, showing the correspondence between narrative structure and the plot. According to Dupin, prior to the arrival of the spirits, the town was fractured and catty, riven by their class, gender, and religious differences. But the crisis erodes the barriers between male and female, noble and bourgeois, the religious and secular-minded. After the expulsion, Dupin sends the women, children, and the elderly to his country residence La Clairière; there, people from different classes reside in the same rooms and work together to complete the chores. When Dupin ventures into the possessed city, he appoints his political, class, and religious opposite Bois-Sombre—a former noble and Catholic monarchist—as deputy mayor. Dupin, an agnostic, also bonds with M. le Curé, the town priest, during their harrowing journey into the city to appease the invading spirits. The experience, Dupin writes, "made us brother and brother. And this union made us more strong" (Oliphant 71). When the gates open and the townspeople joyfully return home, they coalesce that evening at a group sing at the cathedral: "with one voice, every man in unison with his brother" (108). The next day, too, "the whole city assisted" at "a great function in the Cathedral" (108). Dupin reluctantly admits, however, that the inhabitants soon forget their newfound faith and camaraderie. Dupin's later decision to compile several accounts into a "true narrative" suggests his desire to resurrect and maintain that fleeting town unity by using a multinarrator structure (10). Just as the individual men's voices blend into "one voice . . . in unison" at the cathedral (108), the different narrators' voices become "one coherent and trustworthy chronicle" (10). And Dupin's "earnest desire to remain in sympathy and fraternity" with those different from him serves as the glue for both the occupied town and the narrative project (110).

The multinarrator structure in *A Beleaguered City*, then, does not generate the "Rashomon effect," named after Akira Kurosawa's film *Rashōmon* (1950) that shows multiple, equally probable explanations for a man's death. The film is based on two of Japanese modernist Ryūnosuke Akutagawa's short stories. "Rashōmon" (1915) provides the movie's frame setting of the city gate, and the main plot and multinarrator structure come from "In a Bamboo Grove" (1922). The latter short story gives narratives, called either "testimonies" or "confessions" in the section titles, from seven characters, including three people who claim to be guilty of the murder of Takehiro, whose body is found stabbed in a bamboo grove. "In a Bamboo Grove" never identifies the real murderer nor presents one of the scenarios as more probable than the others. Robert Anderson defines the "Rashomon effect" as not only "the differences in perspective found in diverse accounts of a single event" but also the narrative's lack of "a position from which to negotiate agreement or disagreement with them" (66, 68). The Victorian multinarrator novel, which Akutagawa was likely familiar with, having majored in English literature and completing a thesis on Victorian artist William Morris, doesn't revel in the fundamental contradictions between narrators as "In a Bamboo Grove" and *Rashōmon* do; in the Victorian multinarrator novel, reality is stable and narrators' accounts largely corroborate, rather than undermine, those of others.

Furthermore, *A Beleaguered City*'s multinarrator structure is more egalitarian than Dupin's own society, suggesting a democratic bent to the structure. As both Esther H. Schor and Elisabeth Jay point out, Dupin and others marginalize and belittle women, including Dupin's own wife and mother, viewing them as angelic but not capable of strength, leadership, or rationality.[2] Dupin excludes the women from the town's decision-making process despite recognizing the limitations of the women's conventional role: "theirs was no easy part. To sit there silent, to wait till we had spoken, to be bound by what we decided, and to have no voice" (Oliphant 49). After the invasion, however, Dupin specifically requests and incorporates women's narratives—their voices—in the official record. Both Agnès and Lecamus recognize that society doubts them and casts them as inferior. Lecamus knows that because others perceive him as "visionary" he is "not supposed to be a trustworthy witness" (13). Agnès yearns for the town to select her as the messenger to the spirits, but she also concedes that "it was better that the messenger should not be a woman; they might have said it was delusion, an attack of the nerves. We are not trusted in these respects, though I find it hard to tell why" (81). The "true narrative" that Dupin collates purposefully includes both of these societally marginalized voices (10); even the mocked religious "visionary" and the sidelined woman are embraced by the narrative's utopia of unity.[3] Dupin's decision to be inclusive may be inspired by the ghostly council meeting overseen by his dead father, who was a prior mayor of Semur. Lecamus, one of the few humans able to stay in the city during the mass expulsion, witnesses and later informs Dupin of the spectral gathering: "There many were assembled as in

---

2. Schor writes that the novella's "differing interpretations articulate the town's complex and often occult relations of class and gender" (98). Jay highlights how "women are marginalized" in the plot and in the narrative (163).

3. Schor also notices that the "multivocal document" "enfranchis[es] a wider spectrum of the community than Dupin does as mayor" (106).

council. Your father was at the head of all. . . . There were the captains of all the bands waiting to speak, men and women. I heard them repeating from one to another the same tale. One voice was small and soft like a child's" (65). Although Dupin's father leads this council, he also allows other men, women, and even children to speak and report. Both men and women hold the rank of "captain." The "small and soft" child's voice participates and is valued equally in this democratic, unearthly venue.

In general, the Victorian multinarrator novel is inclusive though does not necessarily bestow each narrator with equal power. These novels feature children narrating alongside adults, women narrating alongside men, and members of the middle and working classes narrating alongside aristocrats and gentry. The Victorian multinarrator novel, then, reflects the period's gradual movement toward a more democratic state marked by expanding rights and protections for women, children, and the middle and working classes effected through the passage of the Reform Acts, the Married Women's Property Acts, the Education Acts, the Chimney Sweepers' Acts, the Factory Acts, and other reforming legislation. Unsurprisingly, however, the white, middle-class, English, and male narrator still occupies a position of privilege in many of these novels by opening them, closing them, narrating most frequently and/or for the longest within them, or serving as chief editor of the compiled narrations. For example, in *A Beleaguered City*, the "bourgeois" Martin Dupin narrates six of the ten chapters, including the first and last ones, while every other narrator only narrates one chapter (Oliphant 3); he also "arrange[s] and edit[s] the different accounts" while the others just contribute their narrations (10). While most Victorian multinarrator novels include a female narrator (Robert Louis Stevenson's *Strange Case of Dr. Jekyll and Mr. Hyde, Treasure Island*, and *The Master of Ballantrae* are notable exceptions), female narrators rarely begin or conclude them. But Dinah Mulock Craik's *A Life for a Life*, which alternates between "Her Story" and "His Story," both starts and ends with Dora's narrative, and Charles Dickens's *Bleak House* ends with the narration of Esther Summerson. Almost every narrator is white; within W. Collins's *The Moonstone*, the narration of Ezra Jennings—whose "gipsy darkness" (this term for the Romani people is now considered derogatory) implies "the mixture of some foreign race in his English blood"—represents a rare exception among Victorian multinarrator novels (326, 371). Adult narrators predominate, and child narrators are generally found only in works primarily directed at a children's audience such as in Stevenson's *Treasure Island*, Dickens's *Holiday Romance*, and Juliana Horatia Ewing's *A Great Emergency*. Middle-class—specifically professional—narrators are most common, while either working-class or aristocratic narrators are infrequent, pointing to the middle class's growth in cultural and political power during the Victorian period, as well as to the increasing visibility and importance of the professions. In Bram Stoker's *Dracula,* which I discuss in the epilogue, the three narrators who narrate most frequently are young professional men and women: Jonathan Harker is a solicitor, Jonathan Seward is a doctor, and Mina Harker is an "assistant schoolmistress" (Stoker 62) who imitates "lady journalists" (62) and becomes the group's "secretary" (251). Professional acumen, ambition, and record keeping skills enable these characters to serve as dedicated, reliable narrators. Of the many narrators in *Dracula,* only Arthur Holmwood is a member of the aristocracy; once he inherits the title upon his father's death and becomes Lord Godalming, he never narrates again. Perhaps there's no room for an obsolete "God"—an entity that his name evokes—in a democratic narrative of eyewitness accounts.

Previous scholarship on Victorian female narrators incidentally addresses multinarrator novels since many of the Victorian period's female narrators are found therein, but such work overstates either these narrators' limitations or power. Alison A. Case illuminates the gendered power dynamics of the eighteenth- and nineteenth-century novel: "A feminine narrator typically provides only the raw material of narrative, which is usually shaped and given meaning by a male 'master-narrator' within the text, or by an authorial or editorial frame" (13). To Case, therefore, male narrators possess greater narratorial power than female narrators. N. M. Jacobs comes to a similar conclusion, claiming that both Emily Brontë's *Wuthering Heights* and Anne Brontë's *The Tenant of Wildfell Hall* are framed by privileged male narrators who structurally "cover[ ]" the female narrators, "those without power" (207). The opposite is true to Lisa Sternlieb, who argues that the seeming artlessness of female narrators functions as a smokescreen for their manipulations: "They achieve power" over the greedy men who aim to possess their writings "not through what they do, but through how they tell" (4). Although I agree that tensions and inequalities between narrators exist, particularly between female and male narrators, these arguments overlook the collaboration, unity, and agreement among narrators despite such friction and differences.

Although *A Beleaguered City* and the Victorian multinarrator novel more generally privilege collaboration between characters and narrators, Dupin constantly worries that collaboration will go bad. Groups can become mobs, and narrative collaboration can be dangerous. The "crowd" of townspeople who loiter outside the city gates threatens to devolve into something alarming, drunken, irrational, and even homicidal (Oliphant 33). Bois-Sombre fears that the crowd will transform into a "chao[tic]" and destructive "mob" (76). Even when the town reaches peak unity—when the townspeople have just returned to the city—Dupin asserts his authority as mayor by shuttering the wine shops and initiating neighborhood patrols to stem the potential danger of the people's unbounded, communal joy. Dupin also wields his mayoral authority over the narrative, not only by "arrang[ing] and edit[ing]" it but also by excluding perspectives that would compromise its order and harmony (10). Dupin admits that other townspeople whom he does not ask to contribute to the narration relay their stories to him, and "in their accounts there are naturally discrepancies, owing to their different points of view and different ways of regarding the subject. But all are agreed that a strange and universal slumber had seized upon all" (103). Dupin glosses over these "discrepancies" and instead stresses that "all . . . agreed" on the occurrence of the "universal slumber" before their readmittance into the city, a fact corroborated by Bois-Sombre's, Agnès's, and Dupin's mother's narratives. Dupin also frames the mass-awakening that follows as a communal, shared experience: "With one impulse all awoke" (103). The "different points of view" hang at the edge of Dupin's official document, cursorily acknowledged but not given narratorial space or weight.

Some Victorian authors and thinkers portrayed collective action negatively, particularly for its presumed tendency to eradicate individual will. Collective action occurred frequently during the period: the Chartist agitation in the late 1830s and 1840s; the demonstrations pushing for the Reform Bill in the mid- to late-1860s; and other strikes and riots (including "Bloody Sunday" in 1887). In Dickens's *Hard Times,* written at least partially in response to a strike he visited in Preston, the unionizing and striking workers (known as the "Hands") are all portrayed as succumbing, hypnosis-like, to the demagogue leader Slackbridge. In defending Stephen Blackpool's refusal to join the union and crowd, his friend Rachael plaintively asks, "Can a man have no soul of his own, no mind of his own?" (233). Dickens illustrates how individuality—soul, mind, free will—is quashed by the unthinking, violent mass. Nicholas Visser confirms that crowds often were depicted as irrational, dangerous, and animalistic in novels by Dickens, George Eliot, and Benjamin Disraeli. Gustave Le Bon's "The Mind of Crowds" (1895) posits that when an individual joins a crowd, "he is no longer himself" (60): He "act[s] in a manner quite different from that in which each individual . . . would feel, think, and act were he in a state of isolation" (57). Once the "collective mind is formed" (55), the individual "los[es] his conscious personality" (59) and becomes vulnerable to the "contagion" of other crowd members' emotions (60). While the Victorian multinarrator novel values the collaboration inherent in the collective narrative, it also shows concerns about forced collaboration and the collective's sway over the individual. Gothic multinarrator novels like *A Beleaguered City* manifest the greatest anxiety over the risky or even detrimental effects of collaboration, as I further analyze in chapter 5 and the epilogue.

The multinarrator structure provides a vivid and dramatic way for character relations in the novel's story to be mapped onto form. Different types of multinarrator structure offer different models of character and narrator interaction; therefore, the tone and nuance of each novel's collaboration varies. While chapter 1 juxtaposes the Victorian multinarrator novel with its eighteenth-century antecedents and modernist descendants, each subsequent chapter focuses on one or more examples of a specific type of multinarrator form: chapter 2, the *back-and-forth*; chapter 3, the *quick switch*; chapter 4, *patchworks*; chapter 5, the *permeable frame*; and the epilogue, *returning* and *nonreturning*. Each chapter explores how that type of multinarration relates to the narrators' relationships in the story; in all cases, the use of the multinarrator structure is inseparable from the plot. The multinarrator structure both complements and builds characters' interpersonal bonds.

Chapter 2 focuses on Dickens's *Bleak House,* which alternates between a heterodiegetic narrator and Esther Summerson, a female homodiegetic narrator.[4] *Bleak House* is an example of what I call a back-and-forth structure, in which two narrators switch at roughly regular intervals; this steady interlacing unites and equalizes the two narrators and narratives even in the face of grave obstacles or differences. In *Bleak House,* Esther has a body and the other narrator does not. Esther, however, often eschews her own body and strives to represent herself as a woman of interiority and depth, not of surface. The other narrator, who focuses on the aristocratic world of Esther's mother Lady Dedlock, narrates surfaces and lacks omniscient powers. And yet, the two narrators cooperate to protect Esther's project of depth-creation, as the other narrator never sees or narrates Esther in his section. Despite their different "narrative postures" (Genette, *Narrative* 244)—one being a character in the story, the other not—and the resulting divergence in embodiment, the two narrators largely correspond in content, tone, and ethics; they even describe characters in similar ways. Their harmonious collaboration embodies the story's prizing of compassionate bonds between people and within communities.

Treasure Island by Stevenson utilizes what I term the quick switch, a single, brief switch in narrators. As I detail in chapter 3, Dr. Livesey narrates three chapters midway through the book while Jim Hawkins narrates the rest; the effect is much different from the slow and steady weaving of two narra-

---

4. Genette defines a heterodiegetic narrator as "absent from the story he tells" and a homodiegetic narrator as "present as a character in the story he tells" (*Narrative* 244, 245). Throughout this book, I use Genette's more precise, yet cumbersome, terms alongside the more accessible, yet problematic, terms third-person narrator and first-person narrator.

tives in the back-and-forth structure. Because of the quick switch's brevity and singularity, the secondary narrator/narrative contrasts with the first, throwing both into relief. In *Treasure Island*, I argue, the quick switch highlights the stylistic and moral differences between Jim, a child, and Dr. Livesey, an adult. Livesey is punishing, greedy, and callous. It follows that he reproves and penalizes the pirates and Jim throughout the novel. Jim, on the other hand, is empathetic, sensitive, and curious. He is skeptical of punishment, adulthood, and the imperialism the treasure hunt evokes. Jim eagerly cultivates a relationship with the narratee and Livesey does not; therefore, the reader's sympathy remains with the primary narrator, Jim, and separates the reader from Livesey's viewpoint. Furthermore, Livesey's very decision to barge into Jim's narrative—a narrative he's asked Jim to write and watches him complete—without warning or permission structurally embodies Livesey's domineering role in the plot.

Chapter 4 reveals the centrality of disability to the plots and structures of W. Collins's multinarrator novels: *The Woman in White*, *The Moonstone*, and *The Legacy of Cain*. All three novels feature many disabled narrators, and their mental or physical impairments shape their narrations, which then are interrupted, incomplete, fragmentary, or collaborative. Both the plots and structures of these novels privilege interdependence, a quality disability studies often associates with disability. The narrative pieces can only attain clarity and truth when assembled into what I call patchworks—hodgepodges of narrative genres and lengths with irregular cutting paces (that is, the duration of the narratives vary). In the plot, characters—many of whom are disabled—must similarly collaborate and rely on one another to overcome the threat and achieve justice. The villain in each novel is able-bodied and independent, spurning interdependence. W. Collins's centering of disability, narrative fragments, and interdependence demonstrates what Tobin Siebers calls "disability aesthetics," an alternative to traditional aesthetics that "prizes physical and mental difference" (19). More broadly, I use this chapter to introduce and model disability narratology.

In chapter 5, I classify *Wuthering Heights*'s frame structure as a permeable frame. Lockwood, the tenant at Thrushcross Grange and the novel's frame narrator, asks his housekeeper Nelly Dean to inform him about the people who live across the moors at the Heights. While Nelly's orally delivered tale constitutes most of Emily Brontë's novel, the narrative continues to switch back and forth between her and Lockwood. These frequent switches are subtle, quick, fluid, and occur unconventionally within chapters, paragraphs, and even sentences. While Lockwood and Nelly try to distance and protect themselves from the unregulated intersubjectivity of Catherine and Heathcliff's gothic romance, the boundaries between the two narrators slowly dissipate. In the story, they become friendly and intimate and less like master and servant; in the structure, their unique handoffs blur the boundaries between them— hence, the *permeable* frame. Nelly and Lockwood, then, are not ultimately removed from the gothic as some critics claim; instead, the gothic exists in the novel's very structure and in the relationship between its two narrators.

The epilogue continues to examine the gothic genre, teasing apart the differences in the seemingly similar multinarrator structures of two monster novels published in 1897: Bram Stoker's *Dracula* and Richard Marsh's *The Beetle*. I isolate two key discrepancies between the novels' structures: *Dracula* features a returning multinarrator structure—meaning narrators narrate more than once—and a fast cutting pace of narratorial switches. *The Beetle,* on the other hand, features a nonreturning multinarrator structure—meaning each of the four narrators narrates only once—and a slow cutting pace of narratorial switches. While *Dracula* switches narrators a staggering ninety-two times, *The Beetle* switches only three times. In *Dracula,* the tightly woven, multithreaded narrative both mirrors and helps forge the intimate, resolute, successful vampire-hunting group. The dissimilar structure in *The Beetle* indicates its feeble and ineffective monster-tracking troupe. In the story, the characters experience horrifying one-on-one confrontations with the Beetle; the structure matches these situations with four isolated narratives that are not intertwined like *Dracula*'s narratives are. In both novels, as in *Wuthering Heights,* the gothic starts to infect the narrative structure, as narrators from *Dracula* and *The Beetle* utilize narrating techniques that evoke the monsters' inhumane tactics.

Although I introduce new terminology to catalogue the variations of multinarrator novels, Victorian authors did not simply choose from a warehouse of prefabricated forms. The Victorians inherited certain multinarrator forms— such as the frame and the epistolary novel—but modified those forms to fit their needs and aims in individual novels. For example, *Wuthering Heights*'s permeable frame both looks to and departs from the typical frame structure; most frame narratives prepare readers for the primary, substantial story that follows, then disappear, only briefly reappearing at the novel's close or not reappearing at all. Lockwood's frame does prepare us for—and facilitates our entrance into—Nelly's oral tale, and yet, he doesn't disappear. He pops up recurrently, if temporarily. The frame's borders become muddled rather than clear-cut, structurally embodying the novel's focus on dissolving boundaries and emphasizing the shifting relationship between Lockwood and Nelly. The twin forces of influence and invention contribute to the development of the multinarrator structure in each text. Many of the authors I deal with read each others' works and sometimes knew each other personally, furthering the possibility that they were affected by prior examples of the multinarrator form. For example, Stevenson, born in 1850 and living until 1894, was familiar with many of the novels I discuss in this book. His library stocked *Wuthering Heights, Bleak House,* and the works of Samuel Richardson.[5] In the middle of reading *The Moonstone* in September 1868, he declares to his mother that he finds it "frightfully interesting" and entreats her to not give the plot away (Booth and Mehew 144). He even writes Margaret Oliphant, admiring how her multinarrator novel *A Beleaguered City* "lodged some three or four [arrows] in my heart" (qtd. in M. Williams vii). Stevenson used multiple narrators not only in *Treasure Island* but also in *Strange Case of Dr. Jekyll and Mr. Hyde* and *The Master of Ballantrae*. *Jekyll and Hyde* is a variation of the framed found manuscript structure common in gothic literature. *The Master of Ballantrae,* primarily narrated by Ephraim Mackellar, twice switches to a secondary narrative, the memoirs of the Chevalier de Burke. Each switch is brief—only a chapter long. In this way, *Master* reads like a variation of the quick switch found in his own *Treasure Island,* which changes to a secondary narrator only once. These three novels do not merely copy previous multinarrator forms but vary them. After all, structure and content must suit. Forms are flexible and adaptable, and authors deployed them uniquely in each novel.

Just as these authors may have been influenced by previous iterations of the multinarrator form, they also may have been influenced by the artistic collaborations in their own lives. Dickens and W. Collins teamed up on the North-Pole-set play *The Frozen Deep* and on various stories for Dickens's magazines. The Brontë sisters and their brother Branwell produced joint imaginary worlds (Glass Town, Angria, Gondal) in their juvenilia, and the three sisters published a book of poems together. Stevenson collaborated some with his wife Fanny and extensively with stepson Lloyd Osbourne on several novels: *The Wrong Box, The Wrecker,* and *The Ebb-Tide*.[6] This experience with collaboration doesn't necessarily make these authors anomalous, especially considering Jack Stillinger's point that once we acknowledge the role of various editors like friends, spouses, publishers, mentors, and even the author himself as he returns to a work over time, we realize that "multiple authorship . . . is quite common" (22). But such real-life collaborations are rarely perfectly

---

5. Information about Stevenson's library comes from "What Stevenson Read—His Personal Library" on the *RLS Website*.

6. V. Smith examines Stevenson and Osbourne's collaborations, detailing how both men claimed to have created the map that inspired Stevenson to write *Treasure Island*. V. Smith reads this real-life collaboration as itself "a map: a guide for a further series of real and fictive adult-child collaborations inside and outside the text of *Treasure Island*" (118).

harmonious and egalitarian. The title of Lillian Nayder's book on Dickens and
W. Collins's collaborations—*Unequal Partners*—underscores how W. Collins,
the younger, more radical, and less established of the two, felt dominated by
the famous Dickens. Victoria Ford Smith traces the evolution of the long-lived
Stevenson–Osbourne partnership; in her analysis, even their positive, early
collaborations evinced an "uneven power relationship" and both men found
aspects of their later collaborations challenging (117). Gordon Hirsch portrays
Stevenson as the governing partner since he heavily revised and underplayed
Osbourne's contributions. While we know little of how Emily and Anne's
youthful collaboration proceeded, according to Charlotte, Emily was horrified when her older sister "accidentally" found her poems: "It took hours to
reconcile [Emily] to the discovery I had made, and days to persuade her that
such poems merited publication" (M. Smith 742). Charlotte's letter suggests
that she, the more ambitious sister, dragged the more reclusive Emily into the
world of collaborative publication. The difficult reality of artistic collaboration
might have influenced these authors' depictions of narrative collaboration in
their texts.

RELIABILITY

Surprisingly—because of the great potential to do otherwise—narrators do
not willfully lie in Victorian multinarrator novels, and they remain reliable
on the axis of reporting. Wayne C. Booth coined the terms "reliable narrator"
and "unreliable narrator," and he "called a narrator *reliable* when he speaks
for or acts in accordance with the norms of the work (which is to say, the
implied author's norms), *unreliable* when he does not" (158–59). Even though
W. Booth cautioned that "unreliable narrators . . . differ markedly depending
on how far and in what direction they depart from their author's norms" (159),
many critics have taken to categorizing narrators as either completely reliable
or unreliable. Phelan provides a helpful revision and expansion of W. Booth's
terms by pinpointing specific types of unreliability and by maintaining that
reliability and unreliability are not "a binary pair" (53); therefore, a narrator
may be reliable in some ways and simultaneously unreliable in others. Phelan
identifies three axes of (un)reliability: reporting ("axis of characters, facts, and
events" [50]), reading/interpreting ("axis of knowledge and perception"), and
regarding/evaluation ("axis of ethics and evaluation"). Narrators can perform
these functions wrongly or badly (misreporting, for example) or can perform
them to a lesser extent than they could or should (underreporting, for example). Phelan also adds that a narrator's (un)reliability may vary throughout

their narration. Narrators do not misreport in Victorian multinarrator nov-els.[7] Narrators can be unreliable on the axis of interpreting (by interpreting an event incorrectly) or on the axis of evaluation (by wrongly esteeming cer-tain characters). For example, in W. Collins's *The Moonstone*, Rosanna Spear-man's letter and Franklin Blake's narrative reveal a tragedy of misevaluation. Rosanna, who is in love with Blake, thinks he finds her distasteful and pre-sumptuous, while Blake, falsely believing that Rosanna stole the titular jewel, treats her coolly to prevent her from unduly incriminating herself; however, the evidence that Rosanna provides of Blake's guilt—his stained nightgown—turns out to be reliable.

Narrators' reliability on the axis of reporting points to the Victorians' desire for and trust in facts. "The ideology of mid-Victorian positivism," Thomas Richards writes, "had also led most people into believing that the best and most certain kind of knowledge was the fact. . . . [G]enerally [the fact] was thought of as raw knowledge, knowledge awaiting ordering" (4). But there was, T. Richards explains, a hitch in the Victorian glorification and proliferation of the fact:

> The problem here of course was that facts almost never added up to any-thing. They were snippets of knowledge. . . . It took a leap of faith to believe that facts would someday add up to any palpable sum of knowledge, and that faith often took the form of an allied belief in comprehensive knowledge. Comprehensive knowledge was the sense that knowledge was singular and not plural, complete and not partial . . . that all knowledges would ultimately turn out to be concordant in one great system of knowledge. (6–7)

The multinarrator novel, I argue, orders and integrates facts into a "system of knowledge" in which "all knowledges . . . turn out to be concordant" (T. Richards 7). A particularly famous attempt to combine "snippets" into more "comprehensive" knowledge is *London Labour and the London Poor*, for which Henry Mayhew travelled the London streets, interviewing laborers about their professions and daily lives; his findings were published in a series of articles in the *Morning Chronicle* and later collected in the first book edition (published serially from 1851–52). Full of statistics, interviews, and drawings, Mayhew often includes lengthy first-person testimonies from the laborers themselves;

---

7. Lonoff makes a similar observation in comparing Robert Browning's multiple narrators in his long poem *The Ring and the Book* with W. Collins's narrators: "Collins's eyewitnesses are generally honest; they reliably report what they hear and observe. . . . Browning's narrators may or may not be honest, and they may or may not report reliably" (149).

the book, therefore, resembles the multinarrator novel. Mayhew's reflection on his project reveals his beliefs about fact, truth, and knowledge:

> The attainment of the truth, then, will be my primary aim; but by the truth, I wish it to be understood, I mean something *more* than the bare facts. Facts, according to my ideas, are merely the elements of truths, and not the truths themselves. . . . A fact, so long as it remains an isolated fact, is a dull, dead, uninformed thing; no object nor event by itself can possibly give us any knowledge, we must compare it with some other, even to distinguish it. . . . A fact must be assimilated with, or discriminated from, some other fact or facts, in order to be raised to the dignity of a truth, and made to convey the least knowledge to the mind. . . .
>
> To give the least mental value to facts, therefore, we must generalize them, that is to say, we must contemplate them in connection with other facts, and so discover their agreements and differences, their antecedents, concomitants, and consequences. (447–48)

The multinarrator novel enlivens the "dead" "isolated fact" by positioning facts "in connection with other facts."

In some cases, one narrative within a Victorian multinarrator novel explicitly cross-references another narrative to verify both the facts and the reliability of the narrators; in this way, to use Mayhew's words, the fact is "raised to the dignity of a truth" (448). In W. Collins's *The Moonstone*, Blake, the novel's editor and one of its narrators, authenticates the reporting of Miss Clack, a narrator who proves unreliable on the axes of reading and evaluating. She fancies herself "a Christian persecuted by the world" (*Moonstone* 271) but continually acts in un-Christian ways, and she misinterprets her romantic infatuation with Godfrey Ablewhite as a platonic spiritual connection. And yet, during a scene in her narrative in which she reports a private conversation between Godfrey and Rachel (overheard while she hides behind a curtain), Blake provides a footnote directing the reader to "See Betteredge's Narrative, chapter viii" (245). Looking back, that earlier chapter includes information about the romantic history of Godfrey's parents that Clack also reports Godfrey sharing with Rachel. The corroborated information is inconsequential, but the verified information is not the point—verifying Clack's reporting reliability is. Even though Betteredge, another narrator, warns us not to believe Clack, and even though she considers him an untrustworthy "heathen" (203), her narrative reinforces facts introduced in his account, shoring up both narrators' reliability. Additionally, throughout his own narrative, Blake encourages us to cross-reference it with the eighth chapter and tenth chapter of Betteredge's earlier account.

Similarly, in *A Beleaguered City,* Dupin, the editor of the communal record, uses a footnote to highlight the similarities between two different narrations and to endorse the reliability of the most eccentric narrator Lecamus. Lecamus knows that he is "without credit among [his] neighbors" because he is "a dreamer" (Oliphant 65) with "curious" spiritual beliefs (13). At one point, when Dupin asks him for his opinion, he responds, "I am called visionary. I am not supposed to be a trustworthy witness" (13). But because Lecamus manages to remain within the city walls when everyone else has been forcibly ejected, Dupin needs Lecamus's account of what occurred inside the city. In his narrative, Lecamus potentially further harms his reliability by admitting to feeling as if he were in a "dream" (60). So, when Lecamus recounts hearing the joyful "pealing of the Cathedral bells," Dupin appends a footnote stating that the "reader will remember" that this event was also described in Dupin's earlier narrative (60). Since sound can travel, the same sound is heard both inside and outside the city walls, linking geographically disparate perspectives. The corroborated detail—the bells suddenly ring with no one there to ring them—is relatively minor, but Dupin takes this opportunity to verify the narrative of the seemingly least reliable narrator by crosschecking it with the authoritative account of the respected town mayor.

In Victorian multinarrator novels, characters who would be unreliable on the axis of reporting cannot narrate. For example, although critics censure Walter Hartright for barring his wife Laura from narrating in W. Collins's *The Woman in White,* Laura's mental instability after her experience in an insane asylum prevents her from being reliable on the axis of reporting. She does not just misinterpret events (which a Victorian narrator can do in the multinarrator structure); rather, she believes that certain events transpired that did not occur in reality. She maintains that she visited, had tea with, and spent the night with her old companion Mrs. Vesey in London before being taken to the asylum. Evidence from both Mrs. Vesey and Fosco prove that Laura did not make that visit. Because of Laura's fake memories, the lawyer Mr. Kyrle advises Walter that Laura would make an unreliable and unbelievable witness in a courtroom. The prologue to *The Woman in White* explicitly compares the multinarrator novel to a courtroom and its narrators to witnesses: "The story here presented will be told by more than one pen, as the story of an offence against the laws is told in Court by more than one witness" (9). Narrators throughout *The Woman in White* and *The Moonstone* identify themselves as "witnesses," linking their narrative productions to courtroom testimony. Because Laura "persisted in asserting that she had been to Mrs. Vesey's" (*Woman* 427), Laura is unreliable on the axis of reporting; for the same reason she would be a bad witness on the stand, she cannot be a narrator. Similarly, a minor character in *The Woman in White*, Sir Percival's servant, is "seriously shaken" by watching a church vestry burn with his employer locked inside it (525). A "medical man" ascertains that the "mental condition of the servant . . . appeared at present to debar him from giving any evidence of the least importance" (525). Walter, therefore, can only guess at the servant's actions and thoughts because "the man's own testimony was never obtained to confirm this view" (525). The servant too is barred from providing evidence in either a legal setting or the novel itself.

Information from a character unreliable (or potentially unreliable) on the axis of reporting may be included in the novel but only if it is presented with disclaimers by a reliable narrator. In *The Woman in White*, Walter summarizes in his own words Laura's "sadly incoherent" memories about her abduction (424); however, he warns the reader not to completely trust her recollections by constantly qualifying them as "confused, fragmentary" (426), "vague and unreliable" (427), "uncertain" (427), and "contradictory" (427). In *The Moonstone*, Mr. Candy falls dangerously ill with a fever the night of the dinner party and jewel theft. A few days later, Blake hears that Candy is "talking nonsense . . . in his delirium" (105). Months later, when Blake starts investigating the theft, propelled by the uncomfortable discovery he may have stolen the stone, he decides to interview the party guests, including Candy. But when Blake questions Candy about that night, it is clear Candy has no memory of it and yet tries to hide "the total failure of his memory" (368). Candy can only chat about recent (less than "a month old") community gossip. Blake soon learns, however, that Candy's assistant Ezra took notes of Candy's incomprehensible, delirious ramblings and then meticulously filled in the blanks to create a coherent sense of Candy's intended meaning. During his fever, then, Candy's memory is accessible, but only through Ezra's ingenious means. Blake quotes from Ezra's proffered notes in his narrative. Candy only acts as a narrator late in the novel through a short letter to Blake that covers a recent event—Ezra's death. Because of his fever and then amnesia, Candy is never able to provide direct narration about the night of the dinner party. Several narrators in *A Beleaguered City, The Beetle,* and *Dracula* cross or come to unnarratable blanks in their stories when they fall unconscious or experience amnesia, both usually in response to traumatic events. These blanks, however, are localized and easily jumped over via ellipsis or occur at the end of the narrators' sections. Candy's amnesia, on the other hand, is too vast to skip over, and Laura misremembers rather than not remembering at all.

Furthermore, in the service of suspense, characters who know too much too soon are also refused the position of narrator, and retrospective narrators must underreport and restrict themselves to sharing only what they knew at the time. Phelan usefully distinguishes between this type of underreporting (meant to not give away the end of the story) and unreliable underreporting (meant to deceive the reader). In *The Moonstone,* Miss Clack retrospectively pens her narrative based on her journal entries from the past. Clack begs Blake to let her share her current knowledge, which would include the identification of the villain, but Blake insists on Clack limiting herself to what she knew at the time. As Dennis Porter argues, there are various "devices of retardation" that result in "the repeated postponement of a desired end" in detective fiction, of which *The Moonstone* is an early example (32). These devices—which include a naive narrator—show that "the art of narrative is an art of misleading or of tactical retreat before an advancing reader" (33). W. Collins's own reviewers noted that his multinarrator structure smartly enabled the creation and maintenance of suspense: "The advantage of this new method is, that the story moves forward without interruption, and that the reader's curiosity is continually teased by a sense of mystery. The witness, relating only what he knows, piques our curiosity by his ignorance even more than he satisfies it by his disclosure" (Page 98). Rachel Verinder, who witnesses the drugged Blake steal the moonstone from her cabinet in her room with her own incredulous eyes, must respond with unbreakable silence if the novel is to continue past chapter 11. Her silence is W. Collins's greatest aid in keeping the secret—that Blake himself stole the moonstone—and in laying the groundwork for one of the greatest peripeteias in Victorian fiction.[8]

THEORIZING MULTINARRATION

Narratology often seems to presume texts with one narrator, and multinarrator setups other than the frame narrative and epistolary novel have been generally overlooked. Phelan proffers the term "serial narration" in the epilogue of *Living to Tell about It* to cover "the implied author's use of more than one character narrator to tell the tale" (197); however, this phrase invites confusion, as many novels were published serially during the Victorian period. Additionally, Phelan's restriction of the term to indicate multiple "character narrators"—Phelan's accessible term for homodiegetic narrators—excludes

---

8. Lonoff similarly argues that because narrators cannot lie and suspense must be fanned, Godfrey and Rachel cannot narrate in *The Moonstone*: "If they were [narrators], then according to Collins's rules, they would have to give away the plot" (154).

examples of multinarration like *Bleak House* that pair a homodiegetic narrator with a heterodiegetic one. Other narratologists show an awareness of multinarrator texts without exploring them in-depth. W. Booth acknowledges that "reliable and unreliable narrators can be unsupported or uncorrected by other narrators . . . or supported or corrected" (159–60). F. K. Stanzel analyzes the two narrators of *Bleak House* at length. Gérard Genette introduces the term intradiegetic narrator to indicate "a narrator in the second degree" (*Narrative* 248). However, I prefer to treat the multinarrator structure as a distinct type of narration rather than as the mere multiplication or addition of basic narrator types. In this way, I share Brian Richardson's frustration with the "basic categories of first and third person narration" (13). I classify *Bleak House* primarily as a multinarrator novel rather than as a novel in which a heterodiegetic/third-person narrator alternates with a homodiegetic/first-person narrator. The distinction is slight but crucial. The simple math approach fails to view a multinarrator novel as a structure beyond the sum of its parts. But the experience of reading a novel with one first-person narrator, like Charlotte Brontë's *Jane Eyre,* differs from reading Esther Summerson's chapters of *Bleak House* because Esther's account neither stands alone nor proceeds seamlessly.

Some scholars have used the work of Mikhail Bakhtin, directly or indirectly, to explicate multinarrator novels, but Bakhtin's key terms have little to do with the type of narrator an author chooses to employ.[9] Heteroglossia and dialogism are properties of language and of the novel whether or not that novel uses multiple narrators. While Bakhtin does acknowledge that "incorporated genres" ("Discourse" 320)—such as "the confession, the diary, travel notes, biography, the personal letter" (321)—can be one way of bringing "speech diversity" (321) to the novel, he also imagines many other avenues to achieve such an end. Polyphony requires a "plurality of consciousnesses" that the author allows to be *"free* people, capable of standing *alongside* their creator, capable of not agreeing with him and even of rebelling against him" (Bakhtin, *Problems* 6). The author talks with rather than merely *about* his heroes. But polyphony can be attained through the use of third-person narrators, and Bakhtin specifies that an author's choice of a first-person narrator does not automatically ensure polyphony:

> This problem lies deeper than the question of authorial discourse on the superficial level of composition, and deeper than any superficially compositional device for eliminating authorial discourse by means of the *Ich-*

9. See, for example, Taylor and Kucich: "Multi-voiced novels are more literally 'polyphonic'" (257).

Erzählung form (first-person narration), or by the introduction of a narrator, or by constructing the novel in scenes and thus reducing authorial discourse to the status of a stage direction. All these compositional devices for eliminating or weakening authorial discourse at the level of composition do not in themselves tackle the essence of the problem; their underlying artistic meaning can be profoundly different, depending on the different artistic tasks they perform. (56–57)

"Thus," Bakhtin continues, "all these compositional devices are in themselves still incapable of destroying the monologism of an artistic world" (57). To Bakhtin, the use of a first-person narrator (and, I would add, multiple narrators) is a "superficially compositional device" that "may in fact not weaken the monologism of the author's position at all" (56–57, 57).

The Victorian multinarrator novel does not attain polyphony as Bakhtin envisions it. The Victorian multinarrator novel possesses a "plurality of consciousnesses," and those consciousnesses are often psychologically distinct and stylistically variant (Bakhtin, *Problems* 6); however, in a polyphonic novel, there is no "single objective world," and each of those consciousnesses has "*its own world*" (6). In the Victorian multinarrator novel, facts remain constant across narrations, and the truth, whether that be the existence of a supernatural creature or the solution to a crime, becomes clearer though multiple narrations; in short, the Victorian multinarrator novel moves toward "the unity of a single world" rather than toward a multiplicity of worlds (15). Many of these novels feature an editor character—or more often, characters—who solicit, arrange, and/or edit the plethora of narratives, suggesting a unity of vision behind the collaboration. In this way, the Victorian multinarrator novel resembles Bakhtin's conception of drama as monolithic: "The rejoinders in a dramatic dialogue do not rip apart the represented world" (17). D. A. Miller takes up this line of reasoning in his Foucauldian and Bakhtinian reading of W. Collins's *The Moonstone*: "The novel is thoroughly *monological*—always speaking a master-voice that corrects, overrides, subordinates, or sublates all other voices it allows to speak" (54). To D. A. Miller, the novel's monology ensures that "all readers . . . pass *the same judgement*" (53). Unlike D. A. Miller, however, I do not find that the novel's monology shuts down ambiguity in the narrative or diversity in reader judgement; case in point: decades of lively critical debate on *The Moonstone,* particularly with regards to its representation of the British Empire.

Of the many subtypes of the multinarrator structure, the embedded frame narrative has received the most theoretical attention. Gerald Prince defines the frame narrative as a "narrative in which another narrative is embedded; a narrative functioning as a frame for another narrative by providing a setting for it" (*Dictionary* 33). A framed narrative, therefore, is embedded, a term that William Nelles defines as "the literary device of the 'story within a story,' the structure by which a character in a narrative text becomes the narrator of a second narrative text framed by the first one" ("Embedding" 134). The classic example of an embedded frame narrative is Mary Shelley's *Frankenstein*. The extradiegetic narrator, the explorer Walton, begins the novel; Walton's narrative includes Frankenstein's intradiegetic narrative, and Frankenstein's includes the creature's metadiegetic narrative. Frankenstein is the creature's narratee; Walton is Frankenstein's narratee; and Walton's narratee is his sister Margaret.

But many multinarrator novels do not embed the subsequent narratives within the first one. To Mieke Bal, the two units involved in narrative embedding must have "a hierarchical relationship" (43): "We can say that a phenomenon is embedded whenever it is composed of two units which are subordinate to each other following a transition" (44).[10] I agree with Bal that Nelly's narrative is embedded within and framed by Lockwood's narrative in *Wuthering Heights*, though, as I mention in chapter 5, I coin the term permeable frame to characterize its unique frame structure. Rosanna Spearman's letter is embedded within Blake's narrative in *The Moonstone*. Dracula's letter is embedded within Jonathan Harker's narrative in *Dracula*. But as Bal herself admits, the concept of embedding "excludes juxtaposition" wherein units are "surrounded by" each other rather than "embedded in" each other (44). And in *Bleak House*, Esther's narrative is not embedded within the other narrator's. Although Nelles claims "that a narrative can have only one extradiegetic narrator, the general narrator" ("Stories" 82), *Bleak House* has two extradiegetic narrators—one homodiegetic and one heterodiegetic. To Bal, in embedding, the first narrator does not so much "*allow[ ]* the second subject to speak" as "*quote[ ]* [the second subject] in his own voice" (54). But the other narrator of *Bleak House* does not quote Esther or give Esther permission to speak. In *Treasure Island*, Dr. Livesey's mid-novel, three-chapter narration is not introduced by, framed by, or embedded within Jim Hawkins's narration. The switch does not engender a movement in narrative levels; instead, as the chapter heading states, "Narrative Continued by the Doctor" (Stevenson, *Treasure* 84). Similarly, in W. Collins's *The Moonstone* and *The Woman in White*, narrators talk about "taking [the pen] up next, in my turn" and "add[ing] these new links to the chain of events" (*Moonstone* 272; *Woman* 127). The narrative is a

---

10. Bal's conception of embedding is incredibly capacious and includes any switch in focalizer, a reference to a memory, or insertion of direct discourse.

relay, a chain, done "in . . . turn"—the narratives are not presented as nested. While every narrative, broadly speaking, metaphorically frames subsequent narratives by influencing how we read those later narratives, not every switch in narrator is an example of embedding.[11] The Victorian multinarrator novel's discomfort with the simple embedded frame narrative shows a desire to move beyond merely hierarchal relationships between narrators and between texts.

While one might argue that the collating figures in many Victorian multinarrator novels establish a kind of singular overarching frame in which every switch of narrator occurs, the collating or editing force behind many of these novels consists of multiple characters. Bernard Duyfhuizen writes that in "'hybrid' narratives, constructed of multiple documents—letters, diaries, transcribed testimony, memoirs, even inset novels . . . an extradiegetic narrator must piece [the narratives] together to frame a coherent narrative" ("Framed" 188). But multiple characters often work together to accomplish this piecing together. Although critics often consider Walter Hartright the "master narrator" of *The Woman in White*, Walter and Marian "consult[ ]" and mutually decide to gather relevant materials (W. Collins, *Woman* 435). Marian also obtains Mrs. Michelson's and Mr. Fairlie's narratives for the narrative project. Similarly, critics treat *The Moonstone*'s Franklin Blake as the novel's "master narrator," and yet, Blake and Bruff "*together* have hit on the right way of telling" the story of the moonstone (W. Collins, *Moonstone* 21; emphasis added). The final narrative in the novel, Murthwaite's letter describing the moonstone's triumphant unveiling in India, is addressed to Bruff, not Blake, highlighting Bruff's importance in obtaining documents. Betteredge's second contribution, positioned late in the novel, is not explicitly requested by Blake; instead, Betteredge seems to write it of his own volition and force it into the novel: "My purpose, in this place, is to state a fact in the history of the family, which has been passed over by everybody, and which I won't allow to be disrespectfully smothered up in that way" (462). Betteredge, then, impinges on and overrides Blake's editorial role. In *Dracula*, while it is Mina's idea to "get all [their] material ready, and have every item put in chronological order" (Stoker 239), Mina and Jonathan together physically "put all the papers into order" (243); the unsigned, brief note that opens the novel is potentially authored by the whole narrating team rather than by a sole narrator.

The assumption that every change in narrator leads to framing or embedding limits our understanding of the multinarrator novel. In *Narrative Dis-*

---

11. Nelles differentiates between two types of embedding: "with a shift in narrator but not in narrative level, and with a shift of both narrator and narrative level" ("Stories" 85). To Nelles, every shift in narrator (whether or not there is a shift in narrative level) qualifies as embedding.

course: Authors and Narrators in Literature, Film, and Art, Patrick Colm Hogan usefully distinguishes between "three forms of multiple narration—embedded, collective, and parallel" (183): "Parallel narrators are individual or group narrators who do not embed one another. An embedded narrator is simply a narrator whose telling of a story is included in the story told by another narrator. A group narrator is a collective rather than an individual" (15). Hogan then divides parallel narration into two categories: conjunctive parallelism and disjunctive parallelism. The former occurs when parallel narrators "are treating the same storyworld" (like William Faulkner's *The Sound and the Fury*), and the latter occurs when parallel narrators "are treating different storyworlds" (like Geoffrey Chaucer's *The Canterbury Tales*) (184). Parallel narration "invite[s] the reader or viewer to relate the individual narratives to one another" (186) and "to look for similarities or contrasts, particularly with an eye on emotional or thematic purposes." After doing such comparative work, a reader will assume that "whatever is common to the different versions is true in the storyworld" (187). Although Hogan's analysis focuses on twentieth-century film and literature, his conception of "conjunctive parallel narration" applies to most of the Victorian multinarrator novels considered in this book. Most of the subtypes of multinarration I have introduced—back-and-forth, quick switch, patchwork, and returning and nonreturning—fit within Hogan's category of "parallel narration."

Narrative Bonds also pays attention to the switches in narrator—how the switch is effected and signaled, how often the narrator switches, and how long each narrative lasts. In *Novel Violence,* Garrett Stewart encourages narratologists to "step back—back to the page" (16) and heed the "surface features" and "textures of execution" in Victorian prose (13). Stewart calls this project "narratography," as opposed to narratology. My interest in the details of how a switch occurs—through punctuation, titles, indentations—aligns with Stewart's focus on the page.[12] Borrowing the language of tagged and untagged (or free) discourse,[13] I propose that *tagged* switches are ones that are clearly indicated via title or header, punctuation (usually quotation marks), or typography. *Untagged* switches are not indicated by such methods; an untagged switch initially may be unrecognized by or confusing to a reader. For example, the first switch to Esther Summerson's narrative in *Bleak House* is untagged.

---

12. Ryan identifies "transition-signaling devices" like the "closing of quotation marks, description of the dreamer's awakening, reference to the story-status of the preceding section" as indications to the reader that a boundary has been crossed (379).

13. In tagged discourse, a "clause ('he said,' 'she thought,' 'she asked,' 'he replied') accompan[ies] a character's discourse (speech or verbalized thought)," but in untagged (or free) discourse, "no tag clauses accompany the utterance or thought" (Prince, *Dictionary* 97).

Chapter 3 is labeled "A Progress," not "Esther's Narrative" as many of her later chapters are. The end of chapter 2 does not hint at such a change, and the "I" of Esther's first sentence likely puzzles the reader. The switch to Dr. Livesey in *Treasure Island*, conversely, is clearly marked by the chapter title: "Narrative Continued by the Doctor" (Stevenson 89). Two chapters later, the chapter title informs us again: "Narrative Resumed by Jim Hawkins" (98). In most Victorian multinarrator novels, switches tend to be tagged and to occur simultaneously with large-scale breaks within the novel—chapter, section, or book. As I discuss in chapter 5, *Wuthering Heights*'s interparagraph and intersentence switches are unconventional. The duration of a narrator's narrative also matters. For example, the brevity of Dr. Livesey's narration in *Treasure Island* (he narrates for three of thirty-four total chapters) affects the meaning and impact of both narrations. Lastly, the number and frequency of switches relates to the novel's rhythm. Film editing uses the terms *slow cutting* and *fast cutting* to indicate different editing pacing—a series of longer or shorter shots, respectively. As I lay out in the epilogue, *The Beetle* switches only three times (at roughly regular intervals), while *Dracula* switches ninety-two times (starting with irregular intervals that become more regular over the course of the novel). The nitty-gritty specifics of narrator switches, which I also call transitions or cuts, reveal much about how the multinarrator form works and how it connects to the novels' content.

The critical consensus aligns the Victorian novel with the omniscient narrator of Dickens and Eliot, but the prevalence of the multinarrator novel disrupts our assumptions about the Victorian novel's conventional form. J. Hillis Miller refers to the omniscient narrator as the "standard convention of Victorian fiction" and "the determining principle of its form" (*Form* 63). Audrey Jaffe agrees that omniscience "dominates nineteenth-century narrative," even in first-person narratives (6). D. A. Miller concurs that "the majority of Victorian novels" are told by an omniscient narrator who "assumes a fully panoptic view of the world it places under surveillance" (52, 23). As Paul Dawson and Jaffe note, it is the modernists who are often credited with rejecting omniscience.[14] Patrick Brantlinger, however, discovers the seeds of that rejection in Victorian literature as well: "Within Dickens's London [omniscient narration] begins to seem more artificial . . . because the idea of a narrative persona knowing everything about such a vast place implies something close to supernatural authority" (17). In the genre of sensation fiction, Brantlinger

---

14. Dawson writes that the modernists rejected the omniscient narrator as "technically obsolete and morally suspect" (3). Jaffe summarizes how "discussions of the transition from the Victorian to the modern novel almost always rely on the idea of the disappearance of the omniscient narrator, defined as absolute authority or knowledge" (4–5).

continues, omniscient narration becomes an active hindrance and is hence avoided. The Victorian multinarrator novel manifests the suspicion of omniscience that Brantlinger mentions by implying that multiple viewpoints are needed to achieve truth and that individual perspectives are inherently limited.[15] Often, because of sickness, sleep, or delusion, characters do not even know what has happened to them without helpful information from other narrations. But Robert Scholes, Phelan, and Robert Kellogg consider the "multiplication of narrators" to be "characteristic of modern fictions" by Joseph Conrad and Faulkner, not of Victorian literature (262). Similarly, B. Richardson sees the modernists as "unexpected precursors" to the postmodernists for their "extreme, unusual, and outrageous acts of narration, often associated with the practices of postmodernism" (137); however, he declines to extend the continuum of influence further back into the nineteenth century even though he identifies texts from that period that use or prefigure later narrative strategies. In chapter 1, I position the Victorian multinarrator novel amidst its antecedents in the eighteenth-century epistolary novel and its descendants in the modernist novels of William Faulkner and Virginia Woolf, explicitly adding the Victorians to the lineage B. Richardson delineates.

---

15. Even J. Miller admits that the "use of Esther Summerson as secondary narrator is an important admission of the failure of Dickens' habitual point of view, the detachment of the spectator from the roof of Todgers'" (*Charles* 177–78). Writing on *The Moonstone*'s "use of multiple narrators," Free asserts that it "wrenches authority away from an individual first-person narrator" and thereby "challenges the (imperially linked) authority of a single, knowing figure" (342).

CHAPTER 1

~

Epistles to Narratives to Monologues

NITIAL REVIEWS of William Faulkner's *The Sound and the Fury* and *As I Lay Dying* repeatedly praised the author's method as "experimental." One reviewer christened *The Sound and the Fury* as "one of the most important experiments in creative form and approach I have read for ten years" (Bassett 90). Another review presented *As I Lay Dying* as evidence of Faulkner's "experiment that has widened the boundaries of modern fiction" (94). This celebration of newness existed alongside an identification of Faulkner's stylistic parent—James Joyce. "Joyce is the ultimate source, obviously," remarked one reviewer (89). Reviews did not extend Faulkner's lineage further back to the multinarrator novels of the nineteenth century. Conversely, several reviewers of Wilkie Collins's *The Woman in White* refuted his assertion of structural novelty by reminding him of the eighteenth-century epistolary novel. Henry James also positions *The Woman in White* within a longer literary tradition: The novel, "with its diaries and letters and its general ponderosity, was a kind of a nineteenth century version of 'Clarissa Harlowe.' Mind, we say a nineteenth century version" (742). This chapter elaborates on James's hypothesis. With the Victorian multinarrator novel at the center of my genealogy, I look forward to modernist texts by Faulkner (*As I Lay Dying* and *The Sound and the Fury*) and Virginia Woolf (*The Waves*) and backward to eighteenth-century epistolary novels with multiple letter-writers by Fanny Burney (*Evelina*) and Samuel Richardson (*Clarissa*). I consider them all "versions" of the same multiperspective impulse even though the modernist texts use multiple monologists, not multiple narrators. Comparing these different versions reveals what is specific to the Victorian multinarrator novel: the investment in realism of method, the emphasis on narratorial bodies, and the centrality of narrative collaboration to the novel's plot.

The author's options within the multiperspective form—especially regarding possible speakers and types of narrative—have increased over time. Writing letters costs money, consumes time, and depends on some level of literacy. The eighteenth-century epistolary novel mostly limits itself to wealthy, leisured, literate, upper-class narrators, seldom using lower-class letter writers. Robert Scholes, James Phelan, and Robert Kellogg's point about soliloquists applies to the epistolary novel as well: "Hamlet is Shakespeare's Great Soliloquizer because he is, as a character, well designed for soliloquies; whereas Othello, for example, is not" (178). Not all characters are "well designed" for letter writing.[1] Although most narrators are able to read and write in the Victorian multinarrator novel as well, the number of literate people dramatically increased over the course of the nineteenth century, as Richard D. Altick details in *The English Common Reader*. Additionally, *The Woman in White* incorporates an illiterate narrator through dictation. The Victorian multinarrator novel is not exclusively devoted to letters; diaries, journals, memos, statements, telegrams, and simple narratives, in addition to letters, are medium options. Characters who are not dedicated letter-writers can narrate through other means. While retreating from the documentary bent of the eighteenth- and nineteenth-century multinarrator novels, the modernist multimonologue novel continues to broaden who can speak. *As I Lay Dying* is told through the illiterate Bundrens, and Addie Bundren speaks from beyond the grave. The developmentally disabled, nonverbal, and illiterate Benjy tells the first section of *The Sound and the Fury*.

The different "versions" of the multiperspective form also privilege and facilitate different kinds of realism. The epistolary novels of S. Richardson and Burney share an investment in what Edward Bloom calls *Evelina*'s "moral realism" (xxix): "Realism . . . becomes a triumph of benevolence with social propriety and unaffected goodness inseparable virtues" (xxiv). While definitions of moral realism vary, they all center a preoccupation with morality and awareness of its complicated functions in personal and social life. Malcolm Bradbury, for example, explains that a novel of moral realism "witnesses . . . the fact that the social and moral world are contiguous: that the social world

---

1. Altman also recognizes how the novelist's "choice of the epistle as narrative instrument can foster certain patterns," including the use of specific "character types" (9).

is properly conceived a moral world" (32). To Lionel Trilling, a novel's moral realism "involve[s] the reader himself in the moral life, inviting him to put his own motives under examination" (215). Alternatively, Victorian multinarrator novels exhibit what Robert Louis Stevenson calls "realism . . . of method" ("Note" 226). In his dissection of his multinarrator novel *The Master of Ballantrae*, Stevenson touches on his preference for this method, which he describes as follows: "not only that all in a story may possibly have come to pass, but that all might naturally be recorded." Ephraim Mackellar, the Durie family servant, narrates the majority of the story about the doomed Durie brothers; love and respect for the younger brother motivates his narration: "The truth is a debt I owe my lord's memory" (Stevenson, *Master* 9). Mackellar twice includes an excerpt from "the complete memoirs of" the Chevalier de Burke to address some of the older brother's adventures at which Mackellar was not present (32). Both Mackellar's and Burke's narratives have been "naturally . . . recorded." The Victorian multinarrator novel tends to explain and justify its own creation. By contrast, the modernist novel, as David Lodge writes, "manifested a general tendency to center narrative in the consciousnesses of its characters" (57); furthermore, the modernists sought "a more realistic mode of presenting the often unorganised and chaotic nature of our thoughts," as Violeta Sotirova observes (39).[2] The books I examine by Faulkner and Woolf aim to achieve what I'm calling a realism of consciousness.

These shifts do not indicate progress; rather, I agree with Wayne C. Booth's statement that "the interest in realism is not a 'theory' or even a combination of theories that can be proved right or wrong; it is an expression of what men of a given time have cared for most" (63). Each brand of realism discussed here brings advantages and disadvantages. Although one might claim that narrators and speakers gain more realistic minds in the modernist novel, they also lose the narratorial bodies so crucial to the eighteenth- and nineteenth-century multinarrator novel. The movement toward representing the self who thinks displaces the self who writes and physically creates a material narrative.

THE EPISTOLARY NOVEL AND MORAL REALISM

The epistolary form, like the Victorian multinarrator novel, foregrounds the writing self. These letter writers know they are writing letters; they frequently

---

2. Also see Auerbach's analysis of Woolf's *To the Lighthouse*: "we are dealing with attempts to fathom a more genuine, a deeper, and indeed a more real reality" (540).

reference the act of writing and that ubiquitous instrument of it—the pen.[3] Evelina repeatedly reflects on the letter she is writing or has just completed: "What a long letter have I written" (Burney 152); gives temporal context to the act of writing: "I am now risen thus early, to write it to you" (231); and links her own body to her writing: "but I blush to proceed—I fear your disapprobation" (370). Clarissa also measures the length of her compositions: "Having written to the end of my second sheet, I will close this letter" (S. Richardson 1: 135); describes the documents' physical appearance: "You will not wonder to see this narrative so dismally scrawled. It is owing to different pens and ink, all bad" (1: 487); and connects her physical condition to her writing: "The pen, through heaviness and fatigue, dropped out of my fingers, at the word *indebted*" (1: 401). On one occasion, after Lovelace rapes Clarissa, her words are scattered on the page, written at odd angles, visually manifesting her frenzy and despair (3: 209).

Unlike the Victorian multinarrator novel, a noncharacter editorial presence scaffolds these eighteenth-century epistolary novels; the novels' characters are not responsible for the collecting, editing, and presenting of the letters. This editorial presence exists, in part, to maintain the moral realism of the novel. Most blatantly, the editor of *Clarissa* adds clarifying and interpretative footnotes; although S. Richardson included more of these notes in the second edition and kept them in the third edition, these additions "further a feature of the text already present" in the first edition (Ross 17).[4] I cite the Everyman edition of the novel, which is based on S. Richardson's third edition.[5] In contrast, similar editorial work is done by a character in W. Collins's *The Moonstone*. Some of the footnotes in *Clarissa* merely encourage the reader to cross-reference the text: "See Mr. Lovelace's Letter (xxxi) in which he briefly accounts for his conduct in this affair" (S. Richardson 1: 7). But other footnotes urgently remind the apparently gullible reader of Lovelace's villainy and manipulative powers. The editor aims to save us from being, like Clarissa's family members, "puppets danced upon Mr. Lovelace's wires" (1: 257). Another

---

3. Fludernik states that "the plot of epistolary narrative includes both the events narrated in the letters and the writing of these letters" (277).

4. S. Richardson added more footnotes because he considered readers' responses to the novel—and particularly to Lovelace—"unsatisfactory" (Kinkead-Weekes 156). In Kinkead-Weekes's analysis, S. Richardson's additions, including the notes, "underline the novel's moral teaching" (156).

5. The four-volume Everyman *Clarissa*, originally published in 1932, does not indicate which edition of the novel it is based on. Shirley van Marter, however, infers that it is "based on some version of the third edition" (108), adding that "since [S. Richardson] added over two hundred pages of text to *Clarissa* by the time of the third edition in 1751, it has generally been assumed that the third, or some combination of the third and fourth, best illustrates his final intention" (108).

footnote presents a hypothetical, erroneous reader reaction to guide us, or shame us, into taking the correct stance: "This explanation is the more necessary to be given, as several of our readers (through want of due attention) have attributed to Mr. Lovelace . . . a greater merit than was due to him" (1: 353). The footnotes remind us that Lovelace acts "artfully" (1: 441, 1: 501). Furthermore, the novel's inclusion of very few of Lovelace's letters to Clarissa implies a judgment upon his iniquitous courtship of her; Janet Gurkin Altman counts that "only 6 of the 537 letters composing S. Richardson's novel are exchanged between the heroine and her tormentor" (22). Feared interpretative confusion over Lovelace doesn't instigate all footnotes, however. For example, one footnote defends Clarissa against the reader's possible "censure[ ]" (S. Richardson 1: 501), and another counsels us to doubt Anna's interpretation of Clarissa's behavior (2: 156). In the novel's postscript, S. Richardson justifies the addition of certain footnotes to convince the reader that Clarissa could never have been in love with someone like Lovelace who is so overloaded with "immoralities": "A few observations are thrown in by way of note in the present edition, at proper places, to obviate this objection, or rather to bespeak the attention of hasty readers to what lies obviously before them" (4: 558, 559). These footnotes, therefore, encourage us to understand the moral stakes of this issue; as S. Richardson explains in the postscript, Clarissa could not have acted so honorably if she had been in love with Lovelace.

Just as the footnotes direct the reader to the preferred moral responses to the characters and plot, S. Richardson's brief preface and lengthy postscript further emphasize his moral intent both in the novel's action and in its epistolary structure. S. Richardson bluntly admits that to "warn and instruct" was the chief purpose of his novel; the story's ability to "entertain and divert" was a clever ruse (1: xiv), a "vehicle to the instruction" (1: xv). Additionally, he constructs Clarissa to be an "examplar [sic] to her sex" (1: xiv). Most importantly, he gives a moral power to writing-to-the-moment, an aspect of his epistolary style that oftentimes strains realism: "All the letters are written while the hearts of the writers must be supposed to be wholly engaged in their subjects . . . with what may be called instantaneous descriptions and reflections (proper to be brought home to the breast of the youthful reader)" (1: xiv). S. Richardson hopes that having the authors write while their emotions are fresh will better enable the story to "affect the reader" (1: xv), particularly "the youthful reader" (1: xiv). To S. Richardson, the novel's epistolary structure helps the novel fulfill its goals: "to warn," "to caution," and "to investigate the highest and most important doctrines not only of morality, but of Christianity" (1: xv). In short, the structure facilitates and furthers S. Richardson's investment in moral realism.

The inclusion or exclusion of certain letters in Burney's *Evelina* not only manifests the novel's hidden editor but also reveals that editor's devotion to upholding the novel's moral realism. Bloom indicates that Burney was "very much in tune with eighteenth-century moralism" and "saw the novel as a preceptive vehicle" (xxiv). The reviewers of *Evelina* recommended the novel to female readers "as conveying many practical lessons both on morals and manners" (Cooke 359). *Evelina* omits many letters that the characters allude to having written or read, but Evelina's and Mr. Villars's letters to one another constitute the main correspondence in the novel, and such correspondence is specifically presented as serving a moral function; it allows Villars to continue dispensing guidance to his young ward from a distance, and it permits Evelina to seek counsel while experiencing her hazardous "entrance into the world" that "parallels the temptation of Eve" (Bloom xx). Evelina addresses her adoptive father and moral mentor with a fervent mix of apology, gratitude, and self-abasement that stresses their roles in her moral education: "Unable as I am to act for myself, or to judge what conduct I ought to pursue, how grateful do I feel myself, that I have such a guide and director to counsel and instruct me as yourself!" (Burney 160). Mr. Villars's letters flood with affection, anxiety, and cautionary wisdom, and he bestows his judgments—approval or censure—upon her actions, motives, and acquaintances. His instructive method vacillates between encouraging her to "learn not only to *judge* but to *act* for yourself" (164)—as she proves capable of doing when she daringly prevents Macartney from committing suicide—and prescribing specific behavior—as he does when he orders her to immediately leave the society of Orville.

The omission of Madame Duval's letters from *Evelina* serves as a moral judgment upon Madame Duval herself. A letter from Madam Duval to Lady Howard kick-starts the novel's plot, but the letter itself is absent, pointing to the selective hand behind the novel's composition. Lady Howard writes the novel's first included letter because she has "just had a letter from Madame Duval" and wants to both inform and seek advice from Mr. Villars with regards to its contents (11). Since Lady Howard appraises Duval's letter as "violent, sometimes abusive," she decides "the letter itself is not worthy [of Villars's] notice"—showing an implicitly moral rationale for suppressing Duval's letter. Instead of quoting from, copying, or forwarding Madame Duval's letter, Lady Howard merely summarizes Duval's intentions for Villars. In fact, no letters to or from Madame Duval are included in the entire novel even though many are referenced in letters the reader does see. Madame Duval's letter—"violent, sometimes abusive"—becomes a metonymy for Madame Duval herself, whom Lady Howard describes as "vulgar and illiterate" (11, 12). Most of the main characters in the novel view Madame Duval as a transgressor who invades spaces—including England, carriages, and Lady Howard's home—where she is unwanted and unsuited. Villars's first description of Madame Duval paints her, through a series of "un-" words, as the opposite of a proper woman: "She is at once uneducated and unprincipled; ungentle in her temper, and unamiable in her manners. . . . [and] [u]nhappy" (13). The less-biased Evelina, upon unexpectedly meeting Madame Duval (her grandmother) for the first time, confirms her guardian's verdict. Evelina writes to Villars that she "will not shock [him] with the manner of [Madame Duval] acknowledging [her], or the bitterness, the *grossness* . . ." (52). Madame Duval forces herself upon others in the plot, as she does with Evelina in this scene, but she cannot force her letters into the novel.

The glaring exclusion of the correspondence between Evelina and her good friend Maria Mirvan also maintains the moral realism of *Evelina*. The novel sets up a prolific correspondence between the two friends. Evelina tells Villars that Maria "made [her] promise to send her a letter every post" (165), and Evelina alludes to Maria's letters in her own to Maria; however, readers only see a few letters from Evelina to Maria and none from Maria to Evelina. Julia L. Epstein imagines the Evelina–Maria correspondence as a missing "second novel . . . over which *Evelina* rests like a palimpsest" (119). Tracy Edgar Daugherty ascribes this absence to Burney's "economy" and "great skill in narrative technique" (48), and *Evelina* does exhibit a tightness that *Clarissa* lacks. But Daugherty's comment does not explain the specific lack of the Evelina–Maria correspondence, particularly considering the fact that Evelina is more honest in her correspondence with Maria than in her communication with Villars.[6] The Evelina–Maria correspondence is minimized, I argue, because it's merely an expressive and not an instructional one. Maria never advises Evelina, and Evelina never seeks Maria's advice. Far from fulfilling the role of sisterly counselor, Maria "neither hopes nor fears . . . as" Evelina does (Burney 122). Miss Mirvan's blank character enables her to serve as Evelina's "second self," as a mirror for Evelina. According to Maria's grandmother Lady Howard, they "love each other as sisters" (21). But she imagines their relationship as "tender and happy," not as improving.

Evelina's and Maria's friendship differs from Clarissa's and Anna Howe's friendship; as a result, Clarissa's and Anna's correspondence is one of the primary letter-sets included in *Clarissa*. Clarissa and Anna continually advise and ask for advice, chastise and commend. S. Richardson even emphasizes this aspect of their friendship in his preface to the novel: "Such instances of

---

6. Epstein agrees that Evelina "divulges her real thoughts and feelings only to Maria" and shares in a more "colloquial and forthright" tone than she employs with Villars (118).

impartiality, each freely, as a fundamental principle of their friendship, blaming, praising, and setting right the other, as are strongly to be recommended to the observation of the younger part (more especially) of female readers" (1: xiv). Their correspondence serves a moral purpose for one another and for the reader—an example to young, female readers of a mutually improving friendship. For example, once Clarissa has fled the safety of her family's house to the dubious protection of Lovelace, she must constantly guard herself against him; however, even in such an overwhelming and precarious situation, she continues to fulfill what Victor J. Lams calls the friends' "judicial responsibility" that "obliges them to give good advice and to disapprove if the friend goes wrong" (143):

> I should think myself utterly unworthy of your [Anna's] friendship did my own concerns, heavy as they are, so engross me that I could not find leisure for a few lines to declare to my beloved friend my sincere disapprobation of her conduct, in an instance where she is so *generously* faulty, that the consciousnesses of that very generosity may hide from her the fault . . . . (S. Richardson 2: 122)

To avoid one's "judicial responsibility" would make Clarissa "utterly unworthy" of the friendship. A "beloved" friend deserves to know if her conduct has been wrong, and a good friend is not afraid or too busy to "declare" her "disapprobation." Although more flippant than Clarissa, Anna echoes Clarissa's promise of being "sincere" by responding: "I give you my sincere thanks for every line of your reprehensive letters" (2: 131). Anna adds that her pain in reading them ("I winced a little") only increases her affection and respect for her friend: "I shall love and honour you still more, if possible, than before." The potentially friendship-breaking cycle of rebukes and penitence actually strengthens the friendship.

THE VICTORIAN MULTINARRATOR NOVEL AND
REALISM OF METHOD

Although the heterodiegetic editor figures of *Clarissa* and *Evelina* function as the ultimate directors of the novels, the homodiegetic characters in the Victorian multinarrator novel collect and collate the various texts into a unified whole. This replacement parallels and enables the shift from moral realism to realism of method. In his note on his multinarrator novel *The Master of Ballantrae*, Stevenson explains his "natural love for the documentary method in narration" ("Note" 226). Although he started drafting the novel with a hetero-diegetic narrator, he revised it with the character Ephraim Mackellar as the primary narrator:

> I was doubtless right and wrong [to revise the book's point of view]; the book has suffered and has gained in consequence; gained in relief and veri-similitude, suffered in fire, force and (as one of my critics has well said) in "large dramatic rhythm." The same astute and kindly judge complains of "the dredging machine of Mr Mackellar's memory, shooting out the facts bucket-ful by bucketful"; and I understand the ground of his complaint, although my sense is otherwise. The realism I love is that of method; not only that all in a story may possibly have come to pass, but that all might naturally be recorded—a realism that justifies the book itself as well as the fable it com-memorates. ("Note" 226)

Stevenson associates the "documentary method" with "verisimilitude," "real-ism," and being "natural[ ]." Although he preferred "for one of my puppets to display himself in his own language" (225–26), he eventually found Mackellar to be an imperfect "spokesman" (225), lacking the gravitas to narrate some of the tragedy; nonetheless, he stuck with the "personification of Mackellar" because of his "natural love for the documentary method" (226).

Victorian multinarrator novels habitually explain how, when, where, and why these narratives were written, revised, transcribed, requested, given, read, and collected.[7] To use Stevenson's words, all is "naturally . . . recorded" by the characters themselves, and the book's very existence is explained and "justifie[d]" by those same characters. For example, in W. Collins's *The Moonstone,* the protagonist Franklin Blake originates the idea, along with his lawyer, to put "the whole story . . . on record in writing" (21). To attain that end, Blake repurposes an "old family paper" as the novel's "prefatory narrative" (22); req-uisitions characters to narrate specific spans of the story (Betteredge, Bruff); compensates characters to pen narratives (as is the case with the impover-ished Miss Clack); obtains or receives other narratives to fill in narrative gaps (Rosanna Spearman's letter, Ezra Jennings's journal, Sergeant Cuff's statement, Mr. Candy's letter); and narrates when appropriate. Blake, therefore, takes over the duties and powers ascribed to author-editor agents in *Clarissa* and *Evelina.* Blake acts like the editor of *Clarissa* does by adding footnotes throughout the novel to clarify issues, defend himself, guide the reader's interpretation, and

---

7. As examined in chapter 5, *Wuthering Heights* is the exception to this rule. The novel neither clarifies how Lockwood's narrative came to be nor clearly indicates that Lockwood's narrative is a written document.

encourage the reader to cross-reference narratives. *The Moonstone* is a particularly strong example of the diegetic creation of the collaborative narrative, though most other Victorian novels I discuss account for the creation of the individual narratives and for how the narratives come to be assembled; however, multinarrator novels like Charles Dickens's *Bleak House* and Stevenson's *Strange Case of Dr. Jekyll and Mr. Hyde* cannot include character-driven compilation of all narratives because the novels include heterodiegetic narrators who do not belong to the characters' world. As if to minimize this strangeness, both novels end with a homodiegetic narrator who consciously writes to an audience. Jekyll's statement, addressed to his friend and lawyer Utterson, ends the novel; its last line emphasizes Jekyll's physical creation of the document: "Here then, as I lay down the pen and proceed to seal up my confession" (Stevenson, *Strange* 62). And in *Bleak House*'s final chapter, Esther Summerson refers to "the unknown friend to whom I write," calling attention to both the act of writing and her audience (Dickens 985).

Clarissa foreshadows this Victorian development when characters in the story, Belford and Colonel Morden, collect and copy many of the letters we presumably read in the novel. The two men create a shadow compilation—similar to, but not the same as—the novel sitting before readers: "The inconsolable mother rested not till she had procured, by means of Colonel Morden, large extracts from some of the letters that compose this history" (S. Richardson 4: 532). Clarissa's mother, however, is only able to obtain "extracts" of "some of the letters"; such wording doubly emphasizes the difference between what Clarissa's mother reads and what the reader of *Clarissa* reads. It is also worth noting that in reading these extracts, Clarissa's family realizes their culpable treatment of her and recognizes "the majesty of her virtue" (4: 533); the letters serve an educational purpose and uphold the moral realism of the novel.

The realism of method foregrounds narrators' bodies since bodies are required to write, speak, record, read, or arrange narratives; therefore, in the Victorian multinarrator novel, narrators' exhaustion, passion, and sickness can affect their narrations, as chapter 4 on disabled narrators in W. Collins's novels will explore further. Marian Halcombe's diary in *The Woman in White*, which deteriorates and abruptly ends as her illness incapacitates her, is a case in point. In *Bleak House*, Esther cannot narrate what happens to her after she traumatically discovers her mother's dead body: "I proceed to other passages of my narrative" (Dickens 916). In *The Woman in White*, Walter Hartright similarly cannot bear to narrate what happens when he discovers that Laura, who has presumably died and been buried, is still alive: "I open a new page. I advance my narrative by one week" (W. Collins 412). In *Dracula*, when Mina

Harker's transition to vampire is nearing completion, she sleeps constantly and stops writing. Vampire-expert Van Helsing worriedly observes, "She make no entry into her little diary, she who write so faithful at every pause" (Stoker 386). Mina does not write again until Dracula has been staked, restoring her humanity. On the other hand, *The Sound and the Fury*'s Jason Compson easily continues his monologue despite his frequently mentioned headaches. He feels like his head is about to "explode right on [his] shoulders" (Faulkner 235–36). But even though his head hurts so badly that he "couldn't think about anything except [his] head," he thinks about many other things besides his head in the monologue (241). The pain is acknowledged, but it doesn't impede the section's progress. *As I Lay Dying*'s Addie Bundren, whose first name puns on "I die," seemingly speaks from her coffin; even her body's death does not prevent her monologuing.

THE MULTIMONOLOGUE NOVEL AND
REALISM OF CONSCIOUSNESS

No critical consensus exists over what to call the characters with first-person sections in Faulkner's *The Sound in the Fury* and *As I Lay Dying* and Woolf's *The Waves*. While some critics do use the term "narrator," others consider "monologist" or "soliloquist" more appropriate. Dorrit Cohn classifies the three brothers' sections in *The Sound and the Fury* as monologues, as does Gérard Genette. Cohn also categorizes most of the *As I Lay Dying* sections as monologues.[8] To Cohn, monologues are "unmediated, and apparently self-generated" and represent "unrolling" and "unsifted" thoughts (15, 175, 194). She positions the monologue "as a variant—or better, a limit-case—of first-person narration" (15).[9] Conversely, Cohn labels the sections in *The Waves* as "soliloquies" because "they are all cast in a uniform idiom" (264). Cohn continues, "Woolf's soliloquies . . . convey the idea that they are subject to poetic license, and that they must *not* be understood as realistic reproductions of the characters' mental idiom" (265). Woolf herself described the novel as "a series of dramatic soliloquies" (qtd. in Hite xli). But Molly Hite regards the terms monologue and dramatic soliloquy ill-fitting even though, to her, the sections

---

8. See Cohn's analyses of the monologues in *The Sound and the Fury* (247–55) and *As I Lay Dying* (205–8).

9. To Cohn, narration is chronologically ordered, retrospective, grammatical, and foregrounds its creation and its audience; a monologue, conversely, is immediate, hyper-emotive, and lacks both an audience (beyond perhaps the monologist) and a "realistic motivation of the text's origin" (175).

convey the characters' "immediate impressions and thoughts" (xli). Patrick Colm Hogan distinguishes first-person narration and interior monologues; the former "is self-conscious" and "often retrospective" and the latter is "un-self-conscious" and "ongoing" (189). Hogan includes both forms, however, under the mantle of "mentalistic narration," of which *The Sound and the Fury* is "a paradigmatic case" (189). Hogan treats Benjy, Quentin, and Jason as narrators but also suggests that Faulkner's novel uses interior monologue as well.

While Cohn distinguishes the Faulknerian monologues from *The Waves*'s soliloquies, I find that none are "unmediated" and all "are subject to poetic license" (Cohn 15, 265). These first-person sections are not simply a "direct, immediate presentation of the unspoken thoughts" of the characters, as Scholes, Phelan, and Kellogg define monologue (177). Even Scholes, Phelan, and Kellogg highlight the mediation in *As I Lay Dying*'s monologues: "Faulkner even abandons any attempt to couch his characters' monologues in native idiom, but clothes all their speech with his own Faulknerian rhetoric" (262). Early reviews of *As I Lay Dying* express confusion about the ambivalent mediation of the narratives. One review complains that Faulkner

> does not seem even to have made up his mind whether his method of labelling chapters under characters is meant to represent the subconscious (or semi-conscious) flow of their minds, or what they actually say to themselves in words or thoughts. If the former, then of course he is justified in using fine language, as a poet is justified in using blank verse to express the exalted emotions of his persons . . . But then why all the colloquialisms and bad grammar? (Bassett 98)

To this reviewer, the "fine language" points to Faulkner's (or the implied author's) poetic presence or lens, while the "colloquialisms and bad grammar" suggest that the language originates with the Bundrens. Like the reviewers of *As I Lay Dying*, reviewers of *The Waves* recognize Woolf's mediation—her poetic license—in presenting the consciousnesses of her characters. One reviewer of *The Waves* identified its method as "artificial" and "absurdly naïve" and concluded that the first-person sections are the characters' minds made hyperconscious, poetic, and articulate via refraction through Woolf's mind (Majumdar and McLauren 270). This reviewer also acknowledges that Woolf's use of the first person is a "device . . . [and] a kind of cheating, since, . . . it gives us just that illusion of intimacy which, in logic, the method cannot for a moment support" (270). This review suggests that the use of the first-person pronoun helps give the illusion of access to the characters' immediate thoughts. I will proceed by using the word monologue to describe the first-person sections in all three novels, even though I believe that monologues can be more mediated than Cohn allows. I also acknowledge that there are substantial differences in how each novel uses monologues. Ultimately, *narrator* doesn't seem like the appropriate term, as, for the most part, these characters do not use language that believably or naturalistically comes from them.

Even though the monologue enables the modernists to better achieve realism of consciousness, it diminishes realism of method. Hogan writes, "interior monologue is considerably more significant for representing the mental processes of the narrator than is ordinary first-person narration" (190). But the monologue cannot explain how that consciousness comes to be articulated and recorded. A reviewer of *The Waves* understands how the "quest for an ultimate personal reality" relies on various antirealistic techniques; he uses the terms "artificial" and "illusion" to describe the novel's method (Majumdar and McLauren 270). The review prefigures what W. Booth later says about realism: "Whatever verisimilitude a work may have always operates within a larger artifice; each work that succeeds is natural—and artificial—in its own way" (59). Similarly, Scholes, Phelan, and Kellogg recognize that Faulkner "has simply ridden roughshod over the question of verisimilitude and presented characters like Jason Compson revealing themselves directly in a way which cannot be accounted for in realistic terms" (262).

The selector and arranger of letters in *Evelina* and *Clarissa* reappears in these modernist novels, though much more covertly, as the selector and arranger of monologues. In the Victorian multinarrator novel, the characters select and arrange the narratives themselves. *Dracula*'s Mina Harker is the narrative director par excellence. But no character is given this responsibility in these three modernist novels. Who assigns Benjy the date of April 7, 1928? Who decides where Jason's monologue starts and stops? Who decides that Quentin's section will follow Benjy's? Robert O. Richardson asserts that "a central intelligence is implicit in the arrangement of the monologues themselves" in *The Waves* (698). And W. Booth claims that the method of *As I Lay Dying*—the "roving visitation into the minds of sixteen characters"—exposes the omniscience that orchestrates that tour and that "has chosen correctly how much to show of each" mind (161).[10]

The modernist multimonologue novel shifts from an emphasis on the writing-self to the thinking-self, and correspondingly, from realism of method

---

10. Similarly, Hogan "assume[s that there is] a nonpersonified narrator who is constant across the voices of the parallel narrators" in *The Sound and the Fury* (187). That nonpersonified narrator "commonly makes use of all his or her verbal resources to articulate the ongoing mental experience of the character/narrator in its various perceptual, imaginative, and emotional facets" (192).

to realism of consciousness. The narratives in the Victorian multinarrator novel foreground their written or spoken mediation, but these modernist novels obscure such mediation—the reader does not know how the monologists' words came to be. None of the first-person sections in *As I Lay Dying, The Sound and the Fury,* or *The Waves* are characterized as being written or spoken. In *The Sound in the Fury,* for example, Benjy does not write or speak, so his section cannot be written or spoken by him. Quentin's section is implicitly contrasted with his written suicide notes, which he frequently pats through his coat jacket. And Jason shows disdain for writing things down: "I make it a rule never to keep a scrap of paper bearing a woman's hand, and I never write them at all" (Faulkner, *Sound* 193). Jason's monologue cultivates a hazy feeling of orality—his first line reads "Once a bitch always a bitch, what *I say*" (180; emphasis added)—but the orality is never confirmed, and no listener is ever identified. All the male speakers in *The Waves*—Bernard, Neville, Louis—possess literary talents, but their monologues are presented as "a unique kind of thought-speech" rather than as writing (McIntire 31). The "book, stuffed with phrases" that Bernard carries with him is not the novel (Woolf, *Waves* 219). Furthermore, the characters' monologues are not presented as being spoken in the conventional sense. As Hite explains, the "speakers 'speak' only metaphorically" in *The Waves* (xlii).[11] In his final section, Bernard does mention an auditor, a person he "scarcely know[s]" whom he meets at a restaurant "for an hour or two" (Woolf, *Waves* 217, 218); however, Bernard's monologue does not resemble an actual oral conversation, and it continues in the same style once he has departed from his acquaintance. This removal or mystification of the written and oral mediums, which are so privileged and necessary in the multinarrator novels of the eighteenth and nineteenth centuries, points to the modernist novel's desire to access and present consciousness more directly; mediation via documentation had once bestowed both realism and authenticity to narratives, but modernist authors view such mediation as a blockage rather than as a channel.

Some responses to these novels evince discomfort with the ontological oddness of these monologues. As an early reviewer of *As I Lay Dying* speculated, "We may I think conclude that Darl is identified in a special sense as the author of the book (not at all however identified with Faulkner himself), that the whole book is Darl's" (Bassett 106). Cohn's interpretation of *The Waves* echoes that reviewer's inference: "*The Waves* as a whole would have to be understood as a single autonomous monologue produced, in chronological

---

11. R. Richardson concurs: "Clearly, neither Bernard nor Neville is 'saying' in the usual sense of that term the speeches attributed to them" (695).

order, by Bernard's creative memory. The speeches of the six figures . . . then appear as interior monologues Bernard invents to articulate his memories" (265). By identifying one of the novel's monologists—Darl or Bernard—as the novel's originator, such responses scramble to discover a more realistic explanation for how the book was created; such responses indicate nostalgia for the Victorian multinarrator novel's realism of method.

Faulkner's *As I Lay Dying* playfully implies its unrealism of method. The figure of the Graphophone—a "talking machine"—becomes a metonymy for *As I Lay Dying*'s obscured narrative structure (190). The second Mrs. Bundren's Graphophone—whose music enchants Cash and attracts Anse to her house to borrow shovels—is presented as modern city technology, a so-called "talking machine" that Cash had been saving up to buy until Anse took his money to help pay for new horses after the river-crossing debacle. This Graphophone uses records as opposed to cylinders and was based on the earlier phonograph, the "wonderful machine" that Dr. Seward uses in *Dracula* to record his spoken diary entries (Stoker 237). *Dracula* foregrounds its recording equipment: the phonograph, Mina's stationary typewriter and portable typewriter, the telegraph, pen and paper. *Dracula* always identifies the medium by which each document is created or transcribed. While Jennifer Wicke classifies *Dracula* "as the first great *modern* novel in British literature" because "it stages the very act of its own consumption" and production via "cutting edge technology" (467, 491, 470), I use the novel's reliance on "cutting edge technology" as evidence of its Victorian origins. *As I Lay Dying*, on the other hand, hides the mechanisms by which it exists, refuses to name the machine by which it talks. On the last page of the novel, Cash reminiscences about his family sitting around the Graphophone and listening to the "new record . . . from the mail order" (Faulkner 261). Cash describes the characters listening to "record[s]" at the same time the reader has just about finished reading through the "order[ed]" "records" of the text. *As I Lay Dying* refers to its own structure only in metaphor. *Dracula*, by comparison, explicitly and repeatedly discusses its own structure, such as when Dr. Seward comments, "And so now, up to this very hour, all the *records* we have are complete and in *order*" (Stoker 251; emphasis added).

COLLABORATIONS

The Victorian multinarrator novel, in both form and plot, centers on collaboration, a focus that differs from the eighteenth-century and modernist examples of the multiperspectival form. *Clarissa* and *Evelina*, as their one-name titles imply, concentrate on their respective main character and present the letters written to, from, and about her. Her death or her marriage—and the trials she must undergo to reach her fated conclusion—inspires the swarm of letters. Before the reader even begins *Clarissa* or *Evelina,* they already know whom the protagonist is. Victorian multinarrator novels are not named after individual narrators. The title of Anne Brontë's *The Tenant of Wildfell Hall* only hints at one of the novel's two narrators (Helen, the new tenant of the hall); the title sets up a mystery that will enthrall Gilbert and the community: Who exactly is this new tenant? But other Victorian novels' titles—*The Moonstone, Dracula, The Beleaguered City*—name the item (the missing moonstone), place (the city that is beleaguered), or threat (Dracula) that instigates the narrative collaboration. And these collaborations—in narrative and in plot—are generally successful, even when the novels question the nature of or reveal the costs of those collaborations. Innocence is restored, the threat is subdued, marriage and family are consolidated, and financial security is assured.

In the modernist multimonologue novel, physical collaboration is impossible, relentlessly suspect, or botched. Witnesses are aghast at the odorous funeral procession for the decomposing Addie Bundren in *As I Lay Dying.* Although the Bundren family—and to a certain extent, the community—rallies to transport Addie to her desired burial plot in Jefferson, the unification is both ridiculous and ridiculed. Burying Addie's body—the ostensible cause that motivates the arduous journey—masks each family member's more selfish reasons for making the trip. In *The Sound and the Fury,* the once grand and wealthy Compson family suffers a slow, spectacular, and public fall, as members are disowned, castrated, and buried. Each brother who narrates—Benjy, Quentin, and Jason—selfishly focuses on his own problems, ignorant or careless of the family's monetary and moral collapse. The six main characters in *The Waves* lose their tight coed community once childhood passes and, after that, reunite only twice.

Loss motivates and organizes these modernist novels, and the novels' narrative structures mirror that loss. The characters in *The Waves* violently mourn Percival's unexpected death in India, which occurs midway through the book. Percival never speaks via monologue; he is "the silent center of the novel" (McIntire 40). Gabrielle McIntire observes, "We quite astonishingly hear only one word from Percival in the entire novel" (39). Percival's silence magnifies his larger-than-life status, his godlike reputation among the others. Bernard cultivates the characterization of Percival as the lost center: "About him my feeling was: he sat there in the centre. Now I go to that spot no longer. The place is empty" (Woolf, *Waves* 110). Meditating on Percival's death, Bernard uses the anaphoric repetition of "you have lost" to amplify Percival's unfulfilled potential: "You have lost something that would have been very valuable to you. You have lost a leader, whom you would have followed; and one of you has lost happiness and children" (111). In *The Sound and the Fury*, each brother responds to Caddy's absence—and to the loss of her innocence, foreshadowed by her muddy drawers—differently: Benjy wails, Quentin neurotically obsesses, and Jason rages. Caddy's narrative silence—she is the only one among her siblings not to receive her own section—mirrors and amplifies her absence in the storyworld. Addie's death propels the entire plot of *As I Lay Dying* (she is the "I" who lies dying), and though one blazing section is told from her point of view, she still receives fewer chapters than every other Bundren family member except Jewel. Although Victorian multinarrator plots often include or are precipitated by loss, their conclusions incorporate various gains that outweigh and eclipse that loss. Although the prized jewel returns to India in *The Moonstone* and Lucy dies in *Dracula*, the novels end with pregnancy and a newborn child, respectively. The rejuvenation symbolized by children minimizes the previously incurred losses, and such losses even help to create and strengthen family and community ties by the novels' ends.

In the modernist multimonologue novel, a prospective mental community replaces the physical community of the Victorian multinarrator novel. While the Victorian multinarrator novel distrusts and fears telepathy, the modernist multimonologist novel yearns for mental communion and exchange. In the former, the villains possess mind-reading abilities, and their powers are portrayed as aggressive and invasive. *The Woman in White*'s Count Fosco's gray eyes are so penetrating that Marian feels "his mind . . . prying into [her own]" and his eyes "reach[ing] [her] inmost soul" (W. Collins 265, 287). Such mental "prying" prefigures his raid on her private diary, a move many critics interpret as a metaphoric rape. In Richard Marsh's *The Beetle*, the title monster is "nothing but eyes" and "seemed to experience not the slightest difficulty in deciphering what was passing through [Holt's] mind" (53, 85); the Beetle also physically molests Holt in addition to invading his mind. Dracula's "blazing. . . . [and] red" eyes herald his ability to entrance others (Stoker 46). He eventually forces a hypnotized Mina to submit to his bite and suck blood from his own breast; this sexually charged blood exchange gives Dracula access to Mina's mind. These villainous mind readers also sexually violate their victims, linking invasion of the mind to invasion of the body.

In these modernist novels, mental exchange, rather than the exchange of material documents, binds characters. Characters such as Darl, Bernard, and Dilsey possess a mind-expansive quality that provides a sense of coherence and stability in otherwise chaotic worlds and splintered texts. Faulkner and Woolf didn't need to make their characters clairvoyant. Many of Darl's clairvoyant passages—describing the encounter between Jewel and his horse and Addie's death scene—could have been more naturally narrated by another character: Jewel in the first case and Dewey Dell in the second. The final section of *The Waves*, rather than being only spoken by Bernard, could have continued the routine cycle of monologues. Faulkner's and Woolf's structural choices, therefore, purposefully construct the mind as expansive, swelling beyond its own time, body, and location to bridge the division between characters.

The Waves celebrates mental community more than physical community. The six monologists, friends since childhood, are sadly aware of their separation from one another. Bernard recalls this painful process of differentiation: "We suffered terribly as we became separate bodies" (Woolf, *Waves* 179). The monologues' insistent speech tags—"said Jinny," "said Louis"—mark each character's monologue as separate, as originating with and belonging to individual characters. And yet, the characters desire to come together in a way that overcomes their "separate bodies." Interestingly, the two times the group physically reconvenes—to say goodbye to Percival before he goes to India and to have dinner in late-middle age at Hampton Court—the characters create a mental community. What the characters actually say to one another—customary greetings and small talk—is absent from the monologues; instead, we read their mental conversation. Each monologue jumps off the previous one and leads into the subsequent one in a way that suggests a cerebral conversation, a conversation that depends on the characters' intimate knowledge of the others' thoughts. For example, during the first of the two gatherings, Louis mentally exclaims that he "hate[s]" all present except for Percival and Susan (92). Jinny, who speaks next, counters Louis's claim as if she had heard it. "But you will never hate me," she assures him, because of her body's ability to "dazzle" others (93). Speaking next, Neville concurs with Jinny's self-assessment, commenting that she does, in fact, "demand[ ] admiration" (93); furthermore, he refers to Jinny as "you" as if he were directly responding to her point. In the same monologue, Neville changes the topic to his own life and professes that in "this pursuit"—the search for love—"[he] shall grow old" (94). Next, Rhoda repeats Neville's language ("pursuit" and "grow old") to reflect on her own personality: "If I could believe . . . that I should grow old in pursuit and change" (94), and so on. Certain words, images, refrains, and topics are tossed around like a ball, linking the monologues and giving them the rhythm of conversation. Even Rhoda, perpetually terrified and secretly flailing, seems soothed by the telepathic nature of these rare meetings; she comments, "There are moments when the walls of the mind grow thin; when nothing is unabsorbed" (164). A few pages later she returns to this metaphor of the walled mind: "The still mood, the disembodied mood is on us . . . and we enjoy this momentary alleviation (it is not often that one has no anxiety) when the walls of the mind become transparent" (168). She imagines the mind's boundaries, which protect it from the external world, becoming both "thin" and "transparent," allowing everything to be incorporated and transmitted. Bernard also takes up the image of dwindling boundaries in his final monologue: "I cannot find any obstacle separating us. There is no division between me and them" (214). The mind's openness is celebrated, not feared.

Bernard epitomizes the desire for and the possibility of mental community by speaking the novel's final section on his own. Of the novel's nine sections, section nine features only Bernard, "sum[ming] up" on the behalf of himself and his friends (176). No other section includes only one monologist, and the final section could have continued the habitual cycle of monologues from multiple characters. Effectively, this structural choice represents Bernard as a mind reader. Bernard's receptivity to "the stimulus of other people," his vigorous imagination, and his ability to "sympathise effusively" make him the character most able to access his friends' minds (57, 55). R. Richardson agrees that Bernard, as "an acute, sensitive, and sympathetic human being," "is using knowledge of his friends' personalities, sensibilities, and social circumstances to render the content and quality of that characters' experience" (700). Conversely, McIntire treats Bernard as a "narrative dictator" who "'takes over' the narration" in his final section (38, 31). But rather than "impos[ing] his single voice on the inexhaustibly plural experience of others to contain the diversity they denote" (McIntire 35), I argue that Bernard opens his mind to multiplicity and celebrates his friends' distinct experiences and personalities.[12]

Much like Bernard in *The Waves*, Darl occupies "a highly privileged position as narrator" within *As I Lay Dying* (Bleikasten 56), and Darl's clairvoyance enables mental communication much like Bernard's extraordinary empathy does. Darl narrates far more than any other character—nineteen of the novel's fifty-nine sections. His clairvoyance also enables him to speak about scenes at which he is not present. As André Bleikasten summarizes, "Darl is the one who sees and knows the most, and it is through him that we are most completely . . . informed" (57). The very structure of *As I Lay Dying*, chopped into small divisions, each topped with the character's name in bolded capital letters, heightens the characters' separateness; the blank spaces at the beginnings and ends of sections simulate an impassable gulf. But Darl routinely crosses the gulf that separates mind from mind. In the opening chapters, Darl

---

12. Furthermore, as R. Richardson points out, Bernard is not the only character "to re-create and share even the most inward of another character's experiences" because Louis and Neville also enact such assimilation on a smaller scale (697).

authoritatively describes Jewel's actions, thoughts, and words, none of which
Darl would be able see, know, or hear by traditional means. Darl narrates
his mother's death scene even though at the time of her death he's on the
road with Jewel and far away from the Bundren household. Darl communicates "without words" with his newly pregnant sister Dewey Dell (Faulkner,
Dying 27). He knows that she is pregnant and that she yearns to ask Dr. Pea-
body for assistance in terminating the pregnancy. Dewey Dell and Darl hold
a conversation "without the words" over whether he will inform Anse of her
pregnancy. The Bundrens' helpful neighbor Tull remarks that Darl "dont say
nothing. . . . I always say it aint never been what he done so much or said or
anything so much as how he looks at you. It's like he had got into the inside of
you, someway" (125). Darl can get "inside of you"—know you or communicate
with you—without using spoken or written language.

In *The Sound and the Fury,* the theme of mental community is not as
prominent, but the loyal Compson servant Dilsey does possess some of the
clairvoyance that Bernard and Darl exhibit. Her connection to the house and
its inhabitants manifests as clairvoyance: "Mrs Compson called her name
again from within the house. Dilsey raised her face as if her eyes could and
did penetrate the walls and ceiling and saw the old woman in her quilted
dressing gown at the head of the stairs, calling her name with machinelike
regularity" (Faulkner, *Sound* 270). In Darl's first section, he walks around the
cotton house yet relays what occurs within its walls as Jewel walks through
it; similarly, Dilsey's "eyes . . . penetrate the walls and ceiling" to see Mrs.
Compson. Later, when Dilsey brings Benjy to her church for the Easter service, the amassed members begin to think and breathe and respond as one:
"Their hearts were speaking to one another in chanting measures beyond the
need for words" (294). Like the wordless communication between Darl and
Dewey Dell and the mental conversations among friends in *The Waves,* the
congregation members "speak[ ] to one another" without words. The scene
uses plural pronouns like "them," "they," and "their" to stress the unity of the
congregation: "a long moaning expulsion of breath rose from *them*," and "*they*
did not mark" (295; emphasis added). This "collective" moment represents the
strongest example of community in the entire novel (294). Once the service
concludes, a lachrymose Dilsey confidently portends, "I've seed de first en de
last . . . I seed de beginnin, en now I sees de endin" (297). The service enables
Dilsey to reach her full clairvoyant potential.

Faulkner's and Woolf's novels have long been described as "experimental." This same term has been applied to Dickens's *Bleak House,* the focus of
the next chapter. The traditional narrative of literary history, however, presents modernism as a radical break with the conventional Victorian period,

particularly with regards to form. Considering the multiperspectival structure as a through line links rather than divides these novels—they are not just silos of experimentalism. The discourse of innovation should exist side by side with the awareness that the novels discussed in this chapter can be viewed as related versions of a similar narrative impulse.

CHAPTER 2

⁓

Depth and Surface

Back-and-Forth Narration and Embodiment in *Bleak House*

THE THIRD CHAPTER of Charles Dickens's *Bleak House* (1853) shocks with the appearance of a homodiegetic narrator, Esther Summerson, who expresses her "difficulty in beginning to write [her] portion of these pages" (27). The previous two chapters were narrated by an unnamed, disembodied, heterodiegetic narrator.[1] From chapter 3 onward, the two narrators take turns narrating, the first narrator in the present tense, and Esther in the past tense. I label this regular alternation between two narrators the *back-and-forth* structure. This multinarrator type binds two narrators together through consistent interweaving. I argue that the noncompetitive and harmonious relationship between these two narrators—along with their shared subject matter, moral vision, and tone—embodies the story's endorsement of sympathy and cooperation. I agree, therefore, with W. J. Harvey that "the narrative method seems . . . expressive of what, in the widest and deepest sense, the novel is about" (91). The two narrators relay Lady Dedlock's fall from a great social height and Esther's (Lady Dedlock's out-of-wedlock daughter) rise and eventual thriving among husband, home, and community. This plot, I argue, follows the shift Nancy Armstrong delineates in *Desire and Domestic Fiction* between the aristocratic woman of surface and the feminine domestic

---

1. Although *Bleak House*'s heterodiegetic narrator is not overtly gendered in the text, most critics (except for Wilt) assume or claim that he is masculine; I use male pronouns in this chapter to more easily differentiate the heterodiegetic narrator from Esther.

ideal of depth. The narrators possess different but complementary perspectives of surface and depth that accentuate this shift. The first narrator, who
principally narrates about the decline of Lady Dedlock and her class, narrates
what he sees and hears—narrates surfaces—rather than omnisciently divulg-
ing characters' interiorities. Conversely, in her homodiegetic narrative, Esther
Summerson creates herself as a woman of depth by confessing her unspoken
thoughts, eschewing her physical appearance, and discouraging other characters and the reader from locating her identity in her corporeal figure. The
other narrator supports Esther in her depth-creating endeavor by refusing to
"see" her in his narrative, in which she would be an externally viewed and
described character.

Furthermore, *Bleak House*'s illustrations—overseen by Dickens and
completed by his long-time collaborator Hablot Knight Browne (known as
Phiz)—harmonize with the two narrators' treatment of their material. I do
not attribute the illustrations to either narrator but to the implied author.[2]
Wayne C. Booth invented the term *implied author*, but the concept has since
undergone much debate and revision; I find James Phelan's modified explanation particularly clarifying: "a streamlined version of the real author . . . that
play[s] an active role in the construction of the particular text" (45). In my
approach, the illustrations come from the same entity that provides chapter
titles; Esther's most recurrent chapter title, "Esther's Narrative," is not written
in the first person and, thereby, not provided by her.[3] Gérard Genette considers intertitles (such as chapter titles) and illustrations as two examples of the
"accompanying productions" that form a text's paratext (*Paratexts* 1). Genette
ascribes illustrations specifically to the author because they "involve[ ] the
author's responsibility, not only when he provides the illustrations himself . . .
or commissions them in precise detail . . . but also, and more indirectly, each
time he accepts their presence" (406).[4] While Genette credits these "accompa-

---

2. Conversely, Jordan dismisses "the notion of Dickens/Phiz as the controlling consciousness responsible for the illustrations," finding it "needlessly restrictive" (27). Instead, Jordan
argues that the illustrations are "externally focalized—that is, as seen by a viewer who stands
outside the depicted scene and who is not a character in the novel" as well as sometimes simultaneously internally focalized through an "unseen, character-based focalizer" such as Esther
(42).

3. Genette comments how "in first-person (homodiegetic) narratives, these clausal intertitles may raise the question (much more often than general titles do) of the identity of their
enunciators. When these intertitles are written in the third person . . . this choice . . . obviously
makes the author the enunciator of the intertitles" (*Paratexts* 301).

4. Using transmedial narratology, Thon considers the existence of narrators in graphic
novels, film, and video games, concluding that "recipients will generally attempt to attribute
(fictional) verbal narration to some kind of (fictional) narrator . . . while attributing (fictional)
nonverbal narration to the work's (hypothetical) author(s) in a majority of cases" (30).

nying productions" specifically to the author, I attribute them to the implied author; narratologists who resist the concept of the implied author, like Genette, often concede its usefulness in certain cases, including collaboratively produced works. For their collaboration on *Bleak House,* Dickens guided and approved Phiz's illustrations,[5] and Phiz adapted them to Dickens's literary style, as Jane R. Cohen has argued. Both Cohen and Michael Steig observe that Phiz's increasing use of dark plates in *Bleak House* reflects the somberness and seriousness of Dickens's subject matter. In the context of Phiz's illustrations for Dickens's *David Copperfield,* Robert L. Patten argues that "book illustrations can expound, elaborate, and enlighten the text" (123). In this chapter, I show how the illustrations "expound, elaborate, and enlighten" both Esther's suspicions of visibility and Lady Dedlock's status as icon. Just as the two narratives complement one another, the illustrations reinforce the two narratives, furthering the novel's investment in harmonious collaboration.[6]

The collaboration between the two narrators even attempts to overcome—or at least allay—their divergent embodiment. F. K. Stanzel considers embodiment the primary difference between heterodiegetic and homodiegetic narrators (which he refers to as authorial third-person and first-person narrators):

> The first-person narrator is distinguished from the authorial third-person narrator by his physical and existential presence in the fictional world. In other words, the first-person narrator is "embodied" in the world of the characters. The authorial third-person narrator may also say "I" in reference to himself, but he is embodied neither inside nor outside the fictional world. Personal features can, of course, become visible in an authorial narrator, as well, that is why the criterion of credibility is applicable to him, too—but these personality features are not linked with the notion of his physical existence and corporeality. (90)

Esther has a body, while the other narrator does not. Esther sometimes downplays her body's presence, but her body's reactions—particularly crying—routinely puncture her narrative. The other narrator sometimes evokes a corporeality he doesn't actually possess. Both narrators, then, evade the limits

---

5. Steig reasons that given the specificity of the installment cover, "Browne must have had quite explicit directions, or at least some explanation of Dickens' purposes" and may have read the first few chapters before finalizing the cover (132).

6. Cohen comments that Dickens's and Browne's "rigorous collaboration" on *Bleak House* was "harmonious" (112): "With this work, the two men reached the height—and the limits—of their collaboration" (114).

of their narratorial type, blurring the binary between embodied and disembodied narrators and softening their dissimilarity.

My reading contrasts with the majority of criticism on *Bleak House*'s dual narrative. Many critics erect a hierarchy of narrators and elevate one narrator and one narrative as more artistic, more realistic, more persuasive, more powerful, or more Dickensian than the other narrator and narrative.[7] Alison A. Case evaluates the two narratives as "far from equal in status": "Esther's narrative is not only technically 'subordinate' to that of the omniscient narrator, hers is also far more limited in scope and vision" (132); the other narrator presents "the more comprehensive view" (133). Stanzel similarly describes Esther's narrative as a "subjectively limited one" that contrasts with the other narrator's "panoramic omniscient perspective" (11).[8] My reading resists this "versus" approach by calling attention to the similarities—in content, tone, and ethics—between the two narrators, as well as to their cooperation, evidenced by their narration of the same plot without rehashing the same events. While I do point out the first narrator's surface-oriented narration and Esther's depth-creating one, I do not situate one narrator as better, more valuable, or more reliable than the other because of that difference in technique. After all, *Bleak House* emphasizes the necessity of recognizing the connections between apparently unconnected things.[9]

Bleak House's employment of the back-and-forth multinarrator structure—in which two narrators regularly alternate with sections of approximately equal length—helps create this connection and balance between the two narrators since no one narrator ever gains preeminence and the narrators are constantly juxtaposed. The back-and-forth structure functions similarly in Dinah Mulock Craik's *A Life for a Life* (1860), even though, unlike *Bleak House*, it has two homodiegetic narrators. *A Life for a Life* features what Craik calls "a double diary" in her preface (iii): initially the alternating diaries of Dora and Max and eventually the letters between them. The two characters meet, fall in love, and eventually marry despite the discovery that years prior, Max killed Dora's brother in a drunken rage. Throughout the narrative, both Dora and Max contemplate destroying their diaries and letters. In the final

---

7. Case, Jadwin, J. Miller (in *Charles Dickens*), Moseley, and Serlen conclude that the heterodiegetic narrator (whom they all call omniscient) prevails over Esther for a variety of reasons. Delespinasse, J. Peters, and Sawicki make the opposite move, claiming that Esther possesses or gains dominance over the other narrator and narrative.

8. See Frank and Eldredge for similar points.

9. Levine approaches *Bleak House* through the lens of networks: "Characters in the novel are linked through the law, disease, economics, class, gossip, the family tree, city streets, rural roads, and even global print and philanthropic networks" (125). Similarly, Buzard comments, "It cannot be safe to say something or someone . . . is not connected" in *Bleak House* (115).

chapter, as the newly married couple sail to Canada, Dora shares that Max has encouraged her "to write an end to [her] journal, tie it up with his letters and [hers], fasten a stone to it, and drop it" into the sea (357). But she doesn't jettison the documents. Dora admits doing so "would feel something like dropping a little child into" the ocean (358). The braided narrative, seesawing between chapters titled "His Story" and "Her Story," becomes a physical manifestation of their union, a metaphorical baby. As soon as Dora accepts Max's marriage proposal, they feel spiritually and physically united. Even after she learns the truth about Max's criminal past, Dora concedes she cannot renege on the engagement: "It would have been like tearing my heart out of my bosom; he was half myself—and maimed of him, I should never have been my right self afterwards" (254). The bundle of their journals and letters, "tie[d]" together, resembles their unalterable bond (357).[10]

In both *A Life for a Life* and *Bleak House,* the two narrators almost equally share the narrating duties. In *A Life for a Life,* Dora narrates for twenty-four and Max for twenty-three chapters. The switches are tagged by chapter titles: "Her Story" and "His Story." Generally, the novel switches narrator every chapter; a few times, either Max or Dora narrates two chapters before a switch occurs. In *Bleak House,* Esther narrates for thirty-three chapters, the other narrator for thirty-four. The switches are not quite as regular as in *A Life for a Life,* but, usually, one narrator narrates for two to four chapters before a switch, creating a tangible, if not strict, rhythm of switches. Furthermore, the cuts to Esther's narrative are usually signaled by the chapter title "Esther's Narrative," showing Dickens's attempt to guide the reader through the transitions after the shock of chapter 3. *Bleak House* was originally published serially in monthly installments, nineteen total, counting the final double issue as one installment. The majority of those installments include both narrators: Thirteen include both narrators, five include only the heterodiegetic narrator, and one includes only Esther. The tendency is for both narrators to narrate within each installment. While the majority of installments (eleven) commence with Esther's narrative, the majority of installments (thirteen) close with the other narrator's narrative. While the other narrator has the privilege of opening the novel, Esther has the privilege of concluding it. A balance exists, therefore, between the narrators and the honored positions of beginnings and endings.

---

10. Linder shows how the "novel's dual structure" ultimately "emphasiz[es] the similarities between male and female self-reflections and identity formation" rather than "uphold[ing] a male/female binary" (205). J. Taylor and Kucich offer a similar argument that "Craik also uses the diary form to stress the similarities between Theodora's and Max's inner lives" (261).

DUAL—NOT DUELING—NARRATORS

The two narrators of *Bleak House* share a world populated with the same char-acters, the same government, the same weather, the same time scheme, and the same overarching plot; therefore, *Bleak House* fits Patrick Colm Hogan's category of conjunctive parallel narration that "occurs when there are two or more narrators telling versions of the same story or treating the same story-world" (184). Even though Hogan claims that "multiple narrations are, in gen-eral, of interest to the degree that they diverge from one another" (184–86), the narrators of *Bleak House* coincide on their attitudes toward those shared items: They describe characters with like language, they admire and despise the same characters, and they concur on moral views. As I argue more broadly in *Narrative Bonds*, the Victorian multinarrator novel optimistically highlights how much remains constant across different narrators' narrations.

The heterodiegetic narrator and Esther describe and value characters in the same way. Richard's legal advisor Vholes serves as a good example of their consensus, though a similar analysis could be done of almost any character. Both narrators compare Vholes to a consuming monster: Esther deems Vholes a "vampire," and the other narrator likens Vholes to a "cannibal" (*Bleak* 924, 622). In both narratives, Vholes gazes at clients as if he wants to eat them; he also speaks in an "inward," inaudible way in both narratives (607, 624).[11] One might contend that the narrators' matching descriptions of characters expose Dickens's limitations as an artist—an inability to complicate his flat characters. But the descriptions sound equally credible within each narrative. Esther's antipathy to Vholes is plausible on account of her motherly feelings toward Richard and her anxiety about how Richard's downfall will affect her beloved Ada. The heterodiegetic narrator's disgust with Vholes also rings true because the lawyer represents hypocrisy and the pointlessness of the Chancery case—two themes about which the narrator rages. The consistency of Vholes's char-acter across the two narratives, then, is both inconspicuous and convincing.

Esther and the heterodiegetic narrator agree on more than just charac-ters. They hold similar views on the moral and ethical issues at the heart of the novel, including charity and Chancery.[12] When the heterodiegetic narrator criticizes how Jo has been ignored by supposed do-gooders, he echoes Esther's

---

11. Hornback, also interested in the "parallels between Esther's narrative and the omni-scient narrative," demonstrates the similarities in the two narrators' descriptions of Woodcourt, Bucket, and Miss Flite (10).

12. J. Peters and Senf agree that the narrators "share a common moral stance" (Senf, "*Bleak*" 22). P. Collins likewise remarks that "the two narrators hold similar ideas and attitudes" ("Some" 135).

concerns about Mrs. Jellyby. Both narrators complain that the home is ignored by foreign-minded philanthropists. Similarly, the other narrator bemoans the pointlessness of Chadband's empty and obtuse attempt to "improve" Jo merely by lecturing at him (*Bleak* 409). Instead, he shows how the real help comes from "the charitable Guster," the fit-prone Snagsby servant who shares her "own supper" with Jo (415). The narrator identifies Guster's small acts of kindness as truly charitable and Christian—the opposite of Chadband's sham assistance. Similarly, when Ada and Esther visit a bricklayer's family with Mrs. Pardiggle, they frown upon her selfish, ineffective, and disingenuous method of doing charity. Esther's compassionate gesture—covering Jenny's dead baby with a handkerchief—resembles Guster's authentic and small-scale goodwill. The other narrator equates the "costly nonsense" of Chancery with the dense, omnipresent, and muddling London fog (14). The case, he remarks, "has passed into a joke" (17). Chancery members "mak[e] a pretence of equity with serious faces, as players might" (14). Esther echoes these sentiments by calling Chancery "a great gaming system" (265) that is treated by insiders more like "a Farce or a Juggler than . . . a court of Justice" (973–74). Both narrators lament—to use the names of Miss Flite's birds—the waste, want, ruin, despair, and folly of the case. One might say that these ideas—concentrating on the home country's needs, valuing a certain model of charity, and critiquing Chancery's devastation—are obvious themes of the book as a whole; indeed, these themes come through as such despite the two narrators. Esther and the heterodiegetic narrator share a value system.

Both narrators employ sarcastic and ironic takes on the social ills and hypocrisies that they witness. Critics have long noticed the heterodiegetic narrator's "scathing irony" (Serlen 565) and "wise, sardonic . . . sarcastic" voice (Moseley 36). Some scholars have also recognized Esther's own subtle brand of critical humor.[13] Other critics find that any evidence of Esther's sharp wit contradicts her character, further proving that Dickens was "simply inconsistent as a female speaker" (A. Taylor 133).[14] But the very note of Esther's humor—its avoidance of the overtly acerbic—matches rather than contradicts her character. Esther's trademark humor aligns with Eileen Gillooly's discussion of feminine humor, which, unlike easily recognized and more aggressive masculine humor, "works with extreme subtlety and delicately nuanced gestures to confound the political and affective meaning of the text" (xix). For example, when Mrs. Pardiggle tells Esther how she encourages her husband to contribute to

---

13. Axton writes, "Esther is a master of ironic commentary; she damns with faint praise, employs paraphrase with devastating effect" (545). Also see Deen, Eldredge, Graver, J. Peters, Rosso, and Zwerdling for more discussion of Esther's critical humor.

14. See P. Collins (in "Some") and Harvey for a similar perspective.

charity just as she directs her children to do so, Esther imagines two harried husbands—Mr. Pardiggle and Mr. Jellyby—sharing a moment: "Suppose Mr Pardiggle were to dine with Mr Jellyby, and suppose Mr Jellyby were to relieve his mind after dinner to Mr Pardiggle, would Mr Pardiggle, in return, make any confidential communication to Mr Jellyby? I was quite confused to find myself thinking this, but it came into my head" (*Bleak* 126). Esther sets up the joke, but she doesn't deliver the punch line. Instead, she retreats with her characteristic "confus[ion]" and disclaims agency for the thought. She lets the humor float up and out, blurring around the edges. She often safeguards her more pointed comments with parentheses, as if the parentheses will prevent or protect her from the fallout of such quips. Other times, Esther deadpans with silence or subtly mocks the status quo with a quick "of course."

Both narrators, therefore, express similar moral values in their narrations; both narrators use sarcasm extensively, although Esther's method is more covert; both narrators tell the same stories with the same characters; and the narrators strikingly coincide on their descriptions and evaluations of those characters. Esther and the heterodiegetic narrator are working together—not against each other in a battle for supremacy. Although Philip Collins bemoans that Dickens "missed a rather obvious trick" by not having Esther and the heterodiegetic narrator perceive characters differently, I think Dickens was purposefully avoiding that trick ("Some" 139).

QUESTIONING OMNISCIENCE

Although many critics proceed on the assumption that the heterodiegetic narrator is omniscient, frequently giving him the moniker of the "omniscient narrator," I argue that this narrator is, crucially, not omniscient.[15] Because most of the heterodiegetic narrator's chapters focus on the Dedlock family and its professional helpers, much of the aristocratic content of the novel is narrated by the heterodiegetic narrator. Such content, however, is not narrated omnisciently but as surface and from the outside. This narrative technique further flattens Lady Dedlock, queen of the fashionable sphere, into an image. On the other hand, Esther's first-person narration enables the production of a deep interiority that contrasts with the façade-oriented heterodiegetic narration.

---

15. P. Collins (in "Some"), J. Peters, and Toker argue that the heterodiegetic narrator is not omniscient. Guerard lists the privileges and limitations of this "roving conductor" narrator: He "can take us anywhere" but "as a rule could *not* go into the consciousness of the characters" (341).

Bleak House's heterodiegetic narrator does not display three of the four elements of omniscience that William Nelles outlines. In his valuable reexamination of Jane Austen's narrators, Nelles reasons that they are not omniscient, although they have frequently been labeled as such, because they don't regularly use the "four primary tools" in the omniscience "toolbox" ("Omniscience" 119): omnipotence, the narrator's awareness of the creation of the narrative; omnitemporality, where the narrator can move throughout time; omnipresence, where the narrator can move throughout space and be in different places simultaneously; and telepathy, reading characters' minds. *Bleak House*'s first narrator does not usually display omnipotence, omnitemporality, or telepathy,[16] though he does exhibit omnipresence. This narrator authoritatively reports in his opening chapter that there is "fog everywhere," followed by an itemized list of disparate places constituting that everywhere (*Bleak* 13).[17] But the heterodiegetic narrator does not admit to inventing or controlling the story he's telling (omnipotence). The narrator's use of the present tense and infrequent anachronies, such as flashbacks or flashforwards, keeps him tethered to the now (omnitemporality). And for the most part, the narrator does not impart characters' minds (telepathy). He often cites characters, groups (like the fashionable intelligence), or common knowledge for the information he reports to the reader. Early in the novel, when the narrator declares that Lady Dedlock "is childless," he reveals his ignorance of the truth (*Bleak* 21). When the narrator seemingly relays characters' thoughts, he prefaces them with the language of speculation: "maybe," "it may be," "seems," "one might guess," or "if." Other times, the narrator hazards an educated guess about a character's interiority based on his external actions or face. Tulkinghorn remains an enigma precisely because he allows no signal of his inner thoughts to broadcast from his body: "One could not even say he has been thinking all this while. . . . He has shown nothing but his shell" (168). The narrator occasionally seems to know Jo's thoughts, but such knowledge is usually conjecture based on imagining himself in Jo's place: "It must be very puzzling to see the good company going to the churches on Sundays, with their books in their hands, and to think (for perhaps Jo *does* think, at odd times) what does it all mean, and if it means anything to anybody, how comes it that it means nothing to me?" (257). Even here, the "perhaps" prevarication reveals that the sentences are only a supposition of Jo's thoughts.

---

16. W. Booth identifies "obtaining an inside view of another character" as the "most important single privilege" a narrator can possess (160).

17. Deen agrees that this narrator "does not have the key to anyone's consciousness" but "his eye is extraordinarily far-ranging" (206).

The omniscient "tools" employed by several characters within *Bleak House* further expose the heterodiegetic narrator's limits. Robyn R. Warhol establishes that Tulkinghorn and Bucket have omnipresent abilities, humanizing the one omniscient tool used by the heterodiegetic narrator ("Describing"). In a similar way, Nelles illustrates how the ability to read minds in an Austen novel is "a human rather than divine pursuit" since many characters can read minds with the same accuracy as the novels' narrators ("Omniscience" 124). Audrey Jaffe and Joan Douglas Peters consider Esther the more omniscient of the two narrators since she pens her story retrospectively, years after it occurs. As she writes, she already knows what will happen, and she occasionally anticipates the future via prolepsis and looks backward via analepsis, calling attention not only to her knowledge but also to her temporal freedom in telling her narrative. Just as the heterodiegetic narrator imaginatively accesses Jo's mind through sympathetically connecting with him, Esther claims that her "understanding. . . . seems to brighten" when she "love[s] a person very tenderly indeed" (*Bleak* 28). For both Esther and the other narrator, knowledge comes through sympathy with others. By comparison, an omniscient narrator's typical telepathy seems easy and unearned—it calls on no effort of sympathetic identification as a pathway to knowledge.

Admittedly, the other narrator sometimes "breach[es] his decorum" by breaking his own rules and becoming temporarily more omniscient (P. Collins, "Some" 132), like when the narrator foretells the death that awaits homebound Tulkinghorn or when the narrator very briefly reads minds without his trademark linguistic hedging. But these moments, generally made for dramatic and ironic effect—such as to highlight Tulkinghorn's arrogant ignorance as he heads to his death—should not earn the narrator the omniscient label. Esther's narration also includes moments of temporarily expanded privileges, though they are rarely discussed by critics. For example, she narrates two scenes in chapter 51—a tense meeting between Woodcourt and Vholes and the subsequent conversation between Woodcourt and Richard—as if she were present even though she wasn't. To use Phelan's terminology, sometimes "disclosure functions" (what the author needs to relay to the reader beyond the limitations of the narrative situation) trump "narrator functions" (what the narrator communicates in accordance with her narrative situation) (12). Esther's narration of the aforementioned scenes reveals the intimacy between Woodcourt and Esther despite Esther's engagement to Jarndyce at the time the scenes occur; Esther feels close enough to Woodcourt to recite his memory of events and conversations as if they were her own—it's as if they share a common memory. The concept of "disclosure functions" also rationalizes the other narrator's instances of uncharacteristic privilege.

SURFACE AND DEPTH

In *Desire and Domestic Fiction,* Armstrong outlines the rise of the domestic woman in literature. This new feminine ideal—first promoted by conduct books and then by novels—was frugal, self-regulating, efficient, active, modest, and the opposite of the shallow and materialistic aristocratic female. Armstrong argues that this female ideal unified the disparate groups that would eventually form the middle class. As this figure gained ground, Armstrong contends, eighteenth-century novels increasingly represented the conflict between classes as gender differences that could be resolved in marriage.[18] Inspired by but distinct from Armstrong's argument, I propose that in *Bleak House* the political contract between the upper and middle classes is not resolved by the sexual contract of marriage but by the generational contract between mother and daughter. The transition from an infirm, barren, and ineffectual aristocracy (Sir Leicester suffers from gout, has no children with Lady Dedlock, and fails to get his party's candidate elected) to a healthy, fertile, and capable middle class is not softened or settled by a marriage of members from different classes but by a natural passing of the torch from mother to daughter, from the aristocracy to the middle class, from the "bored to death" Lady Dedlock to her diligent, house keys-loving daughter, Esther Summerson (*Bleak 27*).[19] Through the story of Esther Summerson, *Bleak House* provides a fantasy of earned and bestowed legitimacy to a once illegitimate class. Esther rises above the "disgrace" of her illegitimacy through her own determination and hard work and through her mother's blessing (30). Society's center shifts from Lady Dedlock, who "has been at the centre of the fashionable intelligence" (22), to Esther, who works at the "centre" "of the whole little orderly system" (603).

The dual narrative highlights the contrast and transition between the aristocracy and the middle class. The external, surface-oriented perspective of the heterodiegetic narrator concentrates on Lady Dedlock and her circle, while the internal perspective of Esther allows her to create psychological depth and avoid the snares of a physically attractive surface. As Armstrong writes, the new ideal woman of the middle class "possessed psychological depth rather than a physically attractive surface. . . . the aristocratic woman represented surface instead of depth, embodied material instead of moral value, and dis-

---

18. By the mid-nineteenth century, Armstrong continues, the middle class no longer needed to portray itself as emergent. *Bleak House,* originally published serially in 1852–53, still concerns itself with resolving the conflict between the middle and upper classes, possibly because it is likely set earlier than its publication date. House writes, "The main story cannot have happened later than 1843–6, and is also assumed to be much earlier" (31).

19. Arac also discusses how *Bleak House*'s plot follows the rise of the middle class and the fall of the aristocracy (122–23).

played idle sensuality instead of constant vigilance and tireless concern for the well-being of others" (*Desire* 20). The novel starts with the heterodiegetic narrator but ends with Esther, a shift that embodies the descent of the moribund worlds of Chancery and fashion and the ascendancy of Esther's middle-class cohort.

The other narrator's first two chapters introduce the Court of Chancery and Lady Dedlock's "world of fashion," which "is not so unlike the Court of Chancery" because they are both "things of precedent and usage" (*Bleak* 20). The title of Esther's first chapter, "A Progress," indicates a forward-bound movement that contrasts with the stagnant, "deadened world" of fashion and the foggy, muddy, plodding Chancery. Esther not only gets the story moving by covering her entire childhood in her first chapter but also ends the novel, narrating its last chapter and word. The novel's double ending, the final chapters from each narrator, concludes with Lady Dedlock buried in the family mausoleum and her broken-down husband soon to follow her—a depressing end pictured in the novel's final illustration—and with Esther married, universally admired, and surrounded by a family and community who depend on and love her. The final words of the double ending—which even rhyme!—further emphasize the rise of one class and the fall of another. The heterodiegetic narrator's chapter on the Dedlocks concludes with the dreary finality of "dull repose" (985), and Esther's final sentence ends with a nonending, an imaginative musing and dash that suspend closure and herald continued development: "even supposing—" (989).

In *Bleak House,* Esther Summerson, the "little housewife" (562), incarnates the domestic ideal that Armstrong discusses. When she arrives at Bleak House as Ada's companion, Jarndyce sends Esther the housekeeping and cellar keys. She frequently rings, kisses, and caresses these keys when she feels less than dutiful to remind herself of the "trust" in her they symbolize (89). The key jingling is just one example of Esther's self-policing, another key aspect to the domestic ideal.[20] Frugality—one of the core traits of the domestic woman—is one of Esther's most prominent housekeeping charms; Jarndyce comments, "There never was . . . such a Dame Durden for making money last" (942). Esther assists Caddy to plan a respectable wedding and fashion a trousseau from a mere ten-pound note. Guppy interrupts Esther's bookkeeping to propose to her. Furthermore, the ideal domestic female is active, and Esther bustles throughout the book doing housework, errands, and favors for others. Esther is a homemaker in the truest sense of the word; after witnessing the

---

20. Hall argues that Esther rigorously polices herself because she is illegitimate and must "keep herself . . . out of trouble" (172). Kennedy contends that Esther's self-policing functions as a critique of the female ideal Esther is struggling to attain.

chaotic Jellyby lodgings, Ada quips that Esther could "make a home out of even this house" (58). And finally, per Armstrong's argument, the men and women of the novel adore this domestic goddess: Esther fields three marriage proposals as well as constant praise from friends and acquaintances for the precise qualities that make her the ideal domestic woman.

While Esther encapsulates the new domestic ideal, Lady Dedlock embodies the model aristocratic female, who, according to Armstrong, was defined by showiness, materiality, wealth, and status. Affluent and beautiful, Lady Dedlock has "conquered *her* world" and is always "looked after by admiring eyes" (*Bleak* 22, 651). Her life is a whirlwind of leisure, entertainment, and traveling: "concert, assembly, opera, theatre, drive" (182). Lady Dedlock also lacks the household management skills that Esther possesses. Many of Lady Dedlock's servants are out of her control: Hortense defies her and tries to frame her for murder, Rosa leaves her to be educated and married, and Mrs. Rouncewell is ultimately more loyal to her son than to her mistress.

Furthermore, just as the aristocratic female was defined by her surface, Lady Dedlock is constantly fetishized as an image. When Weevle rents out Nemo's old room in Krook's shop, he decorates the dwelling with "a choice collection of copper-plate impressions from that truly national work, The Divinities of Albion, or Galaxy Gallery of British Beauty, representing ladies of title and fashion" (330). We later learn that Lady Dedlock's portrait is one orb in this illustrious galaxy.[21] Lady Dedlock's impressive portrait at Chesney Wold, "a perfect likeness," charms and dazes Guppy (110). The grand portrait in Chesney Wold so resembles Lady Dedlock that it starts to stand in for her when she is absent. Sir Leicester, often abandoned by the restless Lady Dedlock but detained at Chesney Wold due to his gout, looks to the painting as Lady Dedlock's substitute: "My Lady is at present represented, near Sir Leicester, by her portrait" (256). After her death he "reposes in his old place before [his] Lady's picture" (983); the best replacement for her presence—during her life and after her death—is her painting.

Lady Dedlock's crystallization into an image and an idol has deadly consequences, which suggests that the aristocratic female's method of representation is dangerous and ineffective. Lady Dedlock eventually crumbles under the weight of such idolatry, the burden of being "set up for the world to respect" on a "gaudy platform" (838, 659). She is eventually smothered by having to live up to the much-circulated image of herself. The illustration titled "Sunset in the long Drawing-room at Chesney Wold" (see figure 1) fea-

---

21. As Oost notes, by this time, "a technological and economic shift" made reproductions of paintings and portraits, as well as portraits themselves, more affordable and more available to the middle classes (150).

FIGURE 1. "Sunset in the long Drawing-room at Chesney Wold." *Albert and Shirley Small Special Collections Library, University of Virginia.*

tures a shadow rising on Lady Dedlock's portrait; once we see this image of her image, Lady Dedlock becomes increasingly associated with shadows until she dies. The heterodiegetic narrator's description of sunset in the drawing room specifies that a "weird shade falls" on her portrait "as if a great arm held a veil or hood, watching an opportunity to draw it over her" (641). As the sun sets, "the shadow" consumes the portrait like "threatening hands raised up" (642). The shadow that ascends over her portrait seemingly infects her; the next illustration that features Lady Dedlock is captioned "Shadow" (see figure 2). She becomes the shadow—Phiz draws her as a semitransparent ghost. The text also emphasizes her ghostliness: The heterodiegetic narrator writes that she is "very pale," and Bucket comments that she "don't look quite healthy" (813, 814). Looking for Lady Dedlock in an earlier scene, Guppy peers "into the shade" of her home's library and nearly mistakes her arrival with that of a ghost (533). Meanwhile, Bucket plans to search through the snowy and "shadowed places" for Lady Dedlock (864). In the accompanying illustration, "The Morning," Lady Dedlock's body is draped on a set of stairs in the shadow of the entrance to the graveyard. Steig comments that her "corpse has been reduced almost to a thing by Browne's treatment of it as part of a pattern of

FIGURE 2. "Shadow." *Albert and Shirley Small Special Collections Library, University of Virginia.*

light and *shade*" (155; emphasis added). Indeed, the play of light and shadow on her body recalls the play of light and shadow on her portrait in the earlier illustration. The Dedlock mausoleum looms large in the novel's last illustration, completing Lady Dedlock's illustrated downfall.

All portraits in *Bleak House,* whether they appear in Esther's or the heterodiegetic narrator's sections, have sinister implications. The Chesney Wold drawing room is described by the heterodiegetic narrator as an illustrated cemetery. The Dedlock family portraits are vivified only for a few moments—in the sunset or when the house is being shown to visitors—only to be killed, over and over again, with the return of darkness. As Regina B. Oost points out, these family portraits "express not power, but decline" (149). Guppy's portrait is "more like than life" (*Bleak* 614), a description that echoes Lady Dedlock's eerie metamorphosis into her portrait. Only Guster admires the Snagsby portraits—"of Mr Snagsby looking at Mrs Snagsby, and of Mrs Snagsby looking at Mr Snagsby" (157)—that exemplify the detrimental cycle of suspicion and surveillance that plagues the Snagsby marriage. The proudly displayed paintings of Mrs. Badger's two previous husbands function like death warrants. Husband number one, Captain Swosser, sat for his portrait while he was ill and possibly dying with "fever" (206). Additionally, in Phiz's illustration of the scene, "The family portraits at Mr Bayham Badger's" (see figure 3), a skull leers in the background of the second husband's, Professor Dingo's, portrait. Notably, the Badgers' walls only hold portraits of the dead husbands and of Mrs. Badger's dead identities as their wives; there is no portrait of Mrs. Badger as Mrs. Badger, a noticeable absence that solidifies the link between portraits and death. There is no mention of the book's virtuous characters—such as Ada, Esther, Jarndyce, and Woodcourt—sitting for portraits or displaying portraits of themselves.

Esther is suspicious of the image, of mirrors, of being reduced to her appearance; thereby, she recoils from being the "unrequited image imprinted on [Guppy's] art" and his "idol" (510, 632). When Guppy proposes to and subsequently stalks Esther, she expresses her nascent skepticism of the image. When he arrives at Bleak House, Esther is embarrassed by his near-obsessive attention: "He looked at me with an attention that quite confused me" (148). Although Guppy has only seen Esther a few times before this meeting, he claims that her "image has ever since been fixed in my breast" (153). In the chapter's illustration, "In Re Guppy. Extraordinary proceedings" (see figure 4), Guppy dramatically bends down on one knee, smart and smiling; Esther, on the other hand, sits demurely and concentrates on writing. The writing table separates them. In the text, Esther indicates that she is engaged in the "business" of bills and bookkeeping when Guppy arrives at the house (148); she also

FIGURE 3. "The family portraits at Mr Bayham Badger's." *Albert and Shirley Small Special Collections Library, University of Virginia.*

admits that she moves behind her desk as a barrier against the animated and tipsy Guppy. This illustration, the only time we visually see Esther in the act of writing, reinforces how her writing functions as protection against Guppy's attempts to crystallize her in an image. Guppy may stare at Esther, but Esther responds by staring at her own writing, resisting Guppy's efforts to make her

FIGURE 4. "In Re Guppy. Extraordinary proceedings." *Albert and Shirley Small Special Collections Library, University of Virginia.*

into the fixed image that he has been carrying around in his heart and mind like a locket.

Guppy's devotion continues to confuse and alarm Esther. She notices him one night at the theatre, and she expresses how uncomfortable his unceasing gaze makes her:

To know that that absurd figure was always gazing at me, and always in that demonstrative state of despondency, put such a constraint upon me that I did not like to laugh at the play, or to cry at it, or to move, or to speak. I seemed able to do nothing naturally. (203)

Guppy's behavior forces Esther to stiffen and freeze in constraint—to become unnatural—as if his stare were forcing his image of her upon her. Guppy's eyes, "always gazing" and present "wherever [she] looked," are omnipresent and relentless, much like the public's interest in Lady Dedlock's actions and movements. Finding herself unable to laugh, cry, move, or speak, Esther temporarily resembles the stoic, taciturn, and reserved figure and manner of her mother, Lady Dedlock. Guppy's relentless attentions, therefore, allow Esther to experience the imprisoning sensation of being treated as a publicly available image. To her discomfort, Esther becomes the play rather than an anonymous audience member who can watch the stage happenings without being watched in return.

The heterodiegetic narrator complies with Esther's own desires to create depth and avoid the image; although the other narrator could watch and describe Esther from the outside, as he does with all the characters in his section, he spares her this treatment. The heterodiegetic narrator maintains a respectful distance from Esther's narrative. While Lisa Sternlieb reads an undesirable neglect in this distance, I find a desirable trust. Sternlieb claims that "the narrator is expert at overlooking Esther's narrative" (84) because he is, figuratively, a bad father like so many of the novel's neglectful parents; in contrast, I interpret such "overlooking" as respect for Esther's capacity to narrate and compliance with Esther's decisions as to her own representation. For all the critical talk about the heterodiegetic narrator's mastery and dominance, the heterodiegetic narrator doesn't retell the events that Esther narrates as if he could narrate them better or more completely. On the whole, *Bleak House* is not a "*repeating* narrative" (Genette, *Narrative* 116). As Genette writes, in such a narrative, "the same event can be told several times not only with stylistic variations . . . but also with variations in 'point of view'" (115). In chapter 51, for example, Esther spends one sentence relaying Jo's death, an event she likely learned about from either Woodcourt or Jarndyce. Jo's heartbreaking death was hauntingly depicted in chapter 47 of the other narration, but Esther's brief and vague description—including calling Jo "poor boy" rather than by his name—softens this rare instance of repetition (*Bleak* 789). Right before he dies, Jo spends a few sentences telling Mr. Snagsby about Esther's visit, but Esther never mentions seeing Jo after her illness. Generally, one narrative takes over where the other leaves off rather than the other narrative rehashing and returning to actions previously narrated. The two narrators, therefore, act like equally important relay runners rather than as a pair of unequal or rival narrators.

One of the oldest and most insistent criticisms of Esther could have been mitigated or prevented by having the other narrator treat Esther differently. Critics complain that Dickens forces Esther to naively, clumsily, and annoy-ingly narrate her own virtues. Dickens's friend and biographer John Forster, who was otherwise very fond of *Bleak House,* articulates this exact critique: "Mr Dickens undertook more than man could accomplish when he resolved to make her the *naïve* revealer of her own good qualities" (P. Collins, *Dickens* 304). Dickens could have taken advantage of his own unique narrative struc-ture to allow the heterodiegetic narrator to see Esther and to disclose her merits to the reader. Dickens, however, decided to undertake "more than man could accomplish" and leave Esther to her own devices. Esther is Esther's own problem. One of the lingering mysteries in the novel's conclusion is whether Esther regains her beauty as her husband Woodcourt smilingly asserts she has. Many critics overrule Esther's own ambiguous words on the matter and prefer to believe Woodcourt's estimation over Esther's.[22] The heterodiegetic narrator could have easily stepped in at this uncertain juncture and provided readers with a definitive description of Esther's appearance, but he doesn't. Since Dickens also chooses not to insert an illustration of the happily married couple, the reader is doubly frustrated in their desire to know the truth about Esther's beauty beyond Esther's vague words on the subject. With Esther's own words is where the novel, time and again, leaves the question of Esther's identity.

Esther's appearance in the heterodiegetic narrative would have problema-tized the very representation of herself she creates for the reader. Since the heterodiegetic narrator narrates surfaces, only occasionally and temporar-ily accessing the depth beneath, including Esther in his purview would have made her a character of surface rather than of depth. The other narrator does tease the reader with an anticipated glimpse of Esther at the end of chap-ter 56 but doesn't deliver on it. Bucket arrives at Jarndyce's home and asks Jarndyce to speak to Esther about whether she can accompany Bucket on his search for Lady Dedlock. Jarndyce goes upstairs to converse with Esther while Bucket waits downstairs; Jarndyce returns to tell Bucket that Esther will join them immediately, but before we can see her quickly descending the stairs, the chapter ends and the next one is narrated by Esther, who takes up the story

---

22. Broderick and Grant, Kearns, and Zwerdling all conclude that Esther has regained her beauty and that she is just too insecure to know it or too modest to admit it.

precisely where the other narrator leaves off. When Esther needs to enter the stage, she will also be the narrator. The only evidence in the novel that the heterodiegetic narrator may have "seen" Esther is the first sentence of chapter 7: "While Esther sleeps, and while Esther wakes, it is still wet weather down at the place in Lincolnshire" (*Bleak* 103). Having narrated chapter 6, Esther finishes that chapter by ringing her housekeeping keys "hopefully to bed"; therefore, the first sentence of chapter 7, which references Esther sleeping and waking, functions as a clear topical transition between Esther's narrative and the heterodiegetic narrative. This handoff marks the novel's first changeover from Esther's narrative to the heterodiegetic narrative. Perhaps experimentally, Dickens made use of a more obvious verbal transition between the two narrators than he ever utilizes subsequently. Although some critics consider this one instance as if it were representative of the relationship between the narrators throughout the book, Dickens never employs such a transition again. In fact, the heterodiegetic narrator never again includes Esther's name unless it is spoken in dialogue by a character, which occurs rarely. Even when characters in the other narration refer to Esther, they often avoid using her name, instead calling her "she" (318), "a subject" (324), and "young lady" (715).

The heterodiegetic narrator, therefore, declines to watch Esther, describe her, or even mention her unless a character does; such behavior aligns with Esther's own refusal to describe her appearance. By contrast, almost as soon as the heterodiegetic narrator introduces Lady Dedlock, he provides a lengthy and detailed physical description of her:

> She has beauty still, and, if it be not in its heyday, it is not yet in its autumn. She has a fine face—originally of a character that would be rather called very pretty than handsome, but improved into classicality by the acquired expression of her fashionable state. Her figure is elegant, and has the effect of being tall. (22–23)

Every aspect of her attractive yet aging appearance—the quality of her beauty, her face, her expression, her figure—is touched on, depicted, and qualified. Her features are described as valuable possessions she has managed to hold onto: She "has beauty still," "has a fine face," and has even "acquired" a certain dignified "expression" over time. At the tail end of the above description, the Honourable Bob Stables, as befits his horse-inspired name, extols Lady Dedlock as "the best-groomed woman in the whole stud" (23), further emphasizing that her outer appearance makes her a prized object. Because the other narrator never introduces Esther into his narrative, she evades a similar physical description, and her value can be found elsewhere.

In her own narrative, Esther avoids explaining her appearance, even after smallpox scars her face. Self-description is an artistic challenge for any first-person narrator, but Esther seems demurely determined not to meet that challenge. In comparison, by *Jane Eyre*'s second chapter, the eponymous heroine, whom Esther resembles in many ways, uses her reflection in the red room mirror to linger on "the strange little figure there gazing at [her]" (C. Brontë 18). In Esther's opening chapter, chapter 3, Guppy conveniently points to a looking glass, "in case [she] should wish to look at [her]self" (*Bleak* 43). Esther "took a peep at [her] bonnet in the glass to see if it was neat." Furtively and quickly checking the neatness of her bonnet yet not inspecting her face, Esther forgoes the first-person narrator's standard device of a mirror to describe her appearance for the reader. Similarly, when her mother's face becomes "like a broken glass to [her]" (292), Esther refuses to exploit the unexpected reflection to communicate her appearance to the reader. When a recovered Esther studies her post-illness face in the mirror, she exclaims, "I was very much changed—O, very, very much" (572), but she tantalizingly avoids clarifying the particulars of that change. Although the disease effaces Esther by removing her previous surface, her habitual evasion of self-description highlights how Esther has always effaced herself by deflecting attention away from her appearance and retreating from visibility.[23]

When most characters first glimpse Esther's altered visage, they behave as if they register no change; their reactions imply that Esther isn't defined by her appearance but by a deeper Esther-ness that remains untouched by the devastating illness. This feedback aligns with Armstrong's contrast between the depths of the ideal domestic female and the surface of the aristocratic female. After Esther has sufficiently recovered, she anxiously meets with Ada but detects nothing in Ada's look but "all love, all fondness, all affection. Nothing else in it—no, nothing, nothing!" (*Bleak* 588). As James H. Broderick and John E. Grant observe, "Ada assures Esther of an identity . . . independent of her appearance" (255). When Richard meets the convalescing Esther, he cheerfully remarks, "Always the same dear girl!" (*Bleak* 591), reiterating the sentiment even once she dramatically raises her veil. Ada's and Richard's equivalent reactions suggest that what defines Esther is not her appearance, face, or surface; what defines Esther to the world is not what defines Lady Dedlock to the world. This is rare for a Victorian heroine, particularly a Dickensian one—even the names of Little Dorrit, Estella, Lucie, Bella Wilfer, and Rosa Bud point to—and, to a certain extent, describe—their appearances. Esther's

---

23. Other critics use the term "effacement" with regards to Esther. Jaffe claims that Esther forms an identity through effacement of both her identity and her knowledge. Eldredge discusses Esther's effacement as the consequence of Esther trying too hard to be perfect and loved.

suitors still love Esther after her illness, and Jarndyce even proposes after her face has scarred. When Woodcourt finally confesses his love to Esther, he echoes the sentiment that Esther hasn't changed: "I learned in a moment that my scarred face was all unchanged to him" (937). Even Guppy, who hastily revokes his proposal after first observing his beloved's transformation, reinstates his offer of marriage when he realizes he still loves Esther despite her marked face.

The illustrations of post-illness Esther do not display her face, showing the implied author's respect for Esther's suspicions of the image and sympathy with her aim to—as Armstrong writes about Samuel Richardson's *Pamela*—redirect desire from "the surface of the female body and into its depths" (*Desire* 120). Even the majority of pre-illness illustrations conceal her face; therefore, the rationale behind the post-illness face avoidance cannot just be Dickens's or Phiz's fear that illustrating Esther's scarred face would be improper. Lynette Felber observes Esther's "vague" appearance in the illustrations, often showing her "from the back or in profile" (14), and John O. Jordan notes "the motif of the hidden face" in the illustrations (35).[24] To be more specific, of the eighteen illustrations in *Bleak House* that include Esther, only eight show her face. Of those eight, six position her in profile and reveal only part of her face. In one of the two illustrations that display Esther's whole face, her small figure is positioned in the background and lacks detail; the other image, which depicts her bashful embrace of Woodcourt's flowers, is the novel's only close-up of Esther's pretty face. The first three illustrations of Esther, however, hide Esther's face from view, just as the last three illustrations of Esther do. In "The little old Lady," the novel's first illustration, the faces of Miss Flite, Richard, and Ada are visible while Esther firmly parks her back to the viewer, a stance that sets the tone for the rest of the novel's illustrations. In "Miss Jellyby," the viewer discerns Caddy's petulant features, but Esther's hair and the angle of her body artfully shroud her face. In "The Lord Chancellor copies from memory," Esther's bonnet and posture screen her face.

Esther's desire to emphasize and protect her own depth, however, leads her to flatten Ada into a surface alter ego. Ada's attractiveness captivates almost every character, especially Esther, who obsessively catalogues her beauty. The litany of cutesy names prefaced by "my" that Esther uses for Ada—"my pet," "my darling," "my love," "my beauty," "my dear girl"—exposes Esther's possessive attitude toward Ada and solidifies Ada's status as "a beautiful golden girl"

---

24. A. Taylor mentions in passing that "most of the illustrations present [Esther] with her back towards us" (137). Steig also comments that after suffering from smallpox, Esther's "scarred face will remain hidden throughout" the remaining illustrations (148).

FIGURE 5. "Sir Leicester Dedlock." *Albert and Shirley Small Special Collections Library, University of Virginia.*

(Eldredge 270).[25] Esther feels maddeningly uncomfortable when Guppy stares at her—both when he proposes and at the theatre—but that distress does not prevent Esther from constantly staring at Ada, even while Ada lies sleeping. In the eight illustrations that include Ada, her whole face (or nearly her whole face) is visible; this visibility contrasts with the illustrations of Esther and implies that Ada is more visually available than Esther. For example, in "Sir Leicester Dedlock" (see figure 5), Esther's back confronts the viewer as she demurely looks down and away from Sir Leicester while Ada sits off to the side with an open book, her whole face visible. In "Light" (see figure 6), Ada—whose face is completely visible—clings to a rakishly indifferent Richard while balancing herself on a messy pile of books. Esther looks on in profile while an extra-wide bonnet ribbon conceals her face. Both illustrations divide

25. Eldredge, Hall, and Michie assess Esther's treatment of Ada as domineering, even voyeuristic.

FIGURE 6. "Light." *Albert and Shirley Small Special Collections Library, University of Virginia.*

Ada from the other characters and particularly from Esther. The illustration "Sir Leicester Dedlock" visually separates Ada from the rest of the company by placing her to the far right in a claustrophobic window seat; by positioning Ada in the cell-like space behind a partially closed curtain and directly underneath a caged bird, the illustration heightens the sense of imprisonment and division in the scene. In "Light," the center bookcase becomes a visual chasm with Ada and Richard on one side and Esther on the other; although Ada looks pleadingly at Esther and Esther reaches out to Ada, the illustration movingly conveys how Ada's marriage has severed her from Esther. Ada's visual availability contrasts with Esther's visual unavailability and seems to physically isolate her more and more from other characters.

Ada functions as Lady Dedlock's false daughter, the more aristocratic girl who is poised to ascend and reign but who must ultimately fall so that Esther can rise as Lady Dedlock's true daughter. Although Esther often tries to mask the social difference between herself and Ada by portraying their relationship as that of intimate friends or sisters, she is hired by Jarndyce to serve as Ada's companion. As Felber reminds us, Ada receives the room with the best view because of "her higher social status as a legitimate child" (15). Lady Dedlock intuits Ada's higher status when she unexpectedly meets with

Ada, Esther, and Jarndyce at the lodge during a rainfall. She asks Jarndyce to introduce her to Ada first, and "she took a graceful leave of Ada" but "none of" Esther (*Bleak* 299). Both Zwerdling and Eldredge note the reversal that happens by the end of the novel: Esther, who was seemingly destined for a less-than-desirable marriage with the fatherly Jarndyce, suddenly marries the young and handsome Woodcourt, while Ada, whose life and romance initially showed so much promise, is now a young widow with a child and returns to live with Jarndyce at Bleak House. In crucial ways, Ada's story and choices resemble Lady Dedlock's, as Gillian West observes. Both receive constant praise for their beauty, have stakes in the Jarndyce and Jarndyce Chancery suit, become romantically involved with military men, and have children by those men whom their lovers never meet. Just as Lady Dedlock falls, Ada must also fall to make room for Esther, the daughter who can fulfill the generational contract by bringing about the social transition to the new type of domestic female.

Esther simultaneously disowns a beautiful surface and embraces character depth—she directs readers to "the depths of her private feelings" in her narrative (Armstrong, *Desire* 122), particularly in the portion that relays her sickbed experience. As she worsens, Esther uses spatial descriptions that indicate she is falling beneath and away from the surface of her normal life. She drifts "far off" from her own self; her ordinary life has "retired into a remote distance" "like an old remembrance" and remains at a "great distance, on the healthy shore" (*Bleak* 555). She is both "*falling* ill" (emphasis added) and feels like she has "*crossed* a dark lake" (emphasis added). A chasm of time ("old remembrance") and increasing metaphoric space both horizontal and vertical separate her regular life—her experiences, habits, chores, and duties—from her inner self. She renders this interior landscape as a deep pit out of which she's scaling "colossal staircases" but is unable to "reach the top"—the surface. Though blindness is a rare effect of smallpox that neither Charley nor Jo experiences during their bouts of the disease, Esther's blindness emphasizes the internal nature of these sickbed hallucinations. Not able to see what goes on around her or watch others, Esther concentrates on herself, orienting the reader's interest toward the hellish depths of her psyche. She recurrently admits that these incidents are enigmatic, personal, and probably not appropriate for the reader's eyes, but she "dare[s]" to record them anyway and welcomes the reader to voyeuristically travel through her diseased inner universe (556).

During this illness, Esther also separates herself from the women of surface in her life: Ada and Lady Dedlock. Esther confesses her desire to be flung off "a flaming necklace, or ring, or starry circle of some kind, of which *I* was one of the beads" (556). Helena Michie—who proposes that Esther becomes a viable self only after her illness visually differentiates her from her mother[26]— perceives the necklace moment as "a prophetic separation from her mother whose association with jewelry begins with her introduction into the text" (206). Furthermore, both Ada and Lady Dedlock are depicted wearing bracelets, another type of circular jewelry. Esther notices Ada sleeping "with a little bracelet [Richard] had given her clasped upon her arm" (*Bleak* 273), and Weevle's portrait of Lady Dedlock features her posed with a bulky fur "and a bracelet on her arm" (510). Ada's bracelet, a present from Richard, prefigures the wedding ring he later gives her, and Lady Dedlock's bracelet symbolizes her status and style. Esther's wish "to be taken off from the rest" denotes her rejection of an identity that forces her to be a beautiful object (556).

The cagey way Esther narrates her romance with Woodcourt also redirects the reader's interest from Esther's surface narrative—her relationship with and engagement to Jarndyce—to a hidden narrative, a bits-and-pieces narrative that only occasionally pierces through to the main narrative. While many critics judge Esther's method of revealing this romance to be awkward and cloying, it again reveals her avoidance of surfaces and preference for the depths beneath. When she confesses her feelings about Woodcourt to the reader, she locates such knowledge "in the secret depths of [her] heart" (573). Esther tends to disclose information about Woodcourt at the very end of chapters (see chapters 13, 14, 17, and 35) and, thereby, out of chronological order: "I have omitted to mention in its place" and "I have forgotten to mention—at least I have not mentioned" (214, 237). Such willful anachronies, to use Genette's term,[27] appear to marginalize the Woodcourt narrative while actually placing it in the privileged position of chapter conclusion. When Esther first meets Woodcourt at a dinner party, she omits him entirely; when she belatedly mentions his attendance at the end of the chapter, she holds back his name; in a later chapter, when she converses with "a medical gentleman" named Woodcourt, we don't know until the end of that chapter that Woodcourt and the mysterious dinner party guest are one and the same (*Bleak* 232). Esther forces the reader to be a detective, reading between the lines and below the surface, so the reader can learn of "the little secret [she has] thus far tried to keep" before Esther acknowledges it halfway through the book (570). After Esther accepts Jarndyce's proposal and burns Woodcourt's flowers, the reader must be even more vigilant for signs that she still loves Woodcourt. Perhaps Esther has

---

26. Gaughan similarly argues that "Esther's fever . . . effectively makes her a new person" (90).

27. Genette defines anachronies as "the various types of discordance between the two orderings of story and narrative" (*Narrative* 36).

learned to be suspicious of straightforward romance from Ada's and Richard's negative example. Their romance ignites quickly and visibly. After just a few days at Bleak House, Esther watches Ada and Richard share a tender moment that seals their inevitable romance. Esther's ominous descriptions of the "picture"—with the lovers' "shadows blend[ing]" on the wall and performing a "ghostly motion"—connect visibility to mortality and prefigure Lady Dedlock's dangerous descent into shadowiness (93).

I read Esther's final paragraphs as a reiteration of the themes already discussed: rejection of the image and endorsement of writing as the best method to create feminine depth. Felber, Jordan, Anny Sadrin, and Judith Wilt revel in the openness of Esther's final sentence and its refutation of novelistic closure;[28] Felber and Sadrin appreciate the feminine energy in the final chapter— the presence of the moon and Esther's two daughters. In the midst of such empowerment, I argue that Esther alludes to her old looks not because she wants them back but because she's pleased that Woodcourt's love isn't based on her appearance: "I have been thinking, that I thought it was impossible that you *could* have loved me any better, even if I had retained [my looks]" (*Bleak* 989). Woodcourt tries to fix the ostensible problem by complimenting her. Many critics follow his lead, but Esther is not looking for a compliment. She immediately deflects attention away from her looks and disowns the praise. Rather than simply call her pretty, Woodcourt informs Esther that she is "*prettier* than [she] ever w[as]" (989; emphasis added). Esther will have none of that. She puts this arc of magically increased beauty—where else?— onto Ada. After suffering through Richard's death, Ada "is more beautiful than ever" (988). The grief has "purified" her face and "given it a diviner quality." Beauty is linked to suffering for both Lady Dedlock and Ada. And so Esther stubbornly claims her happiness by maintaining that she "did not know that" she was pretty again (989); thankfully, she can still avoid that fate! In her final paragraph, Esther disposes of the beauty Woodcourt assigns her. She distributes it left and right and leaves no amount of beauty to settle on her: "But I know that my dearest little pets are very pretty, and that my darling is very beautiful, and that my husband is very handsome, and that my guardian has the brightest and most benevolent face that ever was seen; and that they can very well do without much beauty in me—even supposing—" (989). Her final sentence implicitly reminds "the unknown friend to whom [she] write[s]"

---

28. Jordan deems these final words the "only trace that remains of that other, more passionate Esther" in her final chapter; he laments that Esther "hides behind a mask of modesty" for the rest of the chapter (78).

(perhaps the heterodiegetic narrator and/or the reader[29]) not to understand her or value her in terms of her appearance (985).

Conversely, the heterodiegetic narrator's final chapter—the novel's penultimate chapter—emphasizes the downfall of the Dedlocks and the decay of Chesney Wold by representing both as fallen images. Previously, Chesney Wold was a tourist attraction, and Guppy requests and receives a tour of the much-lauded residence. But now, Chesney Wold "is shut up, and it is a show-house no longer" (983). It becomes "a vast blank of overgrown house," "abandoned to darkness and vacancy" (984, 985). The impressive façade of a "show-house" is replaced with a "blank"—Chesney Wold is no longer a visible object in the "darkness." Paralleling his habitation, Sir Leicester is "shrunken," "invalided, bent, and almost blind," and he sits by all that remains of his wife—her portrait (983, 981). To the last, relying on hearsay ("The story goes" and "The truth is said to be" [981]) and on the external appearances of characters and of the house, the heterodiegetic narrator conveys that the aristocratic world of glamorized surfaces has failed and decayed "even to the stranger's eye" (985). This descent, however, is tempered by the same values of compassion and community that prevail in Esther's narrative. George, accompanied by Phil, tends to the ailing Sir Leicester instead of joining his brother's steel factory. George tells his brother, "I am able to be of some trifle of use to Sir Leicester Dedlock since his illness" (957); taking this position also allows him to be close to his aging mother, the Chesney Wold housekeeper, who is "harder of hearing now" (982). And even though George's brother initially scoffs at George's decision, the brothers, long estranged, shake hands and reconcile, in mutual respect for their different paths.

ESTHER'S "LITTLE BODY" AND NOBODY

Esther may be "effaced" in her avoidance of the image, but she is not a disembodied narrator. Although Esther shows uneasiness when her "little body" appears in her narrative and claims that it "will soon fall into the back-ground now" (*Bleak* 40), this moment "reminds us of [her body's] presence" (Michie 203). Anne Robinson Taylor argues that Dickens "refus[es] to let [Esther] experience herself as a person of flesh and blood" (136), but Esther does reference her body, often isolating and naming specific body parts: her waist, lap, hands, arms, breast, bosom, heart, neck, head, hair, forehead, face, cheek,

---

29. Jordan ruminates that this "unknown friend" could be us (the readers), her mother, or "Esther herself. Her narrative may be addressed to an 'unknown' part of herself that she realizes must be left behind if she is to move forward in her life" (75).

lips, and eyes. She reports her body's actions including blushing, trembling, laughing, shuddering, kissing, walking, and writing. She not only talks about what she sees but also what she hears, smells, touches, and feels. Her human body requires respite, and she mentions feeling tired, falling asleep, occasionally dreaming, and then waking. Because Esther possesses a body, she is vulnerable to the contagion that emanates from Tom-all-Alone's and catches the smallpox after she interacts with sick Jo and nurses Charley through her bout of the illness.[30]

Throughout the narrative, Esther habitually narrates her crying fits—a safe, feminine way to give reign to the language of the body. She cries when she first meets Jarndyce in the carriage to Greenleaf; after Guppy's proposal; when Jarndyce gives her Charley as a "present" (*Bleak* 385); when she learns about Woodcourt's heroism at sea; when she reads the proposal letter from Jarndyce; when she first sees her scarred face in the mirror; when Lady Dedlock divulges her identity; when she leaves a married Ada at Richard's squalid apartment; when Woodcourt finally proposes; when Jarndyce transfers her to Woodcourt in front of the new Bleak House; and as she writes her narrative. These tears function as an outlet for various unspoken and even unacknowledged desires: her attraction to Woodcourt, her anxiety over Guppy's and Jarndyce's romantic overtures, and her obsession with beautiful Ada. Esther portrays these crying sessions as periods when her body is in control. She "cannot quite help" the tears, and they "will have their way" (31, 987). She feels "bound to confess that [she] cried," as if imprisoned by the waterworks (962). Allan Conrad Christensen, reading *Bleak House* in terms of contagion, reads this lachrymose Esther as an "underground self": "the sick Esther who threatens with her contagion to contaminate the story of the healthy Esther" (224, 222). While I agree with his reading of Esther's doubleness, I highlight how this "underground self" is strongly related to bodily response. Esther worries that her body impedes her narration. Confessing that she "cannot quite help" crying while writing her narrative, she notes that she can only "go on again properly" once she has "wiped [the tears] away now" (*Bleak* 31). Esther thinks her sobs prevent her from being a "proper[ ]" narrator. They detour her from the past to the "now" of narrating and block the movement of her story. Esther's promise to the reader that her "little body will soon fall into the back-ground now" (40) seems predicated on a belief that a narrator should not be distracted by her body. Esther largely skips over her reaction to

30. Arac discusses how the "simultaneously scientific and moral" references to disease in *Bleak House* "combin[e] the medical dangers of disease and the political dangers of revolution" (131). Burgan, Choi, and Christensen also examine *Bleak House* in terms of contagion and disease.

her mother's death, implying that she is still too physically and emotionally affected by it to narrate it: "I proceed to other passages of my narrative" (916). In these moments, she seems frustrated that she cannot behave as a heterodiegetic narrator would, unhampered by a body.

The other narrator doesn't have a body, and yet he tries to imagine himself having one. When Warhol mentions that this narrator is like Esther's father Nemo in being "Nobody," she doesn't intend the pun that I want to emphasize (*Gendered* 153). The narrator can see what Bucket does when he is alone and locked in Lady Dedlock's room. Precisely because he is a nobody (with no body), the heterodiegetic narrator can see that "which nobody *does* see" (*Bleak* 861).[31] In a different piece, Warhol calls attention to how many of the spaces in *Bleak House* "are characterized by smell, touch, sound, and even taste" and therefore are "registered not just by the eyes but by multiple parts of the body, from the nose to the skin to the mouth" ("Describing" 612). Warhol shows how the other narrator "intermittently adopts the viewpoint of characters on the scene in order to build up the visual and visceral details of the space as the characters experience them" (616); however, to my view, sometimes the narrator seems to be doing the smelling, hearing, tasting, and feeling himself rather than reporting a character's sensations. Warhol's analysis of chapter 2, "In Fashion," reveals that the narrator's sensory descriptions of drenched Chesney Wold go beyond what Lady Dedlock, the presumable focal character of the scene, would notice, although Warhol does not acknowledge this reasoning. For example, the narrator, not Lady Dedlock, seems to feel the humidity, so heavy that the "shot of a rifle loses its sharpness in the moist air" (*Bleak* 21). The heterodiegetic narrator also occasionally uses first-person plural pronouns to suggest that he inhabits "this world of ours" (20): "street mud . . . collects about us" (163) and people are "dying thus around us, every day" (734). When Lady Dedlock's "empty rooms . . . mournfully whisper what your room and what mine must one day be," the narrator uses "mine" to claim not only that he inhabits a room but also that he will eventually die (890). Such phrases indicate that he is a mortal body amongst other mortal bodies, susceptible to dirty streets and human finitude. Just as Esther's posture of effacement doesn't erase her body, the other narrator's linguistic, imaginative embodiment doesn't actually create one—the contagion of Tom-all-Alone's cannot reach him. Yet, both narrators yearn to sometimes approximate the embodiment of the other narrator, tempering this disparity in their narrating positions.

---

31. Guerard writes that this narrator "is not at all an embodied person (named or unnamed) but rather a personalized, often suave and ironic watching consciousness" (341).

Peter K. Garrett deems *Bleak House* "the most extraordinary formal experiment of the whole period" ("Double" 15). And yet, as *Narrative Bonds* shows,
many Victorian novels use multiple narrators. What does make *Bleak House*
"extraordinary" is that it contains Genette's "two types of narrative: one with
the narrator absent from the story he tells . . . the other with the narrator
present as a character in the story he tells" (*Narrative* 244–45). By yoking the
two together through the novel's back-and-forth structure, Dickens doesn't
eradicate all variance between these "two very different situations" (*Narrative*
244) but does provocatively show how aligned they can be, how integrated
they can be, and how equally valued they can be. In a novel all about connection and cooperation, particularly between entities that seem distant, disparate, or unrelated, the very multinarrator structure embodies those themes.
The novel's supportive, uniting impulse contrasts with the multinarrator novel
explored in the next chapter: *Treasure Island*. In Robert Louis Stevenson's
adventure novel, the two narrators do not align in tone, morality, or outlook,
even though both are homodiegetic narrators.

~

CHAPTER 3

The Quick Switch

The Child's Resistance to Adulthood in
Treasure Island

WHILE READING *Bleak House,* readers become accustomed to the handoffs between the two narrators. They start to expect the return of Esther's self-deprecating pen once the other narrator has relayed several chapters. The back-and-forth form consists of a comfortable, predictable alternation between two narrators. In *Dracula, The Woman in White,* and *The Moonstone,* the reader never expects to stay with one narrator for long because the beginning of those novels explicitly inform the reader that the text will feature multiple narrators. The multinarrator form in Robert Louis Stevenson's *Treasure Island* proceeds differently. Protagonist Jim Hawkins narrates most of the adventure novel (91 percent of the chapters), but chapters 16 through 18 are narrated by Dr. Livesey, one of the adult organizers of the treasure expedition. After this mid-novel switch, Livesey does not narrate again. Jim narrates the other thirty-one chapters of the novel— fifteen before and sixteen after Livesey's three-chapter narration. I label this sole, brief switch in narrators the *quick switch.* Texts employing this structure, unlike the other Victorian multinarrator texts I discuss, retain the sense of possessing a primary narrator. The quick switch is the inverse of the typical frame story. A frame narrative tends to be slim, quickly introducing the main, more substantial narrative; in the quick switch, on the other hand, the switch to the second narrator is short-lived and occurs midway or later in the text. A traditional frame narrative influences how we read the framed story that follows; likewise, in the quick switch, we read the second narrative in light of the first one. In the Victorian quick switch examples I examine, the second narrative is markedly unreliable on the axis of reading (interpretation) or regarding (ethics) but not on the axis of reporting (of facts).[1] The primary narrator and/ or reader recognizes the second narrator's unreliability because of the second narrative's contrast with the primary narrative. Because the second narrative is short in the quick-switch structure, the reader's trust and sympathy remain with the primary narrator. The quick switch functions this way not only in *Treasure Island* but also in Charles Dickens's *Little Dorrit* (1857) and Juliana Horatia Ewing's *A Great Emergency* (1874).

In his three chapters, Dr. Livesey recounts how the group of gentlemen (as opposed to the group of pirates) relocates from the swamp-anchored ship to the rudimentary island stockade while under pirate fire. Jim is not with either group, having slipped away from the ship to explore the island. When Livesey hears "the cry of a man at the point of death" emanating from the island, he assumes Jim has died (*Treasure* 85). The doctor's section ends as Jim, "safe and sound, come[s] climbing over the stockade" (97). David D. Mann and William H. Hardesty, III, rationalize the quick switch to Livesey's narration as the "solution to [the] technical problem" of how to relay what happens to the gentlemen's party when Jim leaves it (378); however, Dr. Livesey doesn't intervene again to report the important developments that transpire during Jim's second absence from the gentlemen group: the gentlemen's abandonment of the stockade and the pirates' subsequent possession of it. Although Patricia Whaley Hardesty, W. Hardesty, and D. Mann write that "having Jim repeat another's account would not do" (5), Jim does repeat Silver's explanation of how the pirates came to control the stockade. Later still, Jim summarizes, in his own words, Dr. Livesey's account of the gentlemen's desertion of the stockade and ensuing relocation to Ben Gunn's mountain cave; therefore, the novel does not insist on firsthand testimony to communicate all significant plot events. Furthermore, rationalizing the temporary switch in narrators by citing its necessity ignores the implications of such a structural solution, no matter what Stevenson's intentions were in employing it.[2]

---

1. This conception of the axes of (un)reliability comes from Phelan, and I discuss its applicability to the Victorian multinarrator novel in the introduction.

2. P. Hardesty, W. Hardesty, and Mann propose that "there is always the possibility that changing narrators was simply the easiest course for RLS, ill and in the process of moving from Scotland to Switzerland" (5). Presumably, these critics are working from the account Stevenson himself gives of writing *Treasure Island* in the essay "My First Book" (1894). The first fifteen chapters came easily, Stevenson recounts, "and then, in the early paragraphs of the sixteenth, [he] ignominiously lost hold" (197). The doctor's narration starts in chapter 16. According to

Most criticism on *Treasure Island* ignores the quick switch altogether.[3]

I argue that by giving the doctor's perspective in his own words, the quick switch manifests the dramatic stylistic and moral contrast between Jim and Dr. Livesey. I challenge Jacqueline Rose's impression that the two characters' viewpoints are indistinguishable.[4] I first look at how the quick switch reveals Dr. Livesey's character; then, I show how Jim's portrayal of Dr. Livesey in the rest of the novel confirms Livesey's self-representation. Even though critics view Livesey as an admirable father figure and able professional mentor to Jim, I maintain that both narratives show a different doctor, one that is slow to pity and swift to punish. Adulthood, modelled by Livesey, is marked by cruelty, greed, violence, and lack of emotion. Jim, conversely, depicts himself as an emotional and empathetic child who is skeptical of avarice. Because the quick switch is brief and startling, our sympathy remains with Jim and his perspective. A structure such as the back-and-forth would be misplaced here, as that structure knits together narrators and their perspectives. The quick switch, conversely, reveals and embodies the power relationships between the two characters. Dr. Livesey's constant surveillance, discipline, and punishment of Jim are evident both in the story and in Livesey's very decision to barge into Jim's narrative. Ultimately, rather than follow Dr. Livesey's example, Jim resists the doctor's version of adulthood by taking refuge in an eternal and haunted childhood.

In other Victorian examples of the quick switch, unlike with *Treasure Island,* the transition to the second narrator is explained in advance and is the result of the first narrator's choice. While Charlie narrates most of Ewing's *A Great Emergency,* chapter 15 mostly consists of an embedded excerpt from his older sister Henrietta's diary. Dickens's *Little Dorrit* is narrated by a heterodi-

---

Stevenson, he was unable to write again until he had travelled to Davos, Switzerland, for the winter. The switch in narrators, therefore, seems to align with Stevenson's geographic relocation. Katz, however, uses evidence from Stevenson's letters to show that Stevenson had in fact "written beyond fifteen chapters when he was at Braemar, another example of the imprecision of certain details in 'My First Book'" (xxi).

3. Sandison, for example, never mentions the quick switch yet relies on Jim's position as the author–narrator of the text to prove Jim's earned and increased authority, maturity, and power. Gubar, one of the few scholars to acknowledge that Jim does not narrate the whole novel, argues that Livesey's narration "presents a major challenge to the idea that [Jim] functions as the undisputed master of his fate" (88).

4. Rose only addresses *Treasure Island*'s quick switch in a brief, footnoted sentence: "The narration of *Treasure Island* shifts to the Doctor in the centre of the book, but this in no sense upsets the fundamental cohesion of its narrative voice" (148). Since Rose specifically argues that the existence of "disparate voices" in *Peter Pan* "set[s] [it] apart" from *Treasure Island,* she must find a way to downplay the existence of "disparate voices" in *Treasure Island* itself (78).

egetic narrator except for one chapter, "A History of a Self-Tormentor," that
is penned by the character Miss Wade. In *A Great Emergency*, Charlie narrates the first three paragraphs of chapter 15, explaining how Henrietta voluntarily lent him her diary so he could read about the titular great emergency he
missed, a house fire; Charlie then chooses to copy the relevant diary entry into
his narrative. In *Little Dorrit*, Miss Wade asks Arthur Clennam, "Shall I give
you something I have written and put by for your perusal[. . .]?" and Arthur
readily assents to the offer; once he has left Miss Wade, and as the chapter
closes, "he unfolded the sheets of paper, and read in them what is reproduced
in the next chapter" (690, 693). Henrietta and Miss Wade willingly hand over
their narratives to Charlie and Arthur. Charlie decides to include the diary
entry in his narrative, and Arthur eagerly inspects the papers from Miss Wade
(though the heterodiegetic narrator must make the decision to include them
in the narrative). In *Treasure Island*, by contrast, the movement to the second narrator occurs more abruptly: Only the chapter title warns of the otherwise unexpected and unexplained switch to Livesey: "Narrative Continued
by the Doctor: How the Ship was Abandoned" (*Treasure* 84). Furthermore,
Treasure Island does not show Livesey presenting his narrative to Jim or asking him if he wants to read it; similarly, Jim is not shown choosing to read or
include Livesey's narrative. These absences, differences from other Victorian
quick switches, make Livesey's narrative feel like an incursion into Jim's—like
a power grab.

Livesey has already flexed his authority by asking Jim to write the narrative and by seemingly watching Jim as he writes it. Jim's first sentence reads,
"Squire Trelawney, Dr. Livesey, and the rest of these gentleman hav[e] asked
me to write down the whole particulars about Treasure Island, from the beginning to the end, keeping nothing back but the bearings of the island" (1).
Jim abides by their instructions, showing no awareness that Livesey will narrate a portion; Jim, after all, was asked to narrate "the *whole* particulars . . .
from the beginning to the end" (emphasis added). Livesey monitors Jim as
he composes. In one of his chapters, the doctor references a detail from Jim's
narrative: "The report fell in at the same instant of time. This was the first
that Jim heard" (92). The doctor must have read Jim's account of the cannonade reported approximately nine pages prior. Additionally, while admiring
how Silver was able to keep up with the able-bodied gentlemen, Jim mentions
that the doctor agrees—in the present tense—with his own written assessment: "The work [Silver] went through . . . was work no sound man ever
equaled; and so *thinks* the doctor" (182; emphasis added). This line suggests
that Livesey is reading over Jim's shoulder and verbally offering commentary
as Jim writes.

In the doctor's narration, his attitude toward Jim is pitiless and apathetic. On the second page of the doctor's narration, he hears a distant bloodcurdling yell and immediately interprets it as Jim's swan-scream: "There came ringing over the island the cry of a man at the point of death. . . . 'Jim Hawkins is gone' was my first thought" (85). Even though the doctor correctly identifies the death yell as emanating from "a man" (the reader knows it issues from an adult sailor who refuses to join the pirate mutiny), the doctor subsequently identifies that mannish voice as coming from a child—Jim. The doctor's deduction overrides the knowledge of his own senses; he pushes to interpret the man's scream as hailing from the boyish Jim. Such a forced misinterpretation implies that the doctor believes that Jim deserves such a fate for deserting the gentlemen to explore the island. Until Jim appears several chapters later, nimbly scaling the wall of the stockade and interrupting the doctor's "wondering over poor Jim Hawkins's fate," the doctor does not spare one more thought on Jim (96). The earlier serialized version of *Treasure Island* states the doctor's feelings even more bluntly: "*But there was no time to cry over spilt milk; if they had begun the killing, it was plain enough they would go on—Hawkins now, the rest of us as soon as possible*" (qtd. in Letley 207). Jim's death is dismissed as "spilt milk," something not worthy of making a man like the doctor "cry."

For most of his section, Livesey eerily imagines Jim to be dead. Livesey mentally concludes, "Jim Hawkins is gone" two pages into his narration (*Treasure* 85), and he doesn't know that Jim is alive until the final sentence of his narrative. Livesey's narration is analeptic—it backtracks several hours to just before he hears the scream (a scream Jim has already narrated).[5] The doctor's section functions as a little pocket of time, a sort of alternate history, in which the scream is believed to come from a dying Jim. As if to exemplify the classic pirate phrase, "dead men tell no tales," a dead Jim in the story is matched in the structure by a replacement narrator. Of course, by the time Livesey writes his narrative, he has long known that Jim did not die and that the scream did not come from him. And yet, Livesey still decides to enter the narrative at this exact moment and to include Jim's hypothetical death—the result of his supposed truancy—in the narrative. The reader, however, is structurally distanced

---

5. Livesey's narration does not fill in a time gap in Jim's narration; rather, it is an analepsis, which Genette defines as "any evocation after the fact of an event that took place earlier than the point in the story where we are at any given moment" (*Narrative* 40). Jim's last chapter before the switch, chapter 15, ends with the following sentence: "I beheld the Union Jack flutter in the air above a wood" (*Treasure* 83). When Jim's narration resumes several chapters later, it picks up exactly where and when it left off. The first sentence of chapter 19 reads, "As soon as Benn [sic] Gunn saw the colours he came to a halt" (98). Livesey's narration is analeptic, backtracking several hours to show the lead up to the moment when the ship captain "run[s] up the colours" at the stockade (95)—the flag that Jim sees from afar in chapter 15 (83).

from the doctor's misinterpretation of the scream as heralding the death of Jim. When the doctor hears "the cry of a man at the point of death," Jim has already heard the same cry ten pages earlier (85). Jim also overheard Silver identify it as coming from the murdered Alan. The reader, therefore, knows that "the cry" does not hail from Jim. When the doctor imagines Jim's death, then, the reader is already assured of Jim's safety; the reader is separated from the doctor's rash judgment.

As readers, we feel intimate with Jim and sympathetic with the attitude he espouses. As a narrator, Jim draws in the reader by directly addressing the reader as "you" over thirty times in his narrative.[6] Jim fits Robyn R. Warhol's category of the "engaging narrator" because he "frequently speaks to 'you'" (*Gendered* 34). Such a narrator, Warhol explains, "strives to close the gaps between the narratee, the addressee, and the receiver. Using narrative interventions that are almost always spoken in earnest, such a narrator addresses a 'you' that is evidently intended to evoke recognition and identification in the person who holds the book and reads" (29). Jim's recurrent direct addresses are conducted casually and effortlessly. The conversational nature of Jim's usage—"I tell you, but Silver was anxious to keep up with us" (*Treasure* 182)— creates the impression that we are Jim's friend and confidant. Other uses of direct address reveal Jim's investment in aiding the "you" to imagine the story: "and I can give you no fairer idea of Ben Gunn's boat than by saying it was like the first and the worst coracle ever made by man" (119). Occasionally, Jim positions the "you" in his own shoes. After hearing the nonstop screeching of Silver's parrot, Jim writes that the parrot shrieked "till you wondered that it was not out of breath" (54). Such subtle substitutions of "you" for "I" help the reader identify with Jim's perspective on events. Jim smoothly trusts the reader to understand his own feelings by frequently using constructions like "as you may believe" and "you will readily believe." When speaking of the people in the neighboring town who refuse to help his mother and him face the soon-to-return pirates, he notes, "You would have thought men would have been ashamed of themselves" (20). The direct address places Jim and the reader on the same moral plane, sharing a reasonable judgment of the neighbors' behavior.

---

6. B. Wall's comment that Jim "builds up no comfortable confiding relationship with his narratee" baffles me (71). B. Wall suggests the horror of the events that Jim relates prevents "friendly sharing" with the narratee (72), but I argue that Jim comes across as friendly and confiding despite the terror his narrative conveys. In contrast to Wall, W. Hardesty and Mann claim that "Stevenson's most considerable achievement in the first part of the novel is, essentially, the creation of empathy with Jim" (98).

The doctor's narration lacks the personal revelations and direct addresses of Jim's narration. As readers, we feel distanced from his attitude. Dr. Livesey never addresses the reader or narratee directly in his three chapters. He provides a few more details on his backstory—he was a soldier, he was wounded—but his interiority remains a mystery. He never pulls in the reader and never really tries to. We are not intimate with this narrator. And since the doctor almost always speaks on behalf of his group—frequently acting as the spokesperson for "us" and "we" and rarely offering anything from the viewpoint of "I" or "me"—the narration feels less like an intimate conversation and more like a communal report being delivered to the reader.

The style and content of the doctor's three-chapter narrative construct adulthood as emotionless and violent; the doctor links childhood, on the other hand, with the emotion that adulthood lacks. While Jim rapidly vacillates between emotional extremes—indescribable horror to joy bordering on ecstasy—the doctor narrates his portion with a levelheaded calm, rarely expressing deep fear or overwhelming enthusiasm. This divergence explains a Victorian reviewer's comment that the change in narrators functions as a breather for the reader, a water break from the relentless dread and danger that constitute Jim's narration:

> As we follow the narrative of the boy Jim Hawkins we hold our breath in his dangers, and breathe again at his escapes. The artifice is so well managed that when, for a few chapters, Jim disappears, and the story is taken up by a shrewd doctor, who is never in much danger, the change is felt as a sensible relief. (Butler 130)

The shrewd doctor, however, is in much danger during his section. In those three short chapters, the pirates aim cannons at his escape boat, flood it, force the gentlemen to flee it, meet the gentlemen with a volley of gunshots as they enter the wood, and let loose a lengthy cannonade at the gentlemen's current shelter, the stockade. A bullet, additionally, "whistle[s] close past [Livesey's] ear" and hits and kills the squire's faithful servant, Tom Redruth (*Treasure* 93–94). And yet the doctor's tone underplays his personal peril. His admissions of heightened feeling are rare and are generally expressed on behalf of a group rather than as a disclosure of personal feeling. The singular outburst of emotion narrated in the doctor's section—the squire's tearful response to the death of his old servant Tom—is described as childlike: "The squire dropped down beside him on his knees and kissed his hand, crying like a child" (94). When lachrymose and demonstrative, the squire is "like a child." When handling and shooting guns, the squire is like an adult. Livesey's "calm and steady" demeanor is indicative of his adulthood, and the squire attains an unruffled and ruthless manner while dealing with weapons (6). He is "cool as steel" as he "looked to the priming of his gun" (91). The squire uses the gun successfully when he becomes weapon-like himself; just as the squire is like "steel," the weapons the men are using (cutlasses, pistols, muskets) would have been made with various metals. Squire Trelawney leaves his blubbering child-ishness behind when he takes the role of the "best shot" of the group (90).

Setting Jim's and the doctor's narratives side by side reinforces Jim's emo-tional depth and the doctor's coldness. Both characters describe the island stockade in their narratives, and their diverging portrayals display Jim's curi-osity toward nature, his sensitivity to environmental violence, and the doctor's indifference to both. Jim's more imaginative language marks his capacity for empathy, while the doctor's lack of such language marks his empathetic fail-ure. The doctor's brief, one-paragraph description focuses on the stockade's characteristics from a strategic point of view. The stockade to the doctor is a thing that he can potentially use, a tactical location from which to safely "sho[ot] the others like partridges" (85). He employs only a handful of meta-phors and similes in his section, and almost all of them, like the above com-parison of the pirates to animals, depict the gentlemen's violence. On the other hand, Jim "beg[ins] to look about [himself]" as soon as he has a chance to do so (100). He spends many full, rich paragraphs describing the architecture of the stockade and the appearance of the surrounding environs. Jim identifies the species of wood the stockade is made from ("unsquared trunks of pine" [100]) and the species of trees in the nearby woods: "all of fir on the land side, but towards the sea with a large admixture of live-oaks" (100–101). The doctor never offers such details because the varieties of wood do not matter in his assessment of the stockade's utility. Jim's continuing description of the scene reveals his mindfulness of environmental devastation:

> The slopes of the knoll and all the inside of the stockade had been cleared of timber to build the house, and we could see by the stumps what a fine and lofty grove had been destroyed. Most of the soil had been washed away or buried in drift after the removal of the trees; only where the streamlet ran down from the kettle a thick bed of moss and some ferns and little creeping bushes were still green among the sand. (100)

Jim repeatedly acknowledges how nature had been violently sacrificed to con-struct the stockade: The trees had been "cleared," "destroyed," "remov[ed]," and reduced to "stumps." The resulting soil had been "washed away or bur-ied." Jim's awareness of the loss that enables gain recurs when he imagines how much "it had cost"—in lives, ships, and "shame and lies and cruelty"—to first collect, later bury, and finally unearth the treasure (185). While the doctor describes the stockade only in terms of gain, Jim understands the loss that underwrites such gain. Jim, therefore, seems to be cognizant of and even in opposition to the colonial investments that Diana Loxley argues were uppermost at the time that Stevenson was writing *Treasure Island*: "As a consequence of British expansionism, colonial territory, rather than being settled, was rapidly carved up in the intoxicated pursuit of new sources of raw material that would yield financial profit" (167).

Looking closely at another striking repetition in the two narratives—Alan's horrifying scream—further contrasts the doctor's hardened attitude toward violence and Jim's capacity to be affected by it.[7] We first hear the scream from Jim's viewpoint. Jim hides in the bushes and eavesdrops on Silver, who is trying to convince the sailor Tom to join the pirate mutiny. The piercing yell sharply interrupts the scene:

> Far away out in the marsh there arose, all of a sudden, a sound like the cry of anger, then another on the back of it; and then one horrid, long-drawn scream. The rocks of the Spy-glass re-echoed it a score of times; the whole troop of marsh-birds rose again, darkening heaven, with a simultaneous whirr; and long after that death yell was still ringing in my brain, silence had re-established its empire, and only the rustle of the redescending birds and the boom of the distant surges disturbed the languor of the afternoon. (*Treasure* 75)

Jim's response is a fusion of pathos and poetry. The lengthening assonance of the "o" sounds in "one horrid long-drawn" and the rhyme of "long" and "drawn" emphasize the lengthy duration of the cry in a manner approaching onomatopoeia. The different vowel sound and harsh end consonant in "scream" heighten the sense of bleak horror in the word itself. Jim expands the moment, fashioning a narrative arc from silence to disturbance to the eventual return of stillness and relative quiet.

On the other hand, the doctor approaches the same scream with stoicism and a hint of arrogance: "There came ringing over the island the cry of a man at the point of death. I was not new to violent death—I have served his Royal Highness the Duke of Cumberland. . . . 'Jim Hawkins is gone' was my first

---

7. Because of this "interference" between the two narratives, Genette would identify the doctor's analeptic narrative as a homodiegetic analepsis. That type of analepsis is an "internal analeps[is] that deal[s] with the same line of action as the first narrative. Here the risk of interference is obvious, and even apparently unavoidable" (*Narrative* 51).

thought" (85). Dr. Livesey calmly specifies the scream as given by "a man at the point of death" (85), categorizing the scream as if he were categorizing butterflies. Although his medical training may contribute to his seemingly dispassionate diagnosis of the scream, he does not imagine the scream as coming from a stranger but from the boy for whom he is responsible and, critics assume, deeply cares about. To the doctor, the scream is a fact. To Jim, the scream is a story. While Jim internalizes the echoing yell—"and long after that death yell was still ringing in my brain" (75)—Dr. Livesey suffers no repercussions beyond a momentary alteration in his pulse. Furthermore, as Alan Sandison mentions, the Duke of Cumberland earned a reputation as a vicious general: "This able general acquired his notorious sobriquet 'Butcher' Cumberland for what were seen as his brutal tactics in the battle of Culloden which ensured the decimation of the Jacobite forces and the disfavour of romantic nationalists like Stevenson" (59). Dr. Livesey does not criticize the Duke's battle tactics or the man himself when he brings up his military service after hearing the shriek. Dr. Livesey also shares that he received a wound at Fontenoy, a battle at which, according to Letley, the Duke "was narrowly defeated by the French" (207). The doctor, therefore, invokes "Butcher" Cumberland and recalls his own injury at a battle at which the "Butcher" is defeated. Because the doctor is not only aligned with brutality but also with the defeat of that brutality, Stevenson seems to suggest his aversion to such violence and to the characters who espouse it.

The quick switch highlights Livesey's contrast to Jim and thereby foregrounds a different side of the man than critics usually notice. Scholars almost universally admire Dr. Livesey's intelligence, maturity, and coolness under pressure. Sandison and Christopher Parkes both consider him a strong role model for the fatherless Jim. Critics often sound like Long John Silver in their assessment of Dr. Livesey: "You're a good man and a true; I never seen a better man!" (*Treasure* 166); however, Dr. Livesey is, like Silver, a man capable of lying, betrayal, and ruthlessness. In the above compliment, Silver inflates his praise to manipulate Dr. Livesey, and the doctor is seemingly affected because he soon promises to "do [his] best to save [Silver]" in return for Silver's promise to protect Jim (168). But several chapters later, Dr. Livesey "cheerily" agrees that he "would have let old John be cut to bits, and never given it a thought" (184). If Silver's word means little, so does Dr. Livesey's. His Silver-like quality is highlighted when he is "named cook" of the stockade, paralleling Silver's employment as the "ship's cook" (101, 38). Later, Jim directly connects the two men when the doctor's physical position mirrors Silver's previous stance: "I saw [Livesey] standing, like Silver once before, up to the mid-leg in creeping vapour" (163). Both men emerge from the same slithering mist with its connotation of moral miasma.

Livesey's encounter with Billy Bones at the Hawkins family inn early in the novel exposes the doctor's callousness. Revealing his poor bedside manner, the doctor menaces Billy: "If you keep on drinking rum, the world will soon be quit of a very dirty scoundrel!" (6); the doctor's name-calling medical counsel almost eagerly portends death. When Billy wields a knife, the doctor retorts: "If you do not put that knife this instant in your pocket, I promise, upon my honour, you shall hang at the next assizes" (6). The doctor, who is also a magistrate, threatens Billy with execution. The doctor then institutes a continuous watch over Billy—a sort of panoptical punishment—when the doctor promises to "have an eye upon [Billy] day and night" (6). Lastly, the doctor warns that if he hears "a breath of complaint against" Billy Bones, he will "take effectual means to have [Bones] hunted down and routed out of this" (6). The doctor requires neither evidence nor a substantial grievance—a mere "breath" of criticism would be enough for the doctor to justify violently "hunt[ing] down" Billy as if he were an animal. Jim behaves differently toward Billy Bones. Even though Jim "had certainly never liked" the pirate, he can still "pity him," and when Billy dies, Jim "burst into a flood of tears" (18).

Throughout the novel, Livesey punishes others through his dual professions of magistrate and doctor. When tending to the ill and wounded pirates on Treasure Island, the doctor envisions himself as the dispenser of justice and punishment. According to Jim's narration, when Livesey arrives at the stockade, he reimagines the space as a prison and the pirates as prisoners by labeling himself the "prison doctor" rather than the "mutineers' doctor" (164). He ironically constructs his medical care of the pirates as punishment. He quips, "I make it a point of honour not to lose a man for King George . . . and the gallows" (164). Livesey nurses the pirates so they can live long enough to be hanged. According to Michel Foucault, doctors' examinations were increasingly regularized in the eighteenth century as part of the wider social implementation of the examination as "a normalizing gaze, a surveillance that makes it possible to qualify, to classify and to punish" (184). Dr. Livesey blurs the line between the punishment of the criminal and treatment of the patient. His examination of the pirates, which he conducts "as if he were paying an ordinary professional visit," enables him to question, prod, ridicule, and command the pirates, as well as force "bad-tasted medicine" down his enemies' throats (*Treasure* 164, 165).

Similarly, the doctor sheds blood as a doctor and as a fighter. When he treats Billy Bones post-stroke, the doctor "open[s] a vein" and releases a "great

deal of blood" (11). He later confesses to Jim that the excessive bloodletting
was not required to save Billy's life and served only to quiet him, making him
less of a nuisance to the inn. Furthermore, Jim witnesses the doctor brutally
slay a pirate in a way that mirrors Silver's murder of Tom. Silver knocks down
Tom, pursues him, and then stabs him to death. The doctor similarly pursues, knocks down, and knifes a pirate: "The doctor was pursuing his assailant
down the hill, and . . . beat down his guard, and sent him sprawling on his
back, with a great slash across the face" (112). Jim twice confirms that the doctor killed the man. When Jim reiterates that "the mutineer, indeed, died under
the doctor's knife," the pun on "doctor's knife" conflates the medical scalpel
and fighting cutlass—they both result in death (115).

Even though the doctor does grudgingly admit that "every step, it's [Jim]
that saves our lives," the doctor nonetheless chastises and punishes Jim several times (168). After Jim joins the gentlemen in a stockade-centered skir-
mish with the pirates following his first disappearance, Dr. Livesey "pulled
[Jim's] ears for [him] into the bargain" (115). In *Thoughts of a Parent on Education* (1837), Mrs. Richard Trench opines that "whipping, caning, slapping,
ear-pulling, [and] hair-dragging" are "uncouth and barbarous" punishments
(69–70, 70). Furthermore, many medical voices from the time, both British
and American, decry the practice of ear-pulling and enumerate the negative
physical consequences of it.[8] Though *Treasure Island* is set earlier than these
sources, it is noteworthy that Stevenson has Livesey act in a way that contradicts contemporary medical practice. When Jim returns to the stockade after
a second disappearance, he is stunned to find the pirates there instead of his
friends, and the doctor is less than comforting when he arrives to treat the
wounded pirates: "As you have brewed, so shall you drink, my boy. . . . this
much I will say, be it kind or unkind . . . by George, it was downright cowardly!" (*Treasure* 167). This severe verbal chastisement makes Jim "weep" (167).
Jim rarely weeps and never again because of someone else's words. Later, the
pirates drag Jim to the treasure site, and Jim faces their rage when they realize the treasure is gone; after experiencing such stress and danger, Jim narrates that the doctor continues the guilt-tripping assault: "I did what I thought
best for those who had stood by their duty; and if you were not one of these,
whose fault was it?" (183). Although Jim helpfully befriends Ben Gunn (who
has already found the treasure) during his first disappearance and beneficially
saves the ship during his second disappearance, the doctor continually berates
Jim for his two disappearances, calling him cowardly and undutiful. Livesey

---

8. See "Pulling the Ears" from the "Questions and Answers" section of the January 1875
edition of the *Herald of Health* (30–31), and Jonathan Hutchinson's *Archives of Surgery* (245–46).

even relays his irritation with Jim to Silver; Silver later divulges to Jim that the "doctor himself is gone dead again you—'ungrateful scamp' was what he said" (150). Although we should always take Silver's claims with a grain of salt, his descriptions of Livesey's annoyance with Jim align with what Livesey himself usually says to Jim. Silver also testifies that the doctor purposefully left Jim out from the treaty the gentlemen made with the pirates: "As for that boy, I don't know where he is, confound him . . . nor I don't much care. We're about sick of him" (151). To exclude Jim from the treaty is an additional punishment for Jim since the omission is unnecessary and spiteful—Livesey has no reason to exclude Jim except to retaliate against him for his absenteeism.

But when other gentlemen, as opposed to pirates or children, make mistakes, all is quickly forgiven; the gentlemen never punish themselves or each other. The gentlemen seem worried that Jim might leak information about the upcoming treasure hunt, but it is the squire who has "been talking" (37). And even though Jim notes that "Doctor Livesey will not like that," the doctor does not offer any reproach of the squire's dangerous blabbing that leads to pirates joining their crew (37). When Supervisor Dance confesses he trampled the pirate Pew—and also boasts of his lack of remorse—Jim witnesses the squire and doctor absolve him of wrongdoing and repeatedly compliment him on his kill: "As for riding down that black, atrocious miscreant, I regard it as an act of virtue" (31). Though Dance had worried about a possible reprimand for his action, none occurs. The squire and doctor treat Silver with a similar generosity when Jim spies the pirate Black Dog patronizing Silver's land establishment. At this point, the doctor and squire believe Silver to be a respectable business owner. Just as the squire and doctor "further complimented" Dance after his trampling of Pew (31), the squire and doctor "complimented" Silver after deeming him innocent of knowingly allowing pirates in his bar (46).

Unlike Livesey, Jim is quick to feel pity for others, especially for those fearing, experiencing, or awaiting punishment. On the island, Jim meets Ben Gunn, a longtime marooned pirate. Jim reflects, "I had heard the word [marooned], and I knew it stood for a horrible kind of punishment common enough among the buccaneers, in which the offender is put ashore with a little powder and shot, and left behind on some desolate and distant island" (79). The reader knows the definition of the word "marooned," so Jim's gratuitous explanation of the term serves to express his compassion for Ben. Jim sympathizes with the effect such an extended and harsh punishment has had on Ben: "I now felt sure that the poor fellow had gone crazy in his solitude" (80). When the gentlemen, treasure in tow, depart the island, they leave three of the remaining pirate-mutineers on the island. Jim labels the sentence "wretched" (189). The marooned pirates' supplications elicit pity and sympathy from Jim:

"They continued to call us by name, and appeal to us, for God's sake, to be merciful, and not leave them to die in such a place" (189). This reportage includes free indirect discourse—the narrator's incorporation of the characters' language without tagging it as such. When Jim writes, "for God's sake," he assimilates the pirates' phrasing; Jim himself would never use such an oath. The employment of free indirect discourse connects the narrator and the narrated, stressing Jim's identification with the marooned men and his susceptibility to their desperate pleas. Even at the end of the novel, after Silver has threatened Jim's life multiple times, Jim still feels compassion for the one-legged buccaneer: "My heart was sore for him, wicked as he was, to think on the dark perils that environed, and the shameful gibbet that awaited him" (162). That Jim describes the gibbet—rather than Silver's behavior—as "shameful" again shows Jim's distrust of extreme punishment and his commiseration with the punished.

Jim tries on the adult punisher role at several points in *Treasure Island,* particularly in his treatment of his mother's new apprentice and in his interaction with Israel Hands; however, these brief efforts cause Jim shame and pain. The squire arranges for "a boy" to help Jim's mother, and when Jim visits her before departing on the expedition, he meets the boy "who was to stay here in [his] place beside [his] mother" (39). Jim owns up to unnecessarily penalizing the new employee: "I had my first attack of tears. I am afraid I led that boy a dog's life; for as he was new to the work, I had a hundred opportunities of setting him right and putting him down, and I was not slow to profit by them" (39). The emotional justification for this behavior—Jim's grief, proleptic homesickness, and loss of position and parent—softens its meanness. Jim, however, does admit that his behavior was shameful; he is "afraid" to reveal his cruel treatment of the boy to the reader. Tellingly, the adult language of money enters the passage; Jim "profit[s]" from his punishing manner. Jim's later cat-and-mouse game with Israel Hands on the otherwise empty ship leads to Jim's accidental killing of the pirate. In general, adult characters openly and proudly own their kills, but Jim dissociates himself from his act of slaying Hands. He shoots his weapons without "[his] own volition" and "without a conscious aim" (142). As Troy Boone argues, Hands seems to be "killed not by Jim but by his own malicious action" (80). Jim's "conceited" manner before the involuntary shooting is reminiscent of Dance's and the squire's glee in Pew's gruesome demise (*Treasure* 142). But when Jim's cocky threats to shoot Hands unintentionally come to fruition, Jim is horrified. He feels "sick, faint, and terrified," must close his eyes to avoid the sight of Israel's dead body, and loses "possession" and "master[y]" of his own self (143). Jim quickly retreats from his experiments with the adult punisher role.

Although Jim may be an adult in age when he narrates, he declines to identify himself as an adult narrator; rather, he positions himself as an eternal boy to better resist the callous adulthood of Dr. Livesey. Jim retrospectively narrates the treasure-hunting adventure, but the distance in time between the narration and the adventure remains unspecified. Because of that vague time span, critics have disagreed over whether Jim the narrator—opposed to Jim the character—is an adult or a child. Wendy Katz describes the book as "adult Jim recalling his youthful adventures" (xxv), but Rose construes *Treasure Island* as "a story told by the child hero" (79–80). In Robert Kiely's view, Jim is a child narrator and *Treasure Island* is a pure adventure story—not a story of Jim's development into an adult. To Sandison, on the other hand, the novel is a bildungsroman. Jim, therefore, is an adult narrator; he must have aged to fit the requisite maturation arc of the genre. *Treasure Island,* however, remains cagey on Jim's age both during the expedition and at the time of narration. The only sentence that positively identifies Jim's age—fourteen years old—appeared in the serial version and was cut by Stevenson when he made revisions for the book edition.[9]

Despite the lack of Jim's exact age in the book version, Jim repeatedly casts himself as a boy in comparison to the grown-up men surrounding him: "There were only seven out of the twenty-six on whom we knew we could rely; and out of these seven one was a boy" (*Treasure* 67). He contrasts himself with the adult pirates: Silver "and I should have to fight for dear life—he, a cripple, and I, a boy—against five strong and active seamen!" (170). During the story, Jim identifies himself as and is identified by others as a boy; in the narrating situation, Jim declines to provide information about his age or the date. This lack of an age allows Jim to occupy the position of "boy" generically and endlessly. By comparison, in R. M. Ballantyne's *The Coral Island* (1858), an adventure novel that influenced *Treasure Island,* the narrator Ralph Rover makes clear that he has grown up and even "retir[ed] from the stirring life of adventure" (106); hence, he's earned the right to entertain and instruct his young readers. The exploits he narrates happened long ago, when he was fifteen: "for I was young at that time" (89). Jim, on the other hand, never positions himself as the wizened, wise seaman. Remaining in the position of a child (even if he is not a child in age) allows Jim to mark his continuing resistance to the greed of the adult world.

---

9. The disclosure occurs during Jim's haughty speech to the pirates when he inadvertently hands himself over to them: "The laugh's on my side. I've as good as hanged you, every man, and I'm not fifteen till my next birthday" (qtd. in Letley 209). The book edition reads, "It is for you to choose. Kill another and do yourselves no good, or spare me and keep a witness to save you from the gallows" (*Treasure* 152).

Jim's lack of interest in locating and possessing the treasure further distinguishes him from the adult greed that surrounds him. When W. W. Robson wonders "Why does the *treasure* count so little, emotionally, in the tale?" he is really wondering why it counts so little for Jim (81). It is the squire and doctor who instantaneously concoct the plan to unearth the treasure after Jim gives them Billy Bones's oilskin packet, which, unbeknownst to Jim, secrets a treasure map. When the doctor hears that pirate Flint is involved, his mind immediately turns to money, asking Trelawney: "The point is, had [Flint] money?" and "Will that treasure amount to much?" (*Treasure* 32). The squire declares, "I'll have that treasure if I search a year" (32), and the doctor excitedly agrees to the journey. They both decide to take Jim along but without asking him if he wants to join them. Early in the novel, when Billy Bones pays Jim a monthly salary of fourpenny to watch for a man with one leg, Jim admits that he "paid pretty dear" for that fee with persistent nightmares about the mysterious amputee (3). Jim knows what it costs to profit. Naomi J. Wood observes, "Jim . . . tells of no personal gain except nightmare" (80). When the pirates tow Jim near the supposed treasure site, they, not Jim, are overcome with the desire to acquire the wealth. Multiple times Jim refers to the "treasure-hunters" and never includes himself in that category. As he approaches the treasure site, Jim feels disturbed, not joyful: "I was haunted by the thought of the tragedy that had once been acted on that plateau, when that ungodly buccaneer with the blue face . . . had there, with his own hand, cut down his six accomplices. This grove, that was now so peaceful, must then have rung with cries" (*Treasure* 179). When Jim finally sees the piles of coin, he replays the treasure's violent history:

> That was Flint's treasure that we had come so far to seek, and that had cost already the lives of seventeen men from the *Hispaniola*. How many it had cost in the amassing, what blood and sorrow, what good ships scuttled on the deep, what brave men walking the plank blindfold, what shot of cannon, what shame and lies and cruelty, perhaps no man alive could tell. (185)

Fittingly, the only aspect of the march to the treasure site that Jim enjoys is the scenic landscape. Otherwise, the trip is literally painful because "Silver plucked so roughly at the rope" that ties Jim to the pirate leader (179).

Throughout the scene when Jim handles the treasure, he expresses no desire to possess, save, spend, or calculate the money. Sorting the treasure is a painful activity; Jim reports, "My back ached with stooping and my fingers with sorting them out" (187). Parkes interprets this scene as Jim's "emerge[nce] [as] an image of a heroic civil servant" (332). The "great pleasure" Jim takes

(342), Parkes alleges, in "counting the treasure" (341) positions him as an eager "clerk in the treasury office" (342). But Jim is not *counting* but *sorting* the coins, and Jim's expressed pleasure is in this activity: "I think I never had more pleasure than in sorting them" (*Treasure* 187). Ever alive to detail, Jim is impressed by "the diversity of coinage" before him, just as he was interested in the diversity of tree species on the island. His descriptions of the coins reaffirm the treasure's connection to death and decay. Jim portrays some pieces as resembling "bits of spider's web," a simile that emphasizes how many men the treasure has entrapped. Additionally, Jim remarks that the coins are as plentiful as "autumn leaves," another simile that associates the money with deterioration. While Jim does express his excitement in looking for the treasure the day before setting sail from Bristow, he evinces no desire to possess it. By comparison, as soon as the doctor and squire realize the importance of the map, they anticipate owning the treasure: "We'll have . . . money to eat—to roll in—to play duck and drake with ever after" (34).[10] These two wealthy men do not even need this hidden money; their dream is a fantasy of excess in which money is something to be played with.

Jim's skepticism of the treasure hunt and mindfulness of the treasure's violent history suggest a critique of the British Empire. Although critics often describe *Treasure Island* as unambiguously pro-empire,[11] Marah Gubar treats *Treasure Island* "as an anti-adventure story" that "reflects and amplifies" "late Victorian anxieties about empire" (70, 81). And Katherine Bailey Linehan and Julia Reid have discovered Stevenson's critical stance toward empire in works written after his move to the South Seas in 1889. I argue that the divergence between Jim's and the doctor's imperial views reflects and integrates the political climate of the campaigns leading up to the 1880 election. Stevenson began writing *Treasure Island* in 1881 while in Braemar, Scotland, not long after the historic 1880 election in which Benjamin Disraeli was defeated and replaced by William Gladstone as Prime Minister. The election was viewed as a public referendum on Disraeli's "grandiose and costly schemes" and "ideas of an expanding militant empire" (Eldridge 118). Because he was campaigning for a Scottish seat in Parliament (Midlothian), W. Gladstone travelled to Scotland in 1879 for a well-received lecture tour during which he endlessly battered Disraeli's foreign policy as leading the United Kingdom into "all manner of

---

10. The phrase "to play duck and drake with" means "to throw away idly or carelessly; to play idly with; to handle or use recklessly; to squander" ("duck and drake"). The *Oxford English Dictionary Online* provides the squire's line as an example for the term.

11. See Boone, Bristow, Loxley, Parkes, and Ward. Deane identifies Jim Hawkins's "evergreen boyishness" as underpinning "a fantasy that enabled and sustained the new imperialist imagination" (701, 690).

gratuitous, dangerous, ambiguous, impracticable, and impossible engagements
. . . in all parts of the world" (W. Gladstone, *Political* 47–48). W. Gladstone
repeatedly attacks the past and future costs—in money, manpower, and inter-
national respect—of Disraeli's "impossible engagements" (48). "Guilty cupid-
ity" motivated missions in Cyprus and Afghanistan, W. Gladstone accuses
(205). He presents unsparing pictures of British destruction and cruelty, particularly in the "wilful, unjust, and destructive" war in Afghanistan (203). In
his famous 1878 essay "England's Mission," W. Gladstone continually characterizes Disraeli's imperial policy as shallow, greedy, and morally vacuous.
These new acquisitions, W. Gladstone tallies, will continue to drain the British
purse and taint its moral prestige. Although W. Gladstone did not oppose the
existence of the British Empire, he did question the expansion of that empire.
He showed an awareness of and aversion to the greed and loss involved in
imperial enlargement, and such rhetoric aligns him with Jim, who repeatedly
muses on the losses incurred by the expedition and expresses discomfort with
its spoils. The adults (including the doctor), on the other hand, evoke Disraeli's profit-driven policies (from W. Gladstone's perspective). W. Gladstone, in
fact, was a fan of Stevenson's work. *Treasure Island* "fascinated" him (Hennessy
180), and he read *Kidnapped* in one sitting (Matthew 276).

Jim further highlights his rejection of adulthood by implicitly contrasting his own interrupted development with Abraham Gray's pronounced and
continued advancement; the traditional bildungsroman arc applies to Gray
but not to Jim. Jim never informs the reader how much money he gets, what
he does with the money, or what he does after the expedition; conversely, on
the final page of the novel, Jim details Gray's continued improvement after
the treasure expedition: "Gray not only saved his money, but, being suddenly
smit with the desire to rise, also studied his profession; and he is now mate
and part owner of a fine full-rigged ship; married besides, and the father of
a family" (*Treasure* 191). Gray develops from a lowly "carpenter's mate" and
pirate conspirator into a loyal member of the gentlemen's party and finally
into a respectable ship owner and family man (96). The contrast between
Gray's rise and Jim's stagnation illustrates Jed Esty's argcument about how
"the perpetuation of adolescence displaces the plot of growth" in the modernist bildungsroman (13). In *Unseasonable Youth,* Esty claims that modernism's
"figure of stunted youth. . . . exposes and disrupts the inherited conventions
of the bildungsroman in order to criticize bourgeois values and to reinvent
the biographical novel" (3). Franco Moretti analyzes a similar shift away from
adulthood and toward childhood in what he terms the "late *Bildungsroman*":
"Youth begins to despise maturity, and to define itself in revulsion from it. . . .
youth looks now for its meaning within itself: gravitating further and fur-

ther away from adult age, and more and more toward adolescence" (*Way* 231). Although Esty and Moretti focus on texts written around and after 1900, *Treasure Island*'s correspondence with their arguments indicates an even earlier transformation in the bildungsroman than they observe.

Although Jim tries to separate himself from the treasure, imperial greed, and adulthood, Silver's parrot, who haunts Jim's dreams at the end of the novel, represents Jim's fear that he has not successfully achieved that separation. Jim and the parrot have much in common. Both are named after pirates. Silver names his pet parrot (though female) Captain Flint "after the famous buccaneer" (*Treasure* 54). Fiona McCulloch reports that Jim Hawkins was also named "after a notorious historical pirate" (74).[12] As if to reference this particular parallel between Jim and the parrot, Silver twice calls Jim "Hawkins" when he introduces Jim to the parrot, even though Silver generally refers to Jim by his first name (*Treasure* 54). Jim and the parrot are both coddled and flattered by Silver. Additionally, the parrot and Jim endure a cage-like existence. While the adults freely travel in preparation for the voyage, Jim lives at the squire's hall "almost a prisoner," guarded by the squire's servant Tom Redruth (36).[13] When Jim first meets the garrulous Captain Flint, Silver keeps the parrot "in a cage in one corner" of the galley (54). Adults also attempt to control the parrot's and Jim's voices. Silver silences the parrot by "thr[owing] his handkerchief over the cage" when he wearies of her refrain (54). Jim writes his narrative because he has been asked to by the squire and doctor; furthermore, the doctor, as already discussed, then interrupts that narrative when it suits him to do so.

The parrot has been "mucked" by her travels (55), and Jim worries about and ultimately resists such a fate. The "wickedness" the parrot has witnessed has caused her, in turn, to exhibit "wickedness" herself (54, 55). Accompanying the pirate Captain England to Africa, New Zealand, India, and South America, she acquires a habit for swearing and repeating "pieces of eight." To explain her unbelievable tongue, Silver tells Jim, "You can't touch pitch and not be mucked, lad. Here's this poor old innocent bird o' mine swearing blue fire, and none the wiser" (55). Her screaming refrain wakes up the sleeping pirates when Jim unknowingly walks into the pirate camp. The parrot's evolution into a profane pirate guard-bird reveals the tenuous line between being innocent and being "mucked." The parrot, rather than Silver, continues to haunt Jim's dreams, exposing his fear of becoming like her: "The worst dreams that ever

---

12. Loman provides more details on the historical Sir John Hawkins; however, Loman does not explicitly classify Hawkins as a pirate.

13. As Gubar points out, the squire basically "draft[s]" Hawkins as an employee on his ship without asking his opinion on the matter (83).

I have are when I hear the surf booming about its coasts, or start upright in bed, with the sharp voice of Captain Flint still ringing in my ears: 'Pieces of eight! pieces of eight!'" (191). Jim had risked becoming as naively greedy as the bird—a witness irreversibly "mucked" by what it sees. Although the parrot may look like "she was a babby," she's "two hundred years old" (55, 54). She is Silver's "old" bird (55). The parrot is an adult—mucked by experience and relentlessly mercenary. Gubar argues that Jim fails in differentiating himself from the parrot, becoming a "helpless pawn" of the adults and submitting to adult coercion and flattery (83).[14] But I contend that his unyielding refusal to return to the island to secure the remaining treasure demonstrates his stand against the adults' philosophy: "Oxen and wain-ropes would not bring me back again to that accursed island" (*Treasure* 191). With these firm words, Jim addresses the squire and doctor; they presumably wish to revisit the island since they direct Jim to withhold "the bearings of the island" from his narrative "because there is still treasure not yet lifted" (1).

Livesey's three chapters are thickly surrounded by Jim's narrative; Livesey's viewpoint, then, is buffered by Jim's more compassionate, less greedy one. Given the brevity of Livesey's section and his indifference to courting the reader, the reader's sympathy stays with Jim, encouraging the reader to see the limitations of Livesey's ideology, just as Jim does. In the quick switches in Ewing's *A Great Emergency* and Dickens's *Little Dorrit,* the reader is also urged to read against the grain of the secondary narrative and to recognize its unreliability. In the former text, Charlie runs away from home in search of adventure; meanwhile, at home, his siblings Henrietta and Rupert save baby Cecil from a fire that engulfs their house. Charlie decides to include Henrietta's diary entry recounting the fire as a self-rebuke for his foolishness: "In my vain, jealous, wild-goose chase after adventures I missed the chance of distinguishing myself in the only Great Emergency which has yet occurred in our family" (Ewing 137). But Charlie and the reader must see through Henrietta's demure, humble writing to grasp how heroically she acted during the blaze. While Charlie tends to brag, Henrietta's entry undersells her own courage and selflessness in the face of great danger. In this way, Henrietta misevaluates her actions. After reading her account, Charlie recognizes this unreliability and proves his discernment and honor by perceiving the "real bravery" shown by Henrietta and Rupert (135). In *Little Dorrit,* Miss Wade's one-chapter self-account elucidates for Arthur Clennam how she came to hate Pet and Gowan (who are now married) and live with Pet's maid Tattycoram. From a young

---

14. Sandison also wonders why "a parrot gets the last word" and "why Jim should be frightened by a parrot" (48, 51). Sandison assumes that because the parrot is Silver's pet, the parrot substitutes for Silver.

age, Miss Wade interprets others' attempts at friendliness as veiled snobbery and spiteful pity; she believes that others are purposefully offending her. The reader realizes that her distorted mindset misconstrues other people, leading to her isolation. The chapter's title, "The History of a Self Tormentor," provided by the narrator or implied author and not by Miss Wade, pushes us to see Miss Wade, and not others, as the principle punisher. Furthermore, Miss Wade's behavior in the chapter preceding her narration also presents her as a "self tormentor": She snipes at Tattycoram, snubbing the one person she claims to love. Tattycoram sees through Miss Wade's savior complex, declaring, "You are as bad as [the Meagles] were, every bit" (Dickens, *Little* 692).[15] Both Henrietta and Miss Wade, therefore, are unreliable on the axes of interpretation or evaluation.

In all three Victorian examples of the quick switch, the second narrator markedly diverges from the first narrator. In *Treasure Island* the narrators differ in age and ideology; in *A Great Emergency* they differ in gender and tone; and in *Little Dorrit* they differ in type (heterodiegetic to homodiegetic). These differences do not cause the narratives to contradict one another on the plane of facts; the facts that Livesey, Henrietta, and Wade provide align with facts established by each primary narrator. Charlie catches the end of the fire, supporting the more thorough account of the event Henrietta gives in her diary; Wade's information about Pet and Gowan reinforces what the heterodiegetic narrator has relayed about those characters. The same, specific sounds—church bells in *A Great Emergency* and cannons and screams in *Treasure Island*—ring out at the same time in both narratives, linking and mutually verifying the two narratives. But because the quick switch is quick, the first narrator ultimately overrides the second, and the reader interprets the second narrator against the first one, amending the secondary narrator's incorrect interpretations or judgments.

---

15. Even if learning about Miss Wade's backstory "temper[s] our distaste for her by providing an account of her personal history," Bock reasons that "our critical judgment of her personality predominates over our sympathetic understanding of her as a victim" (113).

~

CHAPTER 4

Disability Aesthetics and Multinarration in Wilkie Collins's *The Woman in White, The Moonstone,* and *The Legacy of Cain*

A THENA VRETTOS declares that "to be ill is to produce narrative" because illness demands to be diagnosed and discussed (2). That may explain why, as Karen Bourrier and Jennifer Esmail observe, so much Victorian literature includes disabled characters; however, fewer Victorian texts feature a disabled narrator. What difference does it make to have the disabled character "produce narrative" herself, for the representation of disability to be self-representation? What characterizes such a narrator's voice? Do disabled narrators in Victorian literature tend to use certain narrative strategies or do their narratives exhibit certain formal characteristics? Martha Stoddard Holmes notes that Wilkie Collins allows some of his disabled characters—mainly Lucilla Finch in *Poor Miss Finch*—to narrate, but Stoddard Holmes doesn't analyze the style or form of Lucilla's narrative ("Bolder"). Julia Miele Rodas provocatively reads Jane Eyre as autistic, though she relies more on Jane's interactions with others in the plot than on traits of Jane's narration to make her point ("On the Spectrum"). One aim of this chapter is to introduce and model a disability narratology that not only centers disability in literary analysis but also pays close attention to the formal and stylistic characteristics of narrations penned by disabled narrators. Vrettos's "tracing [of] how hysteria informs" Lucy Snowe's "acts of narration" in *Villette* (50) comes nearer to the disability narratology approach I use here to study the disabled narrators of W. Collins's multinarrator novels. Critics such as Casey A. Cothran, Lillian

Craton, Kate Flint, Teresa Mangum, Mark Mossman, and Stoddard Holmes have considered W. Collins's frequent, and sometimes progressive, portrayal of disabled characters. Scholars have also spent much ink parsing W. Collins's "novelty of form" (*Woman* 3) in *The Woman in White* and *The Moonstone*; they tend to agree that his multinarrator structures assert the ultimate subjectivity of knowledge, memory, and narrative.[1] In this chapter, I bring together these two approaches—narratology and disability studies—to connect W. Collins's narrative structures and representations of disability; this fused approach reveals that the novels' preoccupation with disability goes beyond plot—it also deeply relates to the novels' form.

I argue that W. Collins's three "novels in testimony" (Emrys 13)—*The Woman in White* (1860), *The Moonstone* (1868), and *The Legacy of Cain* (1888)—not only illustrate W. Collins's investment in showing how disability affects characters and their narrations but also employ what Tobin Siebers calls disability aesthetics. Many of these novels' homodiegetic narrators experience disability; disability influences both the content and shape of their narratives, resulting in texts that are fragmented, wandering, interrupted, pained, or collaboratively created—conditions that subvert more conventional representations of authorship, narrative progression, and closure. While these narrators don't always celebrate their disabilities or appreciate how those disabilities affect their narrations (potentially suggesting the novels' negative attitude toward disability), their productions—despite being fragmented or interrupted—are appreciated by other characters and essential to the search for justice, meaning, and resolution in each novel. W. Collins, as the implied author of the novels, enacts disability aesthetics by creating a narrative structure that centers disabled voices, values fragmented or incomplete productions, and necessitates collaboration and interdependence between numerous texts and characters. Collins sets up a plot and structure in which a team of characters, many of whom are disabled, must work together to defeat the villain—a character who, in all three novels, is able-bodied/minded and ruthlessly independent. Disability studies scholars champion interdependence and argue that it productively reveals and undercuts "the false and unrealizable Western ideal of personal autonomy, self-sufficiency, and independence" (Mitchell and Snyder, "Narrative" 129).[2] Notably, it is the able-bodied/minded villains of these three W. Collins novels—*The Woman in White*'s Count Fosco,

---

1. See Hutter (192), Shuttleworth (197), J. Taylor (202), and Thoms (159).

2. Importantly, this focus on interdependence does not mean that individual disabled people are weak, powerless, and helpless (which are damaging stereotypes about disabled people); rather, as Stoddard Holmes writes, "disability produces an important reminder of the reality that almost all lives *are* based on interdependence and mutuality" (*Fictions* 187).

The Moonstone's Godfrey Ablewhite, and *The Legacy of Cain*'s Helena Grace-dieu—who hold such "false and unrealizable Western ideal[s]."

The plot and structure of W. Collins's three novels evoke what Siebers calls "disability aesthetics." To Siebers, this alternative to traditional aesthetics "prizes physical and mental difference" and "refuses to recognize the representation of the healthy body—and its body's definition of harmony, integrity, and beauty—as the sole determination of the aesthetic" (19, 3). Siebers grounds this concept in the modern art of the early twentieth century in its preoccupation for rendering "bodies previously considered to be broken, diseased, wounded, or disabled" (35). Emily B. Stanback discovers it at work in the Romantic period as well, particularly in the Romantics' interest in poetic fragments. She is alert to the "relationship between disabled bodies and . . . textual qualities" such as "irrationality, inarticulacy, decay, disfigurement, fragmentation, and distortion at the level of the word, line, sentence, stanza, and genre" (44). While W. Collins's "novels in testimony" (Emrys 13) unite disparate narratives into a coherent whole, potentially suggesting a traditional aesthetics, the multinarrator form does not "cure" or "fix" disability—it does not erase the markers of disability and fragmentation in the individual narratives; furthermore, the final collective narratives are asymmetrical patchworks—another aspect of Collins's disability aesthetics. The seams between narrations are visibly marked by descriptive tagged switches between narrators; the narratives are of different sizes and genres; the cutting pace is irregular; and gaps in the story persist despite employing multiple narrators. A useful contrast to what I'm calling W. Collins's "patchworks" would be Anne Brontë's *The Tenant of Wildfell Hall* (1848), an incredibly balanced and symmetrical frame novel. Gilbert Markham narrates for approximately one hundred pages before and one hundred pages after Helen Graham's diary. Helen's diary sits neatly in the heart of the novel, lasting only slightly longer than Gilbert's total page count.

Collins's fictional portrayals of disability are extensive and varied, reflecting the Victorians' interest in what Craton calls the "odd body." According to Craton, odd bodies became prominent in the nineteenth century because a "wide range of social developments converged to give new authority to the concept of normalcy, and thus new significance to representations of abnormality" (30).[3] In the appendix to *Fictions of Affliction: Physical Disability in Victorian Culture*, Stoddard Holmes provides a list of "Physically Disabled Characters in Nineteenth-Century British Literature," and characters from

---

3. Shuttleworth makes a similar point: "Victorian psychiatry sought to demarcate the boundaries of sanity and insanity, of pathological and acceptable behavior, thus conferring the authority of science on bourgeois norms of respectability" (192).

W. Collins's novels populate every category in her list: blind characters, deaf characters, "crippled" characters, people of small and large stature, people with facial "disfigurements," multiple disabilities, and chronic illness or unspecified disabilities (197–99). In considering which W. Collins characters qualify as disabled, I have adopted Rosemarie Garland-Thomson's conception of disability as a "broad term within which cluster ideological categories as varied as sick, deformed, abnormal, crazy, ugly, old, feebleminded, maimed, afflicted, mad, or debilitated—all of which disadvantage people by devaluing bodies that do not conform to cultural standards" (356). This "broad" conception of disability also resonates with how Victorians would have approached it, as Bourrier and Esmail explain: "Victorians did not use the term 'disability' as a sharply defined medical and legal term in the way that we do in the twenty-first century," and disability would have "encompasse[d] physical, sensory, and cognitive differences" (444). Even though Stoddard Holmes focuses on physical disabilities in her book, she acknowledges that the Victorians did not distinguish as clearly between body and mind—and physical and mental disabilities—as we do now. The narrators I discuss in W. Collins's novels, therefore, have a variety of disabilities: deformed characters like Rosanna Spearman, chronically ill characters like Frederick Fairlie and Ezra Jennings, and cognitively or intellectually disabled characters like Eunice Gracedieu and Anne Catherick. Some characters, like Marian Halcombe, are only temporarily disabled, but many disability theorists emphasize that disability is not always a permanent state; as Siebers affirms, "all people, by virtue of being human, move in and out of disability identity" (45).

W. Collins's own body—odd from birth, frequently diseased and disabled during his life—may have prepared him or predisposed him to write about disabled characters. As Catherine Peters details in her biography of W. Collins, "As an adult he was oddly disproportioned, with a bulging forehead, head too large for his body, short arms and legs" (20). W. Collins seemingly inherited his father's gout and suffered bouts of it from the early 1850s until the end of his life. To treat it, W. Collins took progressively large—dangerously large, eventually—doses of laudanum. During these attacks, his eyes were increasingly and painfully engorged with blood, which made reading and writing impossible. Portions of No Name and The Moonstone had to be dictated to his doctor and daughter, respectively. Additionally, W. Collins himself was so ill while composing The Woman in White that he couldn't leave his house (C. Peters 209–10). In his letters, W. Collins frequently describes his symptoms and laments how they slow his writing, curtail his social life, limit his food and drink intake, and either require travel (to healthier locales) or prohibit movement. For example, in a letter written to Paul Hamilton Hayne in 1884, he confides, "Gout and work and age . . . try to persuade me to lay down my pen" (Baker and Clarke 467). W. Collins knew from his own experience, as well as from witnessing how the illnesses of his father and brother curtailed their artistic ambitions, how disability could influence one's artistic pursuits.

THE WOMAN IN WHITE

Even on the level of plot, disability is central to *The Woman in White*. Sir Percival's secret lies at the heart of the novel: His parents weren't married when he was born, technically disqualifying him from inheriting the title and estate. This scandal has remained under wraps because Percival's father led a very secluded life due to his physical deformity; because of his lifestyle, the community incorrectly assumes that his marriage to Percival's mother occurred but happened privately. Sir Percival institutionalizes the "half-witted" Anne Catherick because she convinces him that she knows the secret of his illegitimacy (*Woman* 535). Laura's uncle and guardian, Frederick Fairlie, doesn't prevent Laura Fairlie's marriage to the shady Sir Percival because Fairlie considers himself a helpless invalid unequal to unpleasant or difficult tasks. Percival's confidante Count Fosco switches Anne's and Laura's identities and confines Laura in an asylum under Anne's name; Anne dies, and the stress of the ordeal disables the already nervous Laura, making her a more perfect doppelgänger of the late Anne and permanently affecting her memory.

Disability is also central to *The Woman and White*'s narratives and overall structure. The doubles Anne and Laura are both associated with fragmented and interrupted narratives; in today's parlance, Anne would be categorized as cognitively or intellectually disabled and Laura as experiencing mental illness or a mental disorder. Fairlie's chronic invalidism forces him to collaborate with his valet to create his unsure, perplexed narrative. When Laura's half-sister Marian Halcombe falls severely ill, her diary becomes fragmented and unreadable. Walter Hartright, Laura and Marian's drawing tutor and Laura's second husband, is traumatized by his time abroad and by the loss of Laura, evidenced by the pained gaps and pauses in his narrative. These characters and others must collaborate in the story and in the narrative to attain truth, closure, and victory over the primary villain, Count Fosco. Fosco—independent and able-bodied/minded—pens a narrative that exhibits the more traditional aesthetics of beauty, completeness, and solo genius. The collective narrative's triumph over the nondisabled Fosco, inclusion of disability, reliance on interdependence, and patchwork quality are all evidence of its disability aesthetics.

Anne Catherick and Laura Fairlie are both described in terms of disability, and Anne's short inset texts and Laura's speech are fragmentary and incomplete. While Walter more obliquely refers to "Anne's mental affliction" (*Woman* 475), Anne's mother more bluntly calls her "weak in the head" (534), "half-witted" (535), and "crazy and queer" (536). Sir Percival labels her an "idiot" (536), and Anne's governess/guardian Mrs. Clements shares that Anne was "slow at her lessons" (474).[4] Anne's texts are defaced and disjointed. Her first letter to Laura, which floridly and "incoherent[ly]" (80) warns her not to marry Sir Percival, is unconventional in form—lacking a proper start and end. The letter "began abruptly, without any preliminary form of address" (79) and "ended, without signature of any sort" (80). The handwriting is "strange" (78) and "feeble and faint, and defaced by blots" (80), indicating not only Anne's poor state of health (she has a fatal heart condition) but also a "defaced" narrative. She writes her next note to Laura on "a strip of paper" and buries it underground (297). "Strip" suggests a torn of piece of paper—a fragment—and the dirt presumably defaces this letter as well. Once Laura is kidnapped by Fosco and forcibly institutionalized in an asylum under Anne's name, she experiences a trauma-induced mental disorder; her symptoms include "weakened, shaken faculties" (434) and being unable to remember or coherently explain what has happened to her. Even prior to this event, Laura is headache-prone and "nervous and sensitive" (39). All that Laura can tell her sister and Walter about her traumatizing abduction and captivity is "presented in fragments, sadly incoherent in themselves, and widely detached from each other" (424). Her mind is frequently referred to as "confused" and her recollections as "fragments" (424), "fragmentary" (426), and "interrupted" (414). Even these fragments disperse when she reaches "a total blank" and remembers nothing (427). Laura's recollection is interrupted, fragmentary, and incomplete. But Anne's letters and Laura's recollections are not dismissed because they are unusual and fragmentary; instead, Marian and Walter investigate the claims, however bizarrely expressed, made in Anne's letter. They also accept much of Laura's account and attempt to corroborate it with other texts and information when the lawyer advises them to do so.

The case of Anne and Laura also shows the limits of W. Collins's inclusion of disabled narrators. As I mentioned in the introduction, when disability prevents a character from being reliable on the axis of reporting or creates an unreadable text, that character is disqualified from narrating. Building on

---

4. Wright explains that to the Victorians, "the nineteenth-century term of 'idiot' referred to persons who were considered as suffering from mental disability from birth or an early age" (*Mental* 9); furthermore, idiocy was perceived as a permanent condition. Relatedly, Talairach-Vielmas highlights the debates over insane asylums that were occurring during *The Woman in White*'s serialization.

Wayne C. Booth's conception of narrator unreliability, James Phelan delineates three axes of un/reliability: "Unreliable reporting occurs along the axis of characters, facts, and events; unreliable reading (or interpreting) occurs along the axis of knowledge and perception; and unreliable regarding (or evaluating) occurs along the axis of ethics and evaluation" (50). Narrators who mis- or under-interpret or evaluate are common in W. Collins's multinarrator novels. In *The Moonstone*, Miss Clack misevaluates Godfrey's character and misinterprets her own feelings for him; however, she remains reliable on the axis of reporting. But narrators who misreport—who lie or convey patently untrue statements—are not permitted. Anne is unreliable because she insists that she knows Sir Percival's secret when she only knows that he has a secret. Laura is unreliable because she stubbornly claims she completed actions—like visiting her old governess—that she did not actually do. Walter calls Laura's misbelief "a flaw in the evidence" (*Woman* 436). According to the lawyer Kyrle, this error would make Laura an unreliable and unbelievable witness in the courtroom. Anne and Laura don't purposefully misreport, as they seem to earnestly believe what they claim; the other characters and the reader, therefore, don't judge them negatively for their misreporting.[5] But since both characters would misreport as narrators, they are thereby disqualified from serving as narrators in any significant or extended way in *The Woman in White*—Laura can only offer her speech and Anne her short inset texts. As I'll discuss below, the unreadable scribbles at the end of Marian's diary, scrawled as she falls into delusion and fever, are not reproduced in the text; instead, they are described by the text's editor in an appended note to the reader: "At this place the entry in the Diary ceases to be legible" (336). A tension exists between W. Collins's desire to represent the voice and narrations of his disabled narrators and for his narrators to be reliable and their texts readable. As reviewed in chapter 1, the Victorian multinarrator novel privileges realism of method and cannot accommodate a narrator unreliable on the axis of facts or unable to produce a readable, material text; the modernist multiperspectival novel, however, differs on both counts.

Frederick Fairlie, Laura and Marian's uncle, is a hypochondriac.[6] Fairlie suffers from weakness, exhaustion, palpitations, nervousness, and sensory

---

5. Furthermore, their misreporting goes hand in hand with misinterpreting—their trauma and disability have affected their knowledge. Phelan acknowledges that "misreporting involves unreliability at least on the axis of characters, facts, and events . . . misreporting is typically a consequence of the narrator's lack of knowledge or mistaken values, and, consequently, it almost always occurs with misreading or misevaluating" (51).

6. Both D. A. Miller and Shuttleworth connect his invalidism with femininity. Miller labels him "an effeminate" (151), and Shuttleworth notes that Fairlie "purposefully installs himself in the female role of nervous helplessness" (212).

sensitivity—but these symptoms lack a specific physical cause. Characters usually encounter him sitting in the same chair in the same room. On one occasion he is seen in a different room and his valet and Kyrle must help him stand (618); he later is "carried from the room" (620). He constantly grumbles about his "miserable health" and "the wretched state of [his] nerves" (338, 43). Because of the lack of evident causes for their symptoms, Victorian hypochondriacs were often "denied the validity of their pain by the medical establishment" (Vrettos 48). In line with such a view, Hartright diagnoses Fairlie with nothing more than "selfish affectation" (*Woman* 43). And although Fairlie is certainly both selfish and affected, he does seem to experience symptoms. Rachel Ablow notes in her examination of hypochondria in *Villette* that Victorians considered "the illness [to be] a disorder of the senses as much as an error of belief. The hypochondriac does not simply think she is ill when she is not. Instead, she *feels* ill in the absence of any verifiable cause" (par. 4). But Hartright's refusal to believe that Fairlie's suffering is real illustrates how hypochondria "inevitably raised questions of authenticity" (Frawley 69). Hypochondria, as Maria H. Frawley writes, "blurred" the "line between imagined and real disease" (70), and Fairlie's sudden death after "the shock" of "paralysis" (*Woman* 626) at the end of the novel suggests that his symptoms were not merely illusory or without cause; his fear of being "hurr[ied] into his grave" was justified (616).

Although Fairlie repeatedly identifies himself as an "invalid" (43, 338), he does not appreciate disability or disability aesthetics. Rather, he seems to have internalized negative stereotypes about disability. He denies his own humanity: "I am nothing but a bundle of nerves dressed up to look like a man" (348). He believes himself helpless, incapable, weak, and susceptible to everything. He mostly lives in isolation, much like Sir Felix, Sir Percival's father, did. Because of his "morbid sense of his own personal deformity," Sir Felix "shunned all society" and "hid[ ] his ugliness and his deformity in the strictest privacy" (456, 456, 531). Fairlie seems to do the same. Far from developing an appreciation for disability aesthetics, however, he surrounds himself with "art-treasures" (339): classically beautiful items like Raphael's *Virgin and Child* and "really fine specimens of English water-colour art" copied from Rembrandt (45). Walter first meets him sitting "amid . . . rare and beautiful objects" (42). Fairlie imagines such traditionally beautiful objects the epitome of "taste" (44, 339) with the power to "improve" the viewer (339).

However, Fairlie's narrative, collaboratively composed with his valet Louis, highlights his invalidism and interdependence. Fairlie feels that both his body and mind are not up to the assigned task of writing his narrative, and so he asks, "Is a man in my state of nervous wretchedness capable of writing narratives?" (338). He agrees to write the narrative, but only with Louis's assistance: "What I can't remember and can't write, Louis must remember, and write for me" (338). Louis's mind and body are crucial in the creation of the narrative. Fairlie frequently "consult[s]" (340) Louis and includes Louis's memories and interpretations in his narrative: "I give the words on the authority of Louis" (341). A few pages in, Fairlie feels too exhausted to go on, and once he rests, he continues by giving dictation to Louis (342). "Louis thinks" continues to punctuate the narrative and we're left unsure of how much Louis may have edited Fairlie's dictation. Throughout the narrative, Fairlie asks questions, some rhetorical and others directed at Louis, as Louis's answer is then recorded. Fairlie's narrative draws attention to its collaborative origin by constantly reminding us of Louis's presence, including through the incorporation of such questions. The recurring questions also indicate Fairlie's unknowing, confused, overwhelmed stance—because of his invalidism, he prefers others answer, help, or act. Of the narrative's first six sentences, three are questions; the narrative also closes with a question. Fairlie's narrative is framed by this questioning posture.

Fairlie's onetime employee, Walter Hartright, narrates five sections of the novel; even though he narrates retrospectively, after outsmarting Fosco and marrying Laura, his narrative still increasingly betrays debilitating stress over relaying his traumatic experiences. Walter's first section covers his growing love for Laura while serving as her drawing tutor at Limmeridge House. This part of the narrative shows few signs of stress even when describing stressful events, such as meeting the strange Anne in the road or finding out that Laura is to marry someone else; when pondering his rival Sir Percival he admits "it is hard to confess this," but he nonetheless barrels on because "I must suppress nothing from beginning to end of the terrible story that I now stand committed to reveal" (82). Later, he cannot keep to this promise to "suppress nothing." A series of subsequent traumatic events—leaving his beloved Laura, barely surviving a dangerous trip to Central America, learning of Laura's marriage and then alleged demise—deeply affects his body, mind, and narratives of that subsequent time. Walter's narrative becomes riddled with gaps, and other narrators are left to explain the physical and mental toll such events have taken on Walter because he can't bear to narrate them himself, even retrospectively. The lawyer Mr. Gilmore, the book's second narrator, describes Walter's transformation after he leaves Laura: He now has a "pale and haggard" face, "uncertain" manner, and speaks "confusedly" (155). A "nervous contraction quivered about his lips and eyes," and a "nervous spasm crossed his face" (155, 156). In short, he resembles the nervous, pale, and confused Anne.[7] The novel's third narrator, Marian, covers Walter's disastrous trip to Central America, during which his compatriots die around him from pestilence, attacks from native inhabitants, and shipwreck; he miraculously escapes death each time. Walter seems too traumatized to narrate either his decline after leaving Limmeridge or his experiences on the ill-fated expedition (beyond a few sentences), much like Laura cannot coherently narrate her harrowing abduction and imprisonment. Although many critics believe Hartright's own interpretation that his adventure has toughened him,[8] when Walter takes up the pen again to narrate events that occur once he returns to England, he indicates that he might not have the physical or mental power to complete his narrative: "This narrative, if I have the strength and the courage to write it, may now go on" (407).

A few pages after such promises of progression, however, his narrative is interrupted; he skips one week of the story because he is unable to explain what happens once he realizes Laura is alive and not dead—no one else fills in this ellipsis. He admits that "[his] heart turns faint, [his] mind sinks in darkness and confusion when [he] think[s] of it" (412). A narrative, Walter asserts, must be "untangled" (412), implying that any attempted narrative of that dark time would be twisted and confused—it would resemble Anne's "incoherent" letters or Laura's "fragmentary" memories (80, 426). His long-winded, three-paragraph refusal to narrate the one-week span accentuates this ellipsis and reminds readers of the previous gaps in his story that others (Gilmore, Marian) supplement. Later in this section, when detailing how he, Marian, and Laura lived together in London, Walter professes that writing of these past "days of doubt and dread" still physically exhausts and mentally drains him: "I have paused and rested for a while on my forward course" (480). In this moment of respite, he proleptically "look[s] forward to the happier time which [his] narrative has not yet reached" to recharge his writerly visit "back again" to his difficult past (479, 480). At the end of his last section, Walter's weakened body overcomes him after "many months" of writing; he admits, "the pen falters in my hand" (627), recalling Marian's feverish loss of control over her pen in a scene I inspect in the next paragraph. Walter has reached the end of his

7. D. A. Miller locates Walter's nervousness in his first meeting with Anne Catherick; this scene reveals "the 'origins' of male nervousness in female contagion—strictly, in the woman's touch" (152). Miller argues that the novel "obsessively repeats and remembers" this meeting (152), and Talairach-Vielmas similarly points out that Walter "becomes monomaniac after his encounter with the woman in white" (44).

8. For example, Shuttleworth writes that the "feminized" Walter must "prove himself in the primeval jungles of South America before returning to display his newly acquired masculinity" (212). Gaylin agrees that Walter comes back from Central America "a virile, empowered" man (313).

story, but he also seems physically incapable of continuing any further. This line also potentially prefigures the "Writer's Cramp" that besets and seemingly kills a character in W. Collins's later novel *The Legacy of Cain* (114). Walter was unsure, after all, that he would have the "strength" to finish the story (*Woman* 407), and his previously experienced "spasm[s]" (156) and "quiver[ings]" still haunt him at its close (155).

Typically, Marian's diary is marked by her ability and control; however, when she becomes deeply ill, her narrative splinters, disintegrates, and then ends. She prides herself on the "reliability of [her] recollection[s]" and the "regularity of the entries in [her] journal" (284). When Fosco reads and then writes in her journal while she is ill and unable to stop him—actions scholars often interpret as textual rape[9]—he applauds her diary as "amazing" and "masterly" in its style, observation, and accuracy (336). But the end of Marian's first section (her narration is divided into two by a book break) foreshadows the dramatic end to her second. In the former, she avails herself of her diary on December 22, Laura and Sir Percival's wedding day, a particularly emotional day given her love for her half-sister and her deep distrust of Percival. The day's entry splits into four short sections (three of which are only two sentences long) timestamped seven, ten, eleven, and three o'clock. Throughout the rest of her diary, Marian rarely partitions a day's entry by hour. The timestamping moves the entry toward a more simultaneous and less retrospective account, evocatively illustrating Marian's "whirl and confusion" (195). Once the wedding has concluded, Marian writes, "They are gone! I am blind with crying—I can write no more—" (195). She equates her overwhelming grief and inability to continue with a disability—"blind"—before abruptly ending the entry with a dash. At the end of her second section, she falls into a deadly fever after spying in the rain on Sir Percival and Fosco. She loses the ability to count the chimes of the clock, feels hot, and suffers from a headache. Her physical and visual capacities become muddled: "I can write, but the lines all run together" (335). As her mind and body break down, so does her writing, as she tends to repeat words or phrases several times in a row in a loop-like manner: "the rain, the rain—the cruel rain"; "So cold, so cold"; "I am shivering again—shivering" (335). The last section in the entry includes six dashes, visually representing a halting, interrupted movement. As with the previous example, Marian marks the time more frequently than she usually does, noting both eight and then nine o'clock, fragmenting the June 20th entry. As the entry stutters to an end, Marian is obsessed with whether she has correctly

---

9. See Case (158), Delafield (123), and D. A. Miller (181). Sternlieb, on the other hand, warns against "conflating Marian's diary and virginal body" and encourages critics to "abandon the notion of this scene as a rape" (59, 58).

assessed the time: "And the strokes of the clock, the strokes I can't count, keep striking in my head—" (335). As the clock strokes elude her control, so do the strokes of her pen, as that long dash concludes the legible part of her diary entry. An editorial note, presumably written by Walter (though potentially by Marian herself), clarifies that "At this place the entry in the Diary ceases to be legible. The two or three lines which follow, contain fragments of words only, mingled with blots and scratches of the pen" (336). The blotted and fragmented entry resembles Anne and Laura's productions, as well as those created by other disabled narrators in these three W. Collins novels.

Other of the novel's narrators, while not disabled, highlight their own mental and physical limitations in their narrations—mastery is impossible for nondisabled and disabled narrators alike. Michelson, the Blackwater Park housekeeper, apologizes for the gaps in her memory. She shares her "regret at [her] own inability to remember the precise day on which Lady Glyde left Blackwater" (398). Hester Pinhorn, Fosco's cook, starts off by apologizing as well: "I am sorry to say that I have never learnt to read or write" (399), and she asks the man to whom she dictates "to put [her] language right as he goes on" (399). Hester's account, like Fairlie's, is collaboratively produced with someone who physically records her verbally conveyed account. Like with Fairlie's dictation scenario, the reader can't be sure how much the transcriber alters Hester's language as she requests he do. Like Michelson, Hester calls attention to the inadequacy of her memory: "But, whatever you do, don't trust *my* memory in the matter" (399). Poor memory is one of the symptoms that marks Anne and Laura as disabled or ill. The commonness of memory lapses, even while their severity varies, is another way that W. Collins "collapse[s] boundaries between the able-bodied and the impaired" (Flint 154). Although each narrator is brought in because of what they can offer and what they know, the novel's introductory paragraphs make clear how each narrator is also defined by limitations: "When [one narrator's] experience fails, he will retire from the position of narrator" (W. Collins, *Woman* 9). Individual limitation—or "fail[ure]"—is built into each narrative and into the novel's very structure.

In a broader sense, the novel's structure relies on the reality of individual limitation and, thereby, on the need for interdependence and collaboration. Alison A. Case, Ann Gaylin, and D. A. Miller apply the phrases "master narrator" or "master storyteller" to Walter because he seemingly compiles the narratives and arguably marginalizes other voices, particularly Laura's.[10] But

10. In the same vein, Perkins and Donaghy accuse Walter of "manipulating the narrative for his own ends" (392). According to Heller, Walter's desire to rise in society and establish himself as a successful "professional man" drives this narrative mastery (112). Case argues that Collins's multinarrator novels reveal a gendered conflict by "mov[ing] toward an opposition

Walter is not as masterful as such critics assume or claim, and the procurement of the narratives is more collaborative than critics acknowledge. Early on, Marian researches her mother's correspondence and reads excerpts to Walter that illuminate Anne's identity—those excerpts are included in the novel. Marian shares her diary with Walter but remains in control of his experience of it; Walter recounts that "she read to me from the manuscript, and I took the notes I wanted as she went on" (*Woman* 436). While Walter obtains narratives from Jane Gould, the doctor, and Hester Pinhorn, Marian acquires narratives from Michelson and Mr. Fairlie. And if Walter relays certain parts of Laura's story to the reader (which critics are quick to point out), Marian relays certain parts of Walter's story to the reader as well—namely, his disastrous trip Central America that she learns about through a prophetic dream and then records in her diary.

The plot of the novel, in addition to its structure, stresses the importance of collaboration and interdependence. The unconventional Marian-Laura-Walter household requires all three members to function. Marian and Laura share a passionate bond; Laura and Walter eventually marry; and Walter and Marian deeply admire and rely on each other. When the three are living incognito in London, Marian and Walter pool their money, make a budget, take care of Laura, and pursue the restoration of Laura's rightful identity. Walter may work to fund their living situation, but he maintains "absolute reliance" on Marian (541). Walter proceeds in the investigation only "after consulting with Marian" (435). Once Walter and Laura marry (after Sir Percival's death), Marian continues to live with the couple, and when Walter travels on business, he corresponds with both his "wife and Marian" (625). After being absent for a few harrowing days, Walter comments, "We had hardly known how close the tie was which bound us three together" (543). Marian echoes that sentiment at the novel's close, pledging to stay with Laura and Walter: "There can be no parting between us, till the last parting of all" (621). She declares to Walter, "My heart and my happiness . . . are with Laura and you" (621). Just as Marian needs the couple, the couple also needs her. The novel's much deliberated final lines indicate that Marian is necessary to their marriage; she serves as "the good angel of [their] lives" (627). Marian functions not only as an angel but also as a second mother to Laura and Walter's child. She holds him at the novel's conclusion and authoritatively deems him *"the Heir of Limmeridge"* (627). Walter, Marian, and Laura embrace interdependence and collaboration to thwart Fosco and earn back Laura's identity. The reassertion of Laura's

---

between a subordinated feminine narrator and a hypermasculine master-narrator who gains a full command of narrative authority and agency" (33).

real identity isn't accomplished through the work of a solitary lawyer; rather, it occurs by group acclamation, when the "audience" of Limmeridge tenants vocally accept her as the real Laura (618), then joining "the throng of villagers" to watch the removal of her name from the gravestone (619). Additionally, Walter compels Fosco to write his confessional narrative—which provides the details of stealing Laura's identity—by leveraging his association with a group: The Brotherhood, an Italian secret society. The Brotherhood fights for the "rights of the people" and challenges those who would hurt the group: "tyranny," "a bad King or a bad Minister," or those who "inflict[ ] injury on the well-being of his fellow-men" (575).

Fosco is the most able character in the novel; he's also the villain. Everyone comments on Fosco's strength—of body, mind, manner—over himself and others. Despite his advanced age and corpulence, his face is without wrinkles, and he walks with "a light jaunty step" (567).[11] As D. A. Miller points out, Fosco lacks nerves or has at least "mastered" them via his cigarette smoking in a novel in which most of the main characters are occasionally or perpetually nervous (150). When he daringly writes a "postscript" at the end of Marian's diary while she's sick, his handwriting is "large, bold, and firmly regular" (Woman 336), contrasting with the "feeble and faint" handwriting of Anne and with Marian's illegible ending to her diary (80). In a novel in which many characters are disabled or fall seriously ill, Fosco is the exception; furthermore, he is positioned as a doctor-chemist figure with the ability to cure or kill at will. Although he successfully oversees Marian's recuperation, he hastens Anne's demise through medicine. He prides himself on his knowledge of chemistry and brands the chemist as a god who can disable minds and bodies. He imagines drugging Shakespeare at work on Hamlet and thereby altering the work produced: "I will reduce his mind, by the action of his body, till his pen pours out the most abject drivel that has ever degraded paper" (602). Fosco here acknowledges a relation between dis/ability and narrative.

Fosco's narrative exhibits the traditional aesthetics that Siebers describes: "harmony, bodily integrity, and health as standards of beauty" (19). Fosco's "untiring pen" that writes for hours and hours in "so large and bold a hand" (Woman 593) contrasts greatly with Walter's own "falter[ing]" pen (627). Even after the writing marathon, Fosco "spring[s] to his feet with the activity of a young man" (594). He represents himself as the unscathed victor in a battle with his task: "The subject is exhausted: the man—Fosco—is not" (594). While other narrators openly admit to and sometimes apologize for their limitations

---

11. Wagner shows how Fosco's fatness serves as a cover for his sophisticated villainy: "To Victorians, fat men were jolly, if somewhat stupid" (50–51).

of skill, body, memory, or literacy, Fosco praises his own narrative as "remark-
able" (613). And he hides, rather than spotlights, two relatively minor memory
lapses (forgetting the name of a servant and being unsure how to spell a person's name) by placing them in parentheses. Otherwise, Fosco boldly asserts
his knowledge of "all": "I have all the dates at my fingers' ends" (607). He
proceeds surely and clearly; he writes with rhetorical flourishes. Unlike other
narrators, whose narratives are interrupted or hastily cut off, Fosco's has no
gaps and offers a sure conclusion and signature. His narrative contrasts with
Anne's letter's lack of a proper start and end (80). He does admit to possessing
one "weakness" in his narrative—his admiration for Marian—but he knows
full well that his reader, Walter, will not find it a weakness at all, but rather an
aggravating strength (611).

Furthermore, in his narrative, Fosco presents himself as someone who
needs no help; similarly, he treats his narrative as a standalone production
that doesn't require other narrations to supplement or extend his own. Even
though he references the intermittent assistance of others—namely his wife
and Madame Rubelle—he reasserts his "natural capacity for grappling, single-
handed, with circumstances" (603). Although he might not always technically work alone, he imagines himself as the "single-handed" mastermind who
occasionally employs other people as merely useful tools. He even binds the
pages of his narrative into a little book: He "strung [the papers] together with
a bodkin and a piece of string; revised them; wrote all the titles and hon-
ours by which he was personally distinguished, at the head of the first page;
and then read the manuscript to me" (594). The activities that would usually
be conducted by others, like editors or printers, he does himself: He writes
(doesn't dictate like Fairlie), edits, compiles the pages, and adds the prefatory
material. Fosco even controls Walter's first experience of the manuscript by
reading the narrative out loud to Walter; Fosco also, therefore, serves as first
reader of the text. Although Fosco may intend for his production to stand
alone, it does not. His narrative is one of many in the novel and is nestled
between two short narratives written by Walter—potentially Walter's way of
cornering Fosco in the narrative just as he has done in the plot.

While Fosco can be charismatic and his narrative is stunning,[12] his fate
suggests W. Collins's disapproval not just of his criminality but also of his
denial of interdependence. Fosco's betrayal of the Brotherhood represents
his desire to be singular, independent, and autonomous—separate from the

---

12. In a contemporary review, Oliphant expressed her awe of this narrative: Fosco's "vic-
torious force and cleverness turn discomfiture and confession into a brilliant climax of self-
disclosure" (Page 113).

group. Fittingly, it is a member of that group—Walter's friend Pesca—who chooses to remain loyal to the group (even though he no longer wholeheartedly believes in its cause) by "forward[ing] the report" that dooms Fosco (622). Fosco's disloyalty to the Brotherhood leads to his demise at the hands of that collective. In the novel's conclusion, Walter witnesses Fosco's dead body displayed on a slab in a Paris morgue, his Brotherhood tattoo covered with a "T" for traitor. The multiplicity of the "French mob" and "great crowd" that jostles to glimpse his naked corpse contrasts with his solitariness (623, 622). The "spectators" have the power—his body is "exposed" to their eyes and comments (623). It is an apt, lonely, and "dreadful end" to his destructive belief in self-sufficiency (623).

Fosco, an able-bodied and able-minded (Marian wonders if he's a mind-reader) criminal mastermind and villain, opposes the Victorian association between criminality and disability. Because of that association, as Bourrier and Esmail point out, "often, a highly visual disability, such as a peg leg or a facial disfigurement, functions to mark out a character as a villain" in Victorian literature (447). Victorian psychiatrists like Henry Maudsley increasingly connected criminality and disability throughout the mid to late nineteenth century. He writes in *Responsibility in Mental Disease* (first published in 1874) that the

> criminal class constitutes a degenerate or morbid variety of mankind, marked by peculiar low physical and mental characteristics. . . . They are scrofulous, not seldom deformed, with badly-formed angular heads; are stupid, sullen, sluggish, deficient in vital energy, and sometimes afflicted with epilepsy. As a class, they are of mean and defective intellect, though excessively cunning, and not a few of them are weak-minded and imbecile. (29–30)

Fosco disagrees that crimes are as easily solvable (and hence, that criminals are as easily findable) as Marian and Laura want to believe. Fosco taunts that there are "resolute, educated, highly-intelligent" criminals who get away with their undetected crimes (233). But other Victorian novels indicate, in line with Maudsley's pronouncements, that criminality is legible on the human body. For example, in Robert Louis Stevenson's *Strange Case of Dr. Jekyll and Mr. Hyde,* Hyde tramples a girl in the street, beats M. P. Carew to death with a cane, and commits other unnamed "monstrous" acts (53). Both Enfield and Utterson describe Hyde as possessing a vague, impossible-to-pinpoint "deformity" (11, 17). When Jekyll first transforms into Hyde, he observes that "evil was written broadly and plainly on [Hyde's] face" and "left on that body an imprint of deformity and decay" (51). Bourrier and Esmail recount how the "early Victorian obsession with phrenology and physiognomy, which were dependent on the assumption that an individual's interior qualities were legible in exterior physical features, gave way at the end of the century to the attempts of Cesare Lombroso and others to identify criminals through photography" (444). Marian, however, does not immediately recognize Fosco as a criminal. She discerns his power to "tame" others but also admits that he "has interested me, has attracted me, has forced me to like him" (*Woman* 217). She is cautious toward him but does not feel the instinctive disgust that Enfield and Utterson do upon coming face-to-face with Hyde.

While Fosco, the able-bodied criminal, pens an aesthetically traditional composition, *The Woman in White* exhibits a "disability aesthetics," not only by including disabled narrators and a near continuous occurrence of sickness and anxiety but also because of its patchwork multinarrator structure—one with cuts, asymmetries, disorders, and gaps. Ten narrators receive section headers such as "The Story continued by Vincent Gilmore, of Chancery Lane, Solicitor" and "The Narrative of Hester Pinhorn, Cook in the Service of Count Fosco" (127, 399). These long and descriptive headers—often indicating the narrator's name, profession, and sometimes the narrative genre—visibly and definitively mark the switches between narrators, clearly setting apart one narrator from the next. Several other narrators—including Anne, Marian's mother, and the lawyer William Kyrle—narrate through inset narratives, usually letters; however, these narratives are not given their own sections and headers. The narratives vary widely in size, from Marian's large chunk to Doctor Goodricke's narrative of several sentences and Jane Gould's of one paragraph. While Walter and Marian narrate for the longest spans, Walter's contribution is split into five sections over the course of the novel, and Marian's is split by an "epoch," or book, break midway through her narrative. No one narrator, then, narrates for too long uninterruptedly. The novel's types of narrative include Marian's simultaneous diary, Walter's retrospective account, Anne's letters, and the lawyer's self-styled "record" (161). The pacing of switches is irregular; the novel shifts from large to short contributions throughout, but not in any regular pattern. Beyond the novel starting and concluding with Walter, there is little other symmetry to the structure. While the section headers indicate that Walter has "begun" (9) and "concluded" (613) the narrative, the other narrators "continue" it, to use the word from several section headers. The word "continue" links the narratives sequentially, and yet, the narratives are not written in the order they are presented. For example, Gilmore's narrative, the second we read, was "in order of time, the last that [Walter] received" (625). Marian's diary entries are composed years earlier than Gilmore's or Walter's accounts, and yet her diary succeeds their narratives. There is a disjunction, then, between when the narratives were written and where they are placed in the novel. Even with all these contributing narrators, additionally, gaps remain, including the one-week ellipsis in Walter's narrative previously discussed. Even in the final pages, Walter admits that the person who killed Fosco "was never traced" (624).

THE MOONSTONE

Critics have noticed the presence of illness and disability in *The Moonstone*, and my interpretation broadens and develops their significance in the novel. Sean C. Grass quips, "*The Moonstone* is really more troubled by illness than by crime" (103). To Laurence Talairach-Vielmas, the novel couches "the invisible curse of the gem as miasmatic infection" since "the household becomes unhealthy" once the stone arrives (78). While writing *The Moonstone*, as W. Collins discloses in the novel's preface, he was hit again with gout, including in the eyes, and was forced to dictate some of the novel (including a portion of Miss Clack's section) to his adoptive daughter Carrie. Mossman foregrounds the numerous "abnormal bodies" in *The Moonstone* (487), and other critics have paid some attention to the connection between nonnormative bodies and odd narratives in *The Moonstone*, particularly in relation to Ezra Jennings and Rosanna Spearman. Citing Rosanna's submerged letter to Blake and the book Ezra insists on being interred with him, Tamar Heller highlights not only the prevalence of "buried writing" in the novel but also how burying the writing of "outcasts" blunts its challenging content (144). As Cothran mentions, uncovering "the narratives of Collins's 'mysterious' (different or differently-abled) characters" enables the other characters to solve the mystery (200). Cothran and Heller focus on Ezra and Rosanna; I build on such scholarship not only by emphasizing the fragmentary shape of Ezra's and Rosanna's narratives but also by showing how other narrators—Gabriel Betteredge, Miss Clack, and Franklin Blake—are also described in terms of disability. The product of an old man, Betteredge's narrative falters and wanders much like Betteredge does; however, suffering from "detective fever" brings an agitated focus to Betteredge's account. Miss Clack, treated by others as a "freak," constructs her narrative as an injured body. Blake, who experiences amnesia, learns to embrace his own mental disorder as well as the perspectives of other disabled characters like Rosanna and Ezra. *The Moonstone*, like *The Woman in White*, maintains that collaboration and interdependence are necessary to discover the truth, identify the criminal, and tell the story. The novel's villain, Godfrey Ablewhite, like Fosco, is set up as nondisabled and resistant to collaboration.

Gabriel Betteredge is seventy years old, and his age does seem to incapacitate him. Old age, disability studies scholars point out, is often accompanied by disability; we all, Garland-Thomson asserts, "evolve into disability" (366). The nineteenth century, Karen Chase shows, experienced a "ripening consciousness of age," one sign and consequence of which was the passing of the Old Age Pensions Act in 1908, which set the age of 70 as determining old age (276). Betteredge highlights his old age, referring to himself as "an old fool," a "sleepy old man," "a slovenly old man," and "an obstinate old man" (*Moonstone* 26, 33, 37, 121). Other characters often find him asleep; he unintentionally dozes; he has trouble sitting down, getting up, and running; he loses his breath easily with exertion; he walks with a "stick" (307). About two-and-a-half years prior to the date of writing, his employer, Lady Verinder, forcefully retired him from his "hard out-of-door work as bailiff" because of his advanced age, reassigning him to house steward, which appears a rather cushy position considering the amount of time he spends reclining in the sun reading *Robinson Crusoe* (26). He ponders—even wishes for—his impending death because he feels "wretchedly old, and worn out" (144).

Betteredge's narrative resembles his aging body. He often presents his narrative as a journey he's taking the reader on, but in his hands, the journey is halting and circuitous, "stopping by the way" to tell characters' backstories and to explain his creation of the narrative itself (34).[13] Like his slowing body, his narrative slowly arrives at his assigned story of the moonstone's arrival and theft. He regretfully notes, "This don't look much like starting the story of the Diamond—does it? I seem to be wandering off in search of Lord knows what, Lord knows where" (23). After another digression, he apologizes for "drift[ing]": "We will change the subject, if you please. I am sorry I drifted into writing about it" (59). He's contrite for "another false start, and more waste of good writing-paper," but these "false start[s]" and the "waste" paper are retained, not erased from the narrative or tossed in the trash (26). Betteredge's "wandering[s]" and "halt[s]" (23, 61) make the story personal, humorous, enjoyable, and informational. Like other narratives discussed in this chapter, Betteredge's is collaborative, as he "consult[s]" his daughter Penelope (27). Penelope checks her own diary to provide her father with specific dates for his story, and those dates spur his memory of past events. Only with "Penelope's help," therefore, does the longest single narrative in the novel come to be (61).

While the beginning of Betteredge's narrative is riddled with wandering "false start[s]," his narrative later suffers from pervasive "detective-fever." His

---

13. J. Taylor also notices Betteredge's "lapses and ramblings of memory" and "necessary digressions that delay the main line of the story" (202, 203).

narrative becomes less digressive once he starts relaying his reconnoiters with
Sergeant Cuff; however, this unnatural energy in his narrative resembles a
feverish rush. When Betteredge and Cuff increasingly suspect Rosanna of the
theft, Betteredge feels that the "disease" of "*detective-fever . . .* had now got fast
hold of [his] humble servant" (131). A few pages later, "the infernal detective-
fever began . . . to burn in me again" (139). Later, he "had another attack of
the detective-fever" (161). Even when Lady Verinder dismisses Cuff, Betteredge senses that Cuff "left his infection behind him. . . . the detective-fever
was beginning to set in again" (192). This "disease" (131) and "malady" (310)
attacks, burns, holds, sets in. It causes Betteredge to act and speak violently
and unadvisedly. Betteredge, in a sense, must reenter this illness to write the
narrative of this time, and his narrative becomes as feverish as his detecting
was. Betteredge even implies a parallel between detecting and storytelling,
as both share an interest in dates, details, and trivia. Although Betteredge
clearly intends a metaphoric meaning to the language of "detective fever," he
does provocatively suggest both that illness can foster unique abilities and that
detecting (and storytelling) drains the body and mind. Betteredge's description of the "celebrated Cuff" implies he has long endured the detective fever
that has transformed him into a "grizzled, elderly man," a near skeleton with
not "an ounce of flesh on his bones" and skin "as yellow and dry and with-
ered as an autumn leaf" (106). Detective work possesses and consumes Cuff,
much like an illness would. His tanned and desiccated skin has long endured
the "burn[ing]" detective fever (139). He looks like death, dressed all in black
like an "undertaker" (106). Cuff retires in the middle of the book to the rejuvenation of his rose garden indicating some truth to Betteredge's assessment
of Cuff.

     Miss Clack, a poor spinster who traffics in tracts, is treated like a "freak."
Miss Clack lacks the physical abnormalities characteristic of most "freaks,"
but as Robert Bogdan writes, "'freak' is a way of thinking, of presenting, a
set of practices, an institution—not a characteristic of an individual" (10). In
an interruptive footnote to the second page of Clack's narrative, Blake constructs Clack's narrative as a disabled and nearly freakish body, one that is
"disfigure[d]" and "mark[ed]" due to Clack's own "peculiarities" of personality
(*Moonstone* 202). The narrative's "value" is as an "exhibition" of Clack; such
language conjures an image of Miss Clack as a "freak" on show for others'
profit and entertainment—such "freaks" were often referred to as "exhibits."
Craton explains how "the freak show helped reinforce the audience's sense of
normalcy" (27), and Godfrey's father casts her as a freakish "Rampant Spinster" in a scene in which the assembled cast of characters consolidates their
own sense of self against her strangeness (*Moonstone* 267). Rachel releases

"a scream of horror," Bruff "mock[s]" her, and Penelope snipes that she's "ashamed" of her (270). Clack is left "reviled," "deserted," and "alone in the room" (271). Additionally, many individuals entered and stayed in the freak show business for the money, and Miss Clack acts in what she views as humiliating ways mainly to earn money: The "unrelenting pecuniary pressure of Mr Blake's cheque obliges" her to continue her "painful" story (220). She constructs herself as Blake's employee—a "poor labourer" (202). Bogdan details how some "exhibits took control in negotiating the conditions of their contract" (268); likewise, Clack exposes her attempt to renegotiate her contract with Blake: She fights to incorporate religious tracts into her narrative (Blake refuses) and she pleads to reference knowledge she didn't have at the time the events took place (Blake refuses).

Clack portrays her resulting narrative as pained and wounded—a disabled body. Desperately needing Blake's money, she agrees to tell the story of Godfrey and Rachel's brief engagement and resulting split even though her unrequited (though unacknowledged by her) love for Godfrey makes the project particularly distressing. She initiates the production with an assertion of the pain and violence it will involve: "I am to re-open wounds that Time has barely closed; I am to recall the most intensely painful remembrances—and this done, I am to feel myself compensated by a new laceration, in the shape of Mr Blake's cheque" (*Moonstone* 202). She imagines the writing of the narrative as a masochistic cutting of a "barely" healed body—it will "re-open wounds." The motivation for her writing—Blake's payment—functions as another blow to an already smarting body; her term, "laceration," suggests a particularly rough and vicious tearing. Her references to her pain are frequent throughout her narrative: "intensely painful remembrances" (202); "painful disclosures" (220); "painfully conscious" (247); "painful family circumstances" (248). Miss Clack does not consider her narrating position one of agency or power but a hellish punishment—a "condemn[ation]" (208). The motivating check functions as a torturing "incubus" (208): the masculine demon that suffocates, and sometimes rapes, female sleepers; the metaphor fashions her body as endangered and suffering and her writing as the product of forced and unwanted pressure. At one point she "write[s] with the tears in [her] eyes" (260), and, at another pleads that she "should like to stop here" but the "unrelenting pecuniary pressure" pushes her on (220). When reporting a physical assault on Godfrey, Clack labels her narrative a "record of violence" (208). Cut, pressured, and "hemmed in" (213) as she is, her narrative causes and is marked by her pain—it is also a "record of violence."

Like Laura Fairlie in *The Moonstone*, Mr. Candy, the local doctor, is largely excluded from narrating because of a mental illness; however, his fragmented speech, similar to Laura's incoherent memories, is not disregarded but recorded and utilized to help resolve mysteries and crimes. Candy becomes deathly ill the evening of the moonstone dinner party, and "he lost his memory in the fever" (327). Even once recuperated of the fever, he remains "a wreck" of his former self (365), unable to do any of his medical work, which his assistant Ezra Jennings entirely takes over. Because of "the total failure of his memory" (368), Candy is unable to narrate except in a short two-page letter sent to Blake that appears late in the novel; the letter only covers recent events that Candy is able to remember—the recent death of Ezra—rather than events from further in the past. Candy's feverish words, however, are crucial to the solution of the moonstone's disappearance. When the strange-looking doctor's assistant Ezra nurses Candy through his severe illness, he jots down "the broken phrases, and even the single words, as they had fallen disconnectedly from Mr Candy's lips" (374). Ezra describes Candy's outpourings as fragmentary: "broken sentences" (375), "broken words" (375), and "disconnected words, and fragments of sentences" (386). These "wanderings," as Ezra also calls them, recall Betteredge's "wandering" beginning to his narrative (374, 23). By valuing and recording—rather than rejecting or ignoring—these seemingly pointless fragments, Ezra resurrects Candy's intended expressions, one of which is an admission of drugging Blake the night of the dinner party, thereby causing Blake's somnambulistic theft of the moonstone. Ezra's own experience of disability likely makes him sympathetic not only to Candy's suffering but also to the possibilities within Candy's fragmented speech.

Just as "attack[s]" of pain interrupt Ezra's life, Ezra values, produces, and is buried with interrupted, unfinished, and fragmentary texts (400). He has "suffered from an incurable internal complaint" for ten years and only survives the "agony" by taking opium; however, the drug has "shattered" his "nervous system" and has led to "nights of horror" (380). Like Ezra, W. Collins became dangerously dependent on opium to alleviate physical suffering. Although Ezra manages to run Candy's medical practice, his journal reveals the chronic, disabling, and disruptive nature of his pain. In writing a letter to Rachel he deals with "interruption from pain" (397); he cuts short a visit to Blake because of an oncoming "attack" (400); he must make a "short entry" in his journal one day because his terrible affliction compels him to "close this book" to take a dose of opium (410); he even has to leave Rachel and Blake during the experiment he has so meticulously organized to suffer an "attack" alone (430). In his journal, he documents recurring lateness to appointments because either the pain or the opium's side effects keep him up all night. The journal form—with frequent, brief entries—is particularly suited to Ezra's tenuous physical condition, and Ezra's entries are particularly short in comparison to other Victorian literary diaries (which will be discussed at more length in the next chapter). Furthermore, he confides to Blake that he has spent years writing a medical treatise that "will probably never be finished; and it will certainly never be published" (374); he is later, at his request, buried with this "unfinished book" (460). He is also buried with his diary, but sans the pages detailing the experiment. He tears out these pages on his deathbed and asks Candy to deliver them to Blake; these are the pages that are included in the novel. In his letter to Blake, Candy explains how Ezra "opened the [journal] volume for this year, and tore out, one by one, the pages relating to the time when [Blake] and he were together" (460). The image of Ezra tearing out the pages "one by one" heightens the sense of fragmentation inherent to Ezra's life and record. This removal also makes his previously complete journal incomplete; rather than jettisoning, destroying, or being embarrassed by the "unfinished book" and partial journal, he prizes them enough to request that they be interred with him. Both the journal excerpt included in the novel and the remaining journal are marked by jagged edges, recalling Clack's evocation of tearing by associating her narrative with "wounds" and a "laceration" (202).

In the second half of the book, Blake discovers that he stole the diamond, but to fully understand how and why he unconsciously did so, he must move closer to a disabled perspective; he accomplishes this shift by accepting his own disability—namely, amnesia—and by learning to accept and rely on the accounts of other disabled characters. One way he accomplishes this sympathy with the disabled perspective is by splicing his own narrative with Rosanna Spearman's letter. Rosanna, one of Lady Verinder's maids, has "no beauty" and is "deformed" with "one shoulder bigger than the other" (35, 36, 35); she is also prone to fainting fits and melancholy.[14] When Blake returns to the Verinder house after a lovelorn stint abroad, he reads the letter Rosanna left for him with her friend Limping Lucy. The short note instructs him how to locate a sealed tin buried in the Shivering Sands that contains not only his stained nightgown (evidence that he stole the moonstone) but also Rosanna's long letter explaining that she hid his damning nightgown out of love for him. While Cothran and Stoddard Holmes (in "Bolder") consider Rosanna's missive in terms of its powerful voicing of sexual desire, I'm interested in the narrative

---

14. Talairach-Vielmas contextualizes these fainting fits: "Rosanna's 'fits'—stereotypical symptoms of hysteria in nineteenth-century neurological discourse—result from her parents' contact with urban life and improper behaviour passed as an infection to the offspring" (83). Heller shows how W. Collins employs the "imagery of defect or disfigurement," particularly with Rosanna, "to describe women's 'self-dependence,' or resistance to conventional roles" (148). Critics interpret Rosanna as the "negative reflection," "double[ ]," or disabled "twin" of the beautiful, upper-class Rachel Verinder (J. Taylor 199; Heller 147; Stoddard Holmes, "Bolder" 70).

presentation of her letter. Rosanna's letter appears as an inset (or embedded) narrative within quotation marks within Blake's narrative; however, Blake continually intercuts fragments of Rosanna's epistle with fragments of his own narrative that relate his sensations in reading it. After reading and reproducing the first four sentences of her letter, in which she confesses her love for him, he drops the letter in surprise and interrupts her letter with a narrative of his reaction to her disclosure. Then he "resumed" the letter for several pages until he "broke off in the reading of the letter for the second time" (*Moonstone* 317, 321) when Rosanna reiterates her hatred of her rival Rachel; Blake interjects again to express his frustration. At this point, he continues to reproduce Rosanna's letter in his narrative, but in the story, Blake refuses to read any further, instead asking Betteredge to read on and report back any relevant information. The arrival of Ezra Jennings interrupts Betteredge's reading. A chapter break ensues, followed by the rest of Rosanna's letter. Blake adds one final interruption to her narrative in the manner of an asterisk that leads the reader to an editorial footnote. In her letter, Rosanna claims that at one crucial moment Blake purposefully turned away from her, and in his footnote, he alleges that he didn't even see her. As editor of the novel, Blake could have chosen to present Rosanna's letter on its own, seamless, perhaps as its own chapter; instead, his decision to braid together her epistle and his retrospective narrative, fragmenting and interlocking the resulting pieces, formally represents his attempt to understand and fuse with Rosanna's perspective. Before Blake reads the letter, he is quick to blame Rosanna for stealing the moonstone and for potentially manipulating the evidence; Betteredge calmly warns him away from these assumptions. After Blake reads the whole letter (done later, at Betteredge's counsel), he summarizes events both from his perspective *and* from Rosanna's, and he acknowledges the truth of both points of view.

Blake and Betteredge's reading of Rosanna's letter is bracketed by the appearance of two disabled characters, further highlighting how Blake must come into sympathy with disability to complete the "toilsome journey from the darkness to the light" (335). Limping Lucy acts as gatekeeper to the letter. This "strange creature" provides Blake with Rosanna's instructions to uncover the hidden letter and nightgown (308). In their encounter, Blake focuses on her disability, noting her "limping" and then obsessively tracking the speed and "sound of the girl's crutch" (308). Blake, however, cannot comprehend Lucy's expressions of anger at and disgust with him; he dismissively labels her as "mad" to dispel them (309).[15] The places where Blake halts in his read-

---

15. In analyzing this scene, Mossman shows how Blake "quickly control[s]" Lucy's "disruption of a normalized visual field" by categorizing Lucy's body and mind as abnormal (489).

ing of the letter—Rosanna's blunt declaration of love for Blake and Rosanna's treatment of Rachel as a rival—reveal his discomfort in the plain, deformed Rosanna possessing and asserting her romantic desire for him, a handsome and upper-class man. But by the time Ezra "interrupt[s]" the scene of reading (326), Blake is more prepared to feel sympathy for this "strange" looking man than he was for the "strange" Lucy (326, 308). As Mossman acknowledges, Ezra does not visually appear disabled as Lucy and Rosanna do, and yet, his black-white hair and ambiguous race and age present him as "a body that is strange, unusual, and provocative" (492). Primed by the back-to-back encounters with disabled women, Blake can embrace rather than dismiss the disabled perspective: "It is not to be denied that Ezra Jennings made some inscrutable appeal to my sympathies, which I found it impossible to resist" (*Moonstone* 369). Blake soon learns that Ezra is not only dying but also in constant pain, kept alive by opium that unfortunately has "shattered" his "nervous system" (380). According to Ezra, to recreate Blake's mental and physical state from the night of Rachel's birthday party to determine if and how he took the moonstone, Blake must (again) quit smoking to cause a "morbidly sensitive nervous condition" (392). Ezra's journal, as discussed, documents his incredible pain, but it also relates Blake's worsening condition. The two begin to mirror each other: they can't sleep, are nervous, and resort to opium for necessary rest.[16] Cothran argues that Blake "develop[s] an ability to see beyond the boundaries of the body" through his tender relationship with Ezra (200); I counter that his sympathy for and mirroring of Ezra reveals Blake's growing acknowledgement of the tenuousness of his own body's ability and control.

Like *The Woman in White*, *The Moonstone* criminalizes ability through the villain, Godfrey Ablewhite, who is so aligned with ability that "able" (and "god") appears in his name. Ablewhite corresponds with Siebers's conception of traditional aesthetics: "harmony, bodily integrity, and health" (19). Betteredge presents Ablewhite as a perfect specimen of manhood in comparison to Blake: "Mr Godfrey was, in point of size, the finest man by far of the two. He stood over six feet high; he had a beautiful red and white colour; a smooth round face, shaved as bare as your hand; and a head of lovely long flaxen hair" (*Moonstone* 66–67). He's tall, well-complexioned, "beautiful," and "lovely." Betteredge adds that he is "the most accomplished philanthropist . . . that England ever produced" (67). He uses his "administrative abilities" to help various

---

Mossman also recognizes that Lucy "rejects her impaired body's status as a marginalized, negative, insignificant object to be either pitied or ignored or dismissed as 'mad'" (490).

16. Critics often represent Ezra as the double or "unconscious" of Blake (J. Taylor 190). He's an "uncanny symbol[ ]," Carens argues, for the foreignness that the English characters attempt to repress (257). In J. Taylor's view, Ezra dismantles binaries as a "cross-category figure" (189).

women's charities (452), and Miss Clack, a member of said women's charities, characterizes him as the "possessor[ ] of exalted ability" (259). Fittingly,
Rachel owns a framed photograph of him "speaking at a public meeting" that
showcases his ability (68).

Far from acting collaboratively or interdependently, Godfrey abuses
or betrays those who depend on him. He refuses to marry his mistress; he
siphons off twenty thousand pounds from the young man whom he serves
as trustee for; and he exploits the Ladies Committees as venues to meet and
attract rich women. Whenever he is engaged to be married, as happens several
times in the novel, his interest in supporting the committees abruptly stops, as
even Miss Clack, his greatest fan, concedes. Ablewhite acts relatively independently, scheming and executing his plan to sell the moonstone almost entirely
by himself with only minor use of the money lender Luker. The Indians only
have to kill Ablewhite to get their hands on the moonstone. Like Fosco, Ablewhite is found dead, by himself and in a disguise, with a voyeuristic audience surrounding his dead body. Blake, Cuff, and Gooseberry, having worked
together to track him, are all present at the unveiling of his masquerade. The
collaboration continues as Blake, too nervous to watch, relies on Gooseberry's
verbal play-by-play as Cuff removes the disguise item by item.

Collaboration and interdependence (as opposed to Ablewhite's able-
bodied independence) are key to success in the novel: to a daring restaging
of Blake's theft, to the Indians' acquisition of the moonstone, to the creation
of the novel itself. Ezra oversees and serves as medical counsel for the "bold
experiment" of recreating the night Blake removed the stone from Rachel's
room (388), but everyone else present also plays a part. Blake completely
trusts Ezra's leadership and advice; Betteredge restores the house to its previous material conditions; Rachel reverts her room to its prior state and reprises
her role in her room; and Verinder family lawyer Bruff offers himself as a witness to the proceedings even though he is skeptical of them. Bruff smartly sets
a watch on Luker at the bank (an idea, he adds, jointly devised by him and
Murthwaite), but a sudden "attack of gout" bars him from continuing with
the investigation (440), much like Fairlie family lawyer Gilmore suffers "an
apoplectic fit" in *The Woman in White* (198). In W. Collins's novels, collaborative networks are so crucial because characters can become sick or otherwise
incapacitated at any moment; every character needs other characters to rely
on or to take their place. When Bruff falls ill, the returned Sergeant Cuff and
the resourceful boy Gooseberry continue the investigation, successfully tracking Ablewhite despite his disguise. Similarly, in *The Woman in White*, when
Gilmore is forced into temporary retirement after being "found insensible
at his desk," Gilmore's partner Kyrle admirably takes over the Fairlie affairs

and assists Walter and Marian (198). The three Indians are successful in the "purpose that unites them" because they work in a group, aided by a "modest little Indian organization" in London (*Moonstone* 290, 289). Cuff deduces that one of the Indians "acting by himself . . . could hardly have smothered Mr Ablewhite" given the latter's superior strength and height (451)—only the Indians together could have neutralized Ablewhite and rescued the stone. When Murthwaite spots the three men at the celebration of the restoration of the stone in India, they are punished for forfeiting their caste by departing in "three separate directions," never to see each other again (471). Forced independence and isolation is a punishment, something they are "doomed" to (471). Aptly, even originating the unique, cooperative structure of the novel is a collaborative effort. Blake and the lawyer Bruff agree that the story must be written down; they "together" concoct the idea of "writ[ing] the story of the Moonstone in turn—as far as [their] own personal experience extends, and no farther" (21, 21–22). Since "personal experience" is always bounded, creating "a record of the facts" of the case requires multiple perspectives (22, 21).

After his extraordinary experiences, Blake appreciates the need for such a collaborative and interdependent structure. Blake suffers from amnesia at several points in the story, linking him to Candy, whose fever leads to a permanent "defect of memory" (367). Sometimes Blake's forgetfulness is a result of drugs but not always; the frequency of his amnesiac episodes signals the existence of a chronic disorder. Rachel must inform him that she "*saw [him] take the Diamond with [her] own eyes*" the night of her birthday party since he has no memory of his drugged actions (347). He also "depend[s] on [Betteredge's] memory" to ascertain his own behavior the night of the party (336). When he spots his name on the nightgown stolen by Rosanna, he loses "[his] thinking and feeling power" and falls into "complete bodily and mental prostration" (315). Blake must trust Betteredge's account of what Blake said and did after this stunning discovery because Blake has "not the faintest recollection" of what happened (315). Later, Blake admits that he is "perfectly ignorant of all that [he] had said and done under the influence of the opium" during the restaging of the birthday evening (431); instead, he leaves it to Ezra's trustworthy journal to describe his words and actions on that night. Blake, therefore, must depend on others—Betteredge, Rachel, Rosanna, and Ezra—to witness, narrate, and communicate his own actions. In a similar way, Ezra becomes the holder of Candy's "lost recollection[s]" through his "manuscript-experiments" in reconstructing the meaning behind Candy's incoherent speech (376). Even one's self remains unknown and inaccessible without the help of others. Blake fully recognizes how personal limitation leads to necessary interdependence.

Like *The Woman in White*, *The Moonstone* exhibits disability aesthetics through its patchwork quality. Eleven narrators receive separate, titled sections; Rosanna's narrative is embedded within Blake's narrative but does not receive its own section header. The lengths of the narratives vary widely: Betteredge's first narrative is the longest uninterrupted narrative at 177 pages long, but the statements of Cuff's assistant and the ship captain are only one-page each; Betteredge's second account lasts only two pages. A diverse set of narrative types—journals, letters, "statements," and Cuff's "report"—are included. Most narratives are retrospective by two years: Betteredge, Blake, Bruff, and Clack write their accounts after the events occur at Blake's request, and they promise to restrain their narratives to what they knew at the time. Ezra's journal, written nearly daily, approaches a more simultaneous account. The novel shifts from a slow cutting pace (featuring long narratives and fewer narrative switches) to a fast cutting pace (with shorter narratives and more frequent narrative switches); eight narrations are included in approximately the last hundred pages of the novel. As the novel approaches its conclusion, more perspectives are required to add quick lights to illuminate the mystery. While it feels like the narratives proceed chronologically (not in the order they were written but in the order of events covered), the narratives sometimes overlap. For example, Clack relays Godfrey and Rachel's fleeting engagement; Bruff, who takes up the pen after Clack, retraces much of the same time, explaining the reasons behind the young couple's engagement and its cancellation. Instead of melding the next link on the proverbial chain of the story, Bruff's narrative rests atop Clack's, not countering her account, but offering additional facts and creating a textual palimpsest. Despite the number of narrators, gaps and questions remain. For example, Ezra proclaims that his "story will die with [him]" (378), and when he does die (buried with most of his journals), Candy reaffirms that assertion: "his story is a blank" (460). The characters and reader never learn what terrible crime Ezra was accused of and why he is "incapable" of clearing his name (379). Betteredge's daughter Penelope similarly refuses a public narrative. She references her diary to provide her father with dates for his narrative, but she declines to narrate herself because "her journal is for her own private eye, and . . . no living creature shall ever know what is in it but herself" (27). Ezra's unknown backstory casts a shadow of mystery over the narrative, and Penelope's diary looms as a shadow text that shapes Betteredge's narrative but never comes into the light itself. And lastly, critics like John Reed have pointed out how the novel is framed by India—the prologue details the stone's journey from India to England, while the epilogue traces the stone's journey back to India. And yet, even here, asymmetry exists. The prologue consists of one narrator—an unnamed Verinder family member—while the epilogue consists of three brief narratives by named narrators.

Ezra's "manuscript-experiments," in which he fills in the blanks in Candy's fever-ridden words, serve as a useful metaphor for the novel itself (*Moonstone* 376). As previously discussed, Candy vocalizes "broken phrases" that come out "disconnectedly" (374); Ezra writes down the bursts of speech and marks Candy's silences with "blank space[s]" on the page (375). Ezra proceeds to test out different words in the blanks until he finds a "natural[ ]" sounding construction (375). As Ezra summarizes, "it is all confusion to begin with; but it may be all brought into order and shape" (374). He assembles "those fragments" of "disconnected expression" into coherent sentences (387). After explaining this process to Blake, Ezra presents him with two manuscripts, one with only Candy's words and another with Candy's words plus Ezra's additions. Blake is impressed with how Ezra has "woven this smooth and finished texture out of the ravelled skein" of Candy's words (388). Importantly, Ezra's second manuscript displays its collaborative nature, color coding Candy's original words in black ink and Ezra's guesses, which he admits are not meant to be Candy's exact words, in red ink. Visually, this knitted creation is less "smooth and finished" than checkered and tenuous. Furthermore, both the yarn and knitter in Blake's metaphor are disabled. Ezra recalls how Candy was "so miserably ill" and "so helplessly dependent upon" him when Ezra archives Candy's speech (376). Ezra, dying and kept alive and alert by opium, spends his "anxious hours" filling in the blanks (375). The novel too, makes sense of the bewildering story of the moonstone's brief time in England by gathering the narratives—"fragments of evidence" in a sense—and positioning them "into order and shape" (305, 374). But this final product, like Ezra's black-and-red creation, does not minimize but rather highlights its patchwork seams, its association with disability, and its collaborative origin.

THE LEGACY OF CAIN

Although critics have started to examine the representation of disability in other W. Collins novels, *The Legacy of Cain* remains unexplored from this angle. In this novel, a murderess, on the eve of her execution, persuades a childless clergyman, Reverend Gracedieu, to adopt her one-year-old child. The prison Governor wonders if the child, later named Eunice, will inherit her mother's murderous tendencies or if her more upright upbringing with

Gracedieu will determine her character. Subsequent to the adoption of Eunice, Gracedieu's wife dies soon after giving birth to their child Helena. The widowed Reverend raises the two children as his own; the children do not know that one is adopted, nor do they (or the reader) know which of them is the eldest. Gracedieu, strained by the secrets he holds, slowly deteriorates mentally and physically. The sisters both fall in love with the same man, Philip Dunboyne, and he weakly vacillates on his choice. The jilted Eunice is tempted by her mother's ghost to smother Helena in her sleep (proving to the reader that she is the murderess's offspring), but her genuine love for Philip enables her to resist her criminal blood. Helena, seemingly inheriting some of her mother's heartlessness, attempts to poison Philip when he returns to Eunice. Helena is convicted, imprisoned, and then exiled to America; Gracedieu dies an "imbecile" (*Legacy* 244); Eunice and Philip marry.

The novel includes four main narrators (more characters narrate through brief inset letters); three are disabled, and their physical and mental conditions impact their narratives and vice versa. The prison Governor (never named) retrospectively narrates period one that explains the last-minute adoption in the prison; episodes of gout pepper his narratives. Period two jumps ahead fifteen years to when the daughters are young women; it features alternating sections of Helena's and Eunice's diaries, followed by a narration from the Governor when he visits the Gracedieu residence and witnesses Reverend Gracedieu's mental unraveling. The diaries reveal two very different daughters: Eunice is a "simpleton" and Helena nearly a prodigy who runs the family household (*Legacy* 57). Journaling, which Eunice undertakes only to please her father, further disables her. Period three includes narrations from Helena's diary, the Governor, and Miss Jillgall—the Reverend's spinster cousin and Eunice's confidante. Miss Jillgall, a hysteric, narrates for a short time, but the Governor takes over when Jillgall's narrative crumbles due to strain. Occasional and brief letters written by Gracedieu, Helena, Philip, Philip's father, and Jillgall's friend Mrs. Tenbruggen are included within the four main narrations. *The Legacy of Cain* lacks a clear editor-character like *The Woman in White*'s Walter (with Marian's help) and *The Moonstone*'s Blake (with Bruff's help), although several lines suggest it is the prison Governor.[17] Like the other

---

17. Caleb, Delafield, Emrys, and J. Taylor also identify the Governor as the editor/collator figure of *The Legacy of Cain*. He does know "the whole ground laid out by the narratives which appear in these pages" (W. Collins, *Legacy* 310); however, at another point, he has been told by an unidentified person about the content of "the pages that have gone before [his]" (185), suggesting that he is not familiar with the pages that precede his own. The Governor also implies that Reverend Gracedieu requested he write a narrative about the events in the prison; however, Gracedieu cannot be the arranger because he loses his sanity and then

two novels, *The Legacy of Cain* is a patchwork of different genres (contemporaneous diaries and letters, retrospective accounts), different lengths (the Governor narrates half the book, Helena and Eunice narrate slightly less than a quarter each, and Jillgall only narrates 6 percent of the pages), tagged transitions (chapter or book titles indicate the narrator), and remaining gaps—for example, Helena's poisoning "notes . . . were not to be found; they had doubtless been destroyed" (*Legacy* 305). A. B. Emrys considers the use of what she calls "the novel of testimony" form in *The Legacy of Cain* disappointing, lacking the character depth, effective reveal of clues, and narrative "interplay" present in *The Woman in White* and *The Moonstone* (67, 68).[18] While it is impossible to rank the novel with W. Collins's masterpieces, I argue that *Cain* is worth studying because its multinarrator setup furthers W. Collins's utilization of disability aesthetics. In this novel, the characters themselves, and not just the implied author, more openly appreciate disability and disability aesthetics. By the end of the novel, Gracedieu, the Governor, Jillgall, Eunice, and Philip all form a household accepting of disability, while Helena, the able-bodied criminal mastermind, is disgraced and alienated.

The few critics who have written on this mostly forgotten novel, such as Amanda Mordavsky Caleb and Jay Clayton, have considered its contribution to debates about inheritance, not in terms of disability, even though disability was relevant to Victorian discussions of inheritance.[19] My research of W. Collins's extraneous papers shows that W. Collins was inspired to write the novel after reading an article in *Frank Leslie's Illustrated Newspaper* about a wife who murdered her husband in New York with their elder daughter's help. In his 1887 notes on "The case of Roxalana Druse," W. Collins assumes that the mother transmitted the homicidal instinct to her eldest daughter. He speculates whether the mother's younger daughter, whom had been adopted by another family, would also inherit the criminal tendency. W. Collins muses on the literary potential of the case before outlining a possible plot

---

life before the story finishes. The Governor never outs himself as the novel's main editor as Walter and Blake do, but he has the necessary access to and knowledge of the texts to plausibly fulfill the editor role.

18. Delafield agrees that "in a documentary sense, the assembly is perhaps less proficient than Collins's earlier novels" (133).

19. Caleb concludes that Collins "rejects the fatalist views of heredity and adopts a notion that recognises all the potential factors that influence a person" (131). Although Helena's and Eunice's mothers are dead, Clayton claims that in the novel "the power of maternal inheritance is greater than any influences that descend from the father, through either nature or nurture." In *Responsibility in Mental Disease*, Maudsley claims "that crime is often hereditary," just as "bodily features" are (28); probing a criminal's family history would reveal "that they spring from families in which insanity, epilepsy, or some other neurosis exists" (32).

in which a married clergyman, without children of his own, raises a niece and the murderess's daughter. This planned storyline resembles *The Legacy of Cain*. As W. Collins's reaction to this crime illustrate, Victorians were particularly concerned about criminality and disability being passed from parents to children. Stoddard Holmes indicates that "disabled women characters almost never become biological parents" in Victorian literature because of "Victorian medical science's concern about the transmission of physical illness and impairment" (*Fictions* 6, 7). Craton mentions how an exhibition of Julia Pastrana—known as the "bear woman" for her hairiness—was closed in 1857 because "a pediatrician claimed the performance could endanger the unborn children of pregnant viewers" (2). In *The Legacy of Cain*, the prison doctor voices his fear of transmitted disability in relation to the killer's daughter Eunice: "I have found vices and diseases descending more frequently to children than virtue and health. . . . Children are born deformed; children are born deaf, dumb, or blind; children are born with the seeds in them of deadly diseases" (26). Critical discussions of inheritance in the novel would benefit from a closer attention to the novel's representations of disability.

Eunice, the daughter of the executed murderess and one of the novel's four narrators, is set up as intellectually or cognitively disabled, even though critics have overlooked this aspect of her character. In her first appearance in Helena's diary, Helena depicts her behaving "slowly and silently and lazily" (49). Others describe her as "slow-minded" (51), "stupid" (51, 84, 121, 179), "simple" (51), "foolish" (138), "infantile" (53), and "a simpleton" (57). In her diary entries, Eunice often applies these same terms to herself and admits that she is "ignorant" and not very "learned" (92, 241). Although she is never designated an "idiot" like Anne is in *The Woman in White*, in the nineteenth century, the above terms would have indicated idiocy, though of a milder form than Anne's. The Victorians acknowledged categories of idiocy ranging from those persons completely unable to care for themselves to those who were slow with learning and completing tasks. An 1898 governmental report reads: "From the normal child down to the lowest idiot there are degrees of deficiency of mental power" (qtd. in David Gladstone 136). David Wright shows how the Victorians considered many different qualities to signify idiocy including childishness out of step with the person's age ("Childlike" 124). Helena refers to Eunice as "infantile" and "childish" (*Legacy* 53, 101), and Eunice appears underdeveloped for her age, seeming the younger sister when she is several years older than Helena. A family's identification of a child as an "idiot," according to Wright, generally related to "the child's ability, or rather, inability to perform duties usually expected of his or her status within Victorian households of various classes" ("Childlike" 130). Helena expresses annoyance that Eunice's "defects"

absolve Eunice from undertaking household chores such as deciding the dinner menu or taking dictation from their father (*Legacy* 52).[20]

Furthermore, Eunice disdains classical beauty and instead possesses
a perspective amenable to disability aesthetics. The Governor recalls that
even as a baby, she was overjoyed with "broken toys" (*Legacy* 192). When
Eunice and her sister hesitate to write their first entry in their new journals,
gifts from their father, Helena blots her "so smooth, so spotless" page in her
"beautiful book" (49, 50). Helena finds the blot so "discouraging" that she
"got up, and looked out of window" (49). But when Helena shows Eunice the
"spoiled page," Eunice exclaims that it "comforts" her and she immediately
and quickly writes her entry (49). The traditional art in London museums
and theatres "disappoint[s]" Eunice (57). Even though her companion likes
a certain famous artist's drawings—"Perfectly beautiful, Eunice, isn't it?"—
Eunice disagrees (57). When a London shop displays a photograph of Venus
de Medici in its front window, Eunice hears the figure hailed as "the classic
ideal of beauty and grace" (92); however, when Eunice encounters the photograph, she is not impressed by the "stumpy little creature" (93). Eunice is not
charmed or impressed by the traditionally beautiful. Rather, she appreciates
"broken toys" and the "spoiled page" (192, 49). Additionally, unlike her sister,
she immediately welcomes and befriends Miss Jillgall despite her ugliness,
hysteric behavior, "funny manner" (105), and "funny little eyes" (97).

Collins's nuanced attention to disability includes acknowledging that narrating takes different energies from and tolls on different characters; Eunice's
journaling detrimentally affects her. Although her father hopes journal writing will cure Eunice of her "defects" (52), the attempt backfires, activating
within Eunice an "excitable" "second self" (50, 200). Although a reader may
assume that Eunice's jealousy of Helena activates this second self, Eunice's
journal writing is what initially animates (or necessitates) the dangerous second self that has previously remained dormant in Eunice's life. As Eunice pre-
pares to write her first diary entry, she "suddenly developed into an excitable
person" and writes hurriedly "without once stopping to consider" her words
(50). Once she hastily finishes her brief entry, Eunice's trademark "old easy
indolent movements" return. This "singular change" in Eunice shocks Helena. As Helena clarifies, "Eunice in a state of excitement is Eunice exhibiting
an unnatural spectacle." This new journal-writing Eunice is almost freakish,
likened to an "exhibiti[on]." When Eunice feels like her normal self—"lazy

---

20. Additionally, D. Gladstone quotes a report from the Western Counties Idiot Asylum
showing that some Victorian women with intellectual disabilities stayed at home, as Eunice
does: "Weak minded girls with a certain amount of intelligence are more amenable to treatment
at home, and in some instances may even be helpful to their mother in small things" (151).

and stupid"—she doesn't write in her diary (56). When she feels reckless and excited, she easily pens pages and pages. The "excitable" second self that the journal activates continues to emerge whenever Eunice writes in her journal. Although Talairach-Vielmas claims that Eunice's journal writing "functions as a means of not drifting into madness," the opposite is true (197). On one occasion, she feels like she is "going mad" and turns to her journal to hopefully provide "harmless employment" (*Legacy* 135); instead, seeing certain names "stare [her] in the face in the lines that [she has] just written" hastens Eunice's madness (136–37).

Eunice's eventual rejection of the journal, and hence, of her father's attempt to normalize her, suggest her bold acceptance of her disability. Eunice only starts writing in a journal because her beloved father asks her to; he hopes that a regular journal writing practice will battle her "lazi[ness]" and instill "good moral discipline" in her (50, 51). As Bourrier and Esmail note, the "medical model of disability that retains currency today—in which disability is understood as a personal, biological issue in need of a cure—gained ascendancy in the nineteenth century" (444). The search for a cure—through journaling and Eunice's self-medication—backfires. Eunice's excitable second self claims ascendancy when Eunice imbibes some of her "father's medicine" (*Legacy* 142) that she tellingly refers to as "composing medicine" (141), a label that links it to her journaling-as-treatment. While she "wait[s] to be composed," she is visited by the ghost of her mother who goads her to kill Helena (141). Eunice wishes that "[her] father's medicine would only help [her]," but that medicine—both the calming drug prescribed for her father and her father's prescription for Eunice to journal—do not quiet or normalize her (142). Because Eunice determines that writing in her journal brings her pain and danger, she quits the activity. Once Eunice has narrated her sleepwalking-come-almost-murder episode, she concludes her journal: "My last words are written. I lock up this journal of misery—never, I hope and pray, to open it again" (146). Eunice finds more power in ending her narration than in continuing it, and she hopes to seal herself off from "misery" by containing her dangerous second self within the diary's lock. In the last page of the diary, Eunice has regained her "better self" and "c[o]me to [her]self" (146). Unfortunately, the other self, once unleashed, cannot be suppressed so easily, and Eunice slips into it even after she terminates the journal. Nonetheless, Eunice never again writes in her journal after this moment. The abrupt cutoff is common in narratives authored by W. Collins's disabled characters, as is the honest admission of the pain caused by and energies required for the creation of narrative. Eunice twice associates her journal with misery: She labels it the "journal of misery" and later mentions "the misery of having written it" (146,

200). Similarly, Miss Clack in *The Moonstone* highlights the pain she feels in composing her narrative.

As Eunice splits into two selves, her memory is affected—she sometimes experiences memory blackouts during or after slipping into her second self, but she sometimes feels assaulted by memories she can't force aside; her narrative, therefore, includes both gaps and obsessive repetitions. After she shares her first kiss with Philip, she "forgot [her] own self" and "cannot remember" how much time she spent calming herself after the passionate encounter (96). Conversely, when she catches Helena and Philip kissing, she involuntarily replays the scene in her mind over and over again: "I remember! oh, how I remember! . . . She kisses him, kisses him, kisses him" (135). No distraction or willpower prevents these "recollections" from "crowding" her (135), just as the phrases "remember" and "kisses him" crowd the page. When her father embarrasses her during a visit to the local school, enraging her almost to violence, she forgets how she acts afterwards: "I don't know what I said, it was all confusion" (113). When the ghost of her mother visits her, the memory of Philip becomes "a blank" (142). After she contemplates smothering Helena, her father appears in the bedroom as Eunice awakens from her homicidal trance: "I remember his leading me away—and I remember nothing more" (146). This sentence is the third-to-last in her final diary entry. Her termination of the diary, then, ends not only with a statement of her misery, as discussed, but also with unknowingness, with a blank that is never filled in.

The Legacy of Cain's insistence that writing is a profoundly physical act—one that can be dangerous and/or painful to the writer—is reinforced by the character of Philip's father, Mr. Dunboyne. This character, who narrates only in the form of embedded letters, possesses a "crippled hand" that has been "attacked by the malady called Writer's Cramp" (253, 114). This condition "change[s]" his handwriting (114). He blames this ailment on "the studious habits of a lifetime." No increasingly interventionist treatments—rest, massage, and electricity[21]—help, and the condition worsens, preventing him from writing and forcing him to dictate his letters. He soon dies. The novel suggests that his life of writing has instigated the writer's cramp and effectively killed him. Fittingly, W. Collins dedicates *Cain* to "Mrs. Henry Powell Bartley," the married name, as C. Peters points out, of his adopted daughter Carrie, who was his longtime secretary and amanuensis (424). In this dedication, W. Collins thanks her for "the pen which has skillfully and patiently helped [him],

---

21. An article from *The Lancet* in August 1890 recommends rest, electricity, and massage as treatments for "tailor's cramp," "writer's cramp," and other "fatigue diseases" arising from the "constant repetition of some muscular movement which constitutes the very essence of the trade" (Poore 327).

by copying [his] manuscripts for the printer" (*Legacy*); W. Collins, who was very ill, presumably was unable to make the copies himself. C. Peters reads this dedication as expressing W. Collins's "feeling [that] he might never write another novel" (424). *Cain* was serialized from February to June 1888 and then published in a three-volume book version in November 1888. W. Collins died in September 1889 and never completed another novel.

Although the Reverend Gracedieu, the girls' father, never narrates in the novel beyond short embedded letters, he is also associated with confused and fragmentary texts like many other disabled characters in W. Collins's novels. He initially experiences "nervous quiverings" (*Legacy* 79), and as the situation intensifies—his daughters sparring over the same man—his anxiety increases, and he transforms into an "imbecile" and "madman" (244, 221). Just as his health is "disordered" and his memory "broken" (150, 159), he creates confused and fragmentary texts. He accidentally tears up an important letter into "fragments" (79). Later, in a fit of "insane violence" (223), he destroys a painting of his late wife and "cut[s] it malignantly into fragments" (221). The painting itself is a text of sorts because it communicates information about the absent woman: Jillgall notices the image's "slanting forehead and the restless look in her eyes," hinting at Mrs. Gracedieu's unangelic true nature (140). At a certain point, Gracedieu can't write at all, "constantly interrupted either by a trembling in the hand that held the pencil, or by a difficulty . . . in expressing thoughts imperfectly realized" (169). Other writings he manages to produce are "incomprehensible," containing only "scattered words" (169). These productions resemble Candy's broken and fragmented outpourings during his illness in *The Moonstone*.

Miss Jillgall, the Reverend's cousin and another one of the novel's four narrators, is a hysteric. Hysteria, "the quintessential female malady" in Elaine Showalter's words, included a "vast, unstable repertoire of emotional and physical symptoms—fits, fainting, vomiting, choking, sobbing, laughing, paralysis—and the rapid passage from one to another" (129). It was often ascribed to women's "unsatisfied sexual and maternal drives" (131), and Miss Jillgall, who is described as extremely ugly, is unmarried and without children. The hysteria may be related to a previous "long and serious illness [that] completely prostrated her" (*Legacy* 72). While experiencing a "hysterical" attack in which she uncontrollably veers between laughs and tears, she confesses to Eunice that she "get[s] rid of these weaknesses . . . by singing to [her]self," suggesting that she frequently deals with these episodes (124). On another occasion, she sings the same song while suddenly deciding to fix a hole in a curtain. At one point, she suffers paralysis, another common symptom of hysteria, and cannot move or talk. In another scene, she "shook and shivered" during a fit (284). At a particularly dramatic moment, she, in her own words, acts "like a madwoman," and a doctor must give her wine to bring her down from her "hysterics" (298).

In Jillgall's four-chapter narrative, which consists of letters she writes to the prison Governor, hysterics both punctuate and shape her narrative. Even though her letters are meant to inform the Governor of any "suspicious circumstance[s]" she observes in the house (281), her body's symptoms work their way into those reports. Her body trembles, cries, knocks, shakes, shivers, and chatters. On one occasion, her body's incapacitation prevents her from immediately writing an emergency note to the Governor since she can only write "as soon as [she] could hold a pen" (285). In a moment of crisis, when Eunice becomes ferocious and terrifies Helena, Jillgall watches, paralyzed and mute. Her description of the scene formally embodies these symptoms: "If I could have moved, I should have fled to the first place of refuge I could find. If I could have raised my voice, I should have cried for help. I could do neither the one nor the other. I could only look, look, look; held by the horror of it with a hand of iron" (289). The anaphoric quality of this passage—repeating "If I could have," "I should," and "I could" at the beginning of successive clauses—creates a linguistic loop of inactivity. In describing her immobility, she uses epizeuxis—repeating "look" three times in a row—as if her description cannot move on from the word, stuck in looking. At the end of Jillgall's narrative, Helena hypocritically accuses Eunice of poisoning Philip and Jillgall of helping her (Helena is the true poisoner); in response, Jillgall experiences another hysteric episode: "I ran out of the room; I rushed headlong down the stairs. The doctor heard me, and came running into the hall. I caught hold of him like a madwoman. 'Euneece!' My breath was gone; I could only say: 'Euneece!'" (298). The short, staccato-like clauses emphasize her hectic, forceful movement—"I ran," "I rushed," "I caught hold"—and her lack of breath. A few sentences later, her narrative abruptly ends. The Governor narrates the subsequent section. He explains that since Jillgall's "method of expressing herself betrayed a gradual deterioration," he will supplant her as narrator and provide the "substance" of Jillgall's narrative (303). The "substance" includes no reference to Jillgall's corporeal reactions to events, which were a crucial effect of her disability on her narrative. The Governor's assumption of narrating duties again points to the limits of W. Collins's inclusion of disabled narrators: Miss Jillgall's narrative reaches a point where her disability impinges too much on the readability of her account for the Governor (and W. Collins) to let it continue.

It can be easy to overlook how the Governor also constructs himself as a disabled narrator, but he does frequently mention his own debilitating, chronic illness. A few days after the prisoner's execution he falls on the stairs, and he experiences a "long illness" that obliges him to relocate to a "milder climate" for more than a year (35). For a year, he is unable to work because of illness and recovery. At the beginning of his second narrative section, he admits that "advancing age and failing health" forced him to resign his high position at the prison (149). At the start of his third narrative section, he spends a paragraph bemoaning that gout, "the most capricious of maladies," prevents him from travelling—and even from writing, it seems—for two months (303). Given that beginnings are privileged narrative positions, opening two of his three sections with candid statements of the existence and effects of his chronic conditions situates those conditions as central to his self and story. Additionally, the Governor's final narrative is essentially collaborative, a mixture of his own and Miss Jillgall's words. Though one could view the Governor as creating a hierarchy between himself and Miss Jillgall through his decision to offer a streamlined version of her increasingly hysterical account, he also stresses his own diseased body directly beforehand, lingering over his two "months of pain aggravated by anxiety" (303). Miss Jillgall's body and narrative "have broken down," but the Governor presents himself as broken down as well. Gout has "attack[ed] him," "subjected" him, and "cruelly la[id] the patient prostrate."

Furthermore, even though the Governor is not formally related to any of the main characters, he situates himself within their community of disability. He resembles Rodas's conception of a "satellite persona": "a (presumably) nondisabled person who appears to construct his or her personal identity around a central nexus of disability" ("Tiny" 93). The satellite, Rodas continues, is "drawn to the implicit power and authenticity of the disabled subject and that he seeks to harness and channel these perceived attributes—motivated in part by the desire to construct himself as a beneficent mediating agent, in part by an unconscious wish to assert his own normative identity" (52). The Governor does seem to perceive himself as a "beneficent mediating agent" to disabled people. He shows patience and kindness in attending to the increasingly ill Reverend Gracedieu. The Governor likes and flirts with the ugly and hysterical Miss Jillgall whom he considers a "queen" of "domestic affairs" (*Legacy* 319). He feels protective and fond of Eunice, treating her like a daughter and believing that she has more "force of character" than her nondisabled husband or sister (310). And yet, unlike Rodas's satellite, in these relationships, he often further establishes his disabled identity, not "his own normative identity" (52). He rejects opportunities of contrasting himself with the disabled characters. He experiences a "tendency to sympathize" with Eunice and her ill health (*Legacy* 152). When the Governor first visits the ailing Gracedieu, he feels overcome by Gracedieu's wandering faculties and simultaneously admits his own weakness: "I was not sufficiently master of myself to be able to speak to him" (154). When he witnesses Gracedieu become confused and frantic, the Governor advises him to "compose [him]self"; he also acknowledges, however, that he "had not been composed enough" himself (156). He directly identifies with Eunice and implicitly identifies with Gracedieu.

The Legacy of Cain also criminalizes ability and independence—characters consistently describe Helena in terms of ability, beauty, and health. Eunice ranks Helena as her "superior": "She is prettier than I am, cleverer than I am, better worth liking than I am" (61). In a parallel manner, Helena judges Eunice "[her] inferior in every respect" (116). The sisters' father trusts only Helena with administrative duties. On one occasion, Helena ably runs a "Girls' Scripture Class" by "advising everybody, governing everybody, encouraging everybody" (87). Like Fosco and Ablewhite, she is a capable leader but is also set apart from the group—she runs but does join the "everybody." With her ability, beauty, and talents, she diverges from the criminal woman type that Victorian psychiatrist Maudsley describes as "ugly in features, and without grace of expression or movement" (30).[22] Rather, Eunice resembles the "children, who become juvenile criminals" who "do not evidence the educational aptitude of the higher industrial classes" and "make slow progress in learning" (30). Talairach-Vielmas provocatively points out that Helena's "self-control may be read as a sign of pathology" (202). In *The Legacy of Cain*, Eunice, who "bears traces of regression" in Talairach-Vielmas's reading (196), earns her happy ending, while the nondisabled woman, Helena, is pathologized.

Like Mr. Fairlie in *The Woman in White*, Helena despises the signs of disability in others and views disability as something that can be overcome with sheer will. She proclaims a disgust of the disabilities that accompany old age: "What a horrid thing old age is to look at! To be ugly, to be helpless, to be miserably unfit for all the pleasures of life—I hope I shall not live to be an old woman" (*Legacy* 52). With such a mindset, she hates the "hideous old maid" Miss Jillgall at first sight (115). She comments that Jillgall's touch nearly makes her faint. Helena considers illness a personal failing. She calls Eunice's ill health "entirely her own fault" (152). She also mocks her sister for being a "simpleton" (57). Eunice admits that her sister "is often hard on [her] when [she] do[es] stupid things" (125). Helena imagines that her father could get better if he just tried harder: "He is able to sit up in an armchair . . . and he

---

22. Maudsley references a prison doctor's observation that out of "thousands of prisoners . . . he had not known one to exhibit any aesthetic talent; he had never seen a pen-sketch, a clever poem, or an ingenious contrivance produced by one of them" (31). In addition to her other skills, Helena possesses artistic talent; Eunice writes, "My sister is a musician" (*Legacy* 63), and Helena mentions "practicing music" (52).

might do more, as I think, if he would exert himself. He won't exert himself. Very sad" (154). What is "sad" to Helena is not her father's distress but her father's lack of sufficient willpower to overcome his disability. She herself experiences "a fit of some sort" and falls to the ground when she realizes Philip has returned to Eunice (266); however, she declares "I am more clever than the doctor" and finds the cause of her fit to not be illness or weakness but "rage." She refuses to discern any modicum of sickness or disability in herself.

At the end of *The Legacy of Cain*, the court convicts, imprisons, and sends Helena to America, flushing out the able woman who is beautiful, clever, and accomplished; the remaining characters thrive in an interdependent community of disability. Across the pond, Helena seemingly reinvents herself, becoming the "leader of a new community" that "asserts the superiority of woman over man" (320). This new position reaffirms her longstanding belief in her own preeminence and fulfills her desire to independently lead others.[23] The novel's conclusion defies Mitchell and Snyder's argument in *Narrative Prosthesis* that once disability has served its purpose of jumpstarting the narrative engine, disabled characters must be killed or cured by the narratives' ends. Except for the older Reverend, the novel's disabled characters are not cured, killed, or exiled—a difference from *The Moonstone* and *The Woman in White*. In *The Moonstone,* Rosanna and Ezra die and Lucy is sidelined. In *The Woman in White,* Mr. Fairlie and Anne die and Laura never fully recovers. But in *The Legacy of Cain*, Eunice, the "simpleton," happily marries her man (*Legacy* 57). *Cain* also inverts the trope that Stoddard Holmes calls the "twin structure": a plot pairs a disabled woman who remains unmarried with an able-bodied woman who does marry ("Twin" 222). Eunice marries the man she passionately loves and the hysterical and ugly Miss Jillgall lives with the newlyweds, presiding over their household like a "queen" since Eunice still seems unable to manage a household (*Legacy* 319). The aging, gouty, retired Governor acts as the surrogate father to the now-parentless Eunice and Philip. He visits them during their honeymoon at the seaside and then every year at Philip's house in Ireland: "I am still strong enough to pass my autumn holidays in that pleasant house" (319). At Eunice and Philip's wedding, Jillgall serves as bridesmaid and the Governor "gave away the bride" (313). Reverend Gracedieu accepted Jillgall into his household when she was destitute and without money, having drained her resources surviving a "long and serious illness" (72); when, in turn, his health fails, she "take[s] care of the good man who had befriended her in her

---

23. As C. Peters notes, Helena "ends as an American feminist. In his last years Wilkie could imagine nothing worse" (425). Caleb confirms that W. Collins meant this outcome to be a penalization: "For Collins it represents not only an exile from her home country but also an adoption of a position of which he did not approve" (131).

hour of need" (314), allowing her to fulfill her "dream . . . to make [her]self useful to others" (161). Just as Eunice, Philip, Miss Jillgall, and the Governor enact interdependence in "that pleasant house," the narratives of *Cain* rely on one another to create meaning and closure.

Helena's attitude toward her diary marks her prideful isolation, while other characters' use of their narratives shows both self-deprecation and the impulse to exchange with and rely on others. The first night of Helena's and Eunice's journaling, Helena points out to Eunice that she "had not turned the key, in the lock which was intended to keep her writing private" (50). Eunice replies that anyone can read her diary, and Helena peruses it soon as her sister falls asleep. When Eunice travels to London to visit friends, the sisters promise they will exchange diaries upon Eunice's return; upon her homecoming, Eunice immediately entrusts her diary to Helena, but Helena refuses to reciprocate. Later, Helena writes that she "protect[s]" her diary "by a lock" (101). Eunice, conversely, does not lock her diary until she decides to no longer write in it (and even then, she voluntarily reopens it to share it with the Governor). In the "second period," the narrative alternates between Helena's diary and Eunice's diary nine times (though not at regular intervals); this fluctuation not only keeps readers guessing which woman is the adopted daughter but also juxtaposes Helena's process of isolation with Eunice's process of networking. Full of pride and belief in her own superiority, Helena sheds potential allies and disparages almost everyone around her, particularly "stupid Eunice" (84). Eunice, less proud and vain than her sister, builds a group of friends and supporters she learns to trust and depend upon: the Straveleys, Miss Jillgall, Philip, the Governor, and the family who employs her as a governess. Even Reverend Gracedieu admits that he prefers Eunice to Helena. The sisters' diverging treatment of their diaries—either perennially locked or open for review—embody Helena's preference for independence and Eunice's for interdependence. As Catherine Delafield points out, however, at the end of the novel, Helena's diary "is read in court, reread in newspaper accounts, and read again by the Governor" (133); Helena's attempt to keep her diary locked and private, therefore, ultimately fails.

Like Eunice's diary, Jillgall's and the Governor's narratives are driven by friendliness, exchange, and interdependence. Jillgall's narrative consists of a series of letters written to the Governor, her "admirable friend" (*Legacy* 290). He comments that during his prostration from gout, he "heard regularly from the friendly and faithful Serena [Jillgall]" (303), and he visits her and Eunice as soon as his health allows. The Governor sees his "old friend" (154) Gracedieu upon the latter's urgent request for "counsel" (150); additionally, the Governor suggests that he writes his own narrative at Gracedieu's "invitation"

(184). Gracedieu, then, is likely the unnamed person "who has claims on" the Governor and who asks the Governor to write about the incidents in the prison (9). Jillgall's letters are written to a friend, asking him for help, and the Governor's narrative is likely written at the request of a friend who also asks for assistance.

In conclusion, Wilkie Collins centers disability in multiple ways in *The Woman in White*, *The Moonstone*, and *The Legacy of Cain*. Disability plays a role in the story, in individual narrations, and in the overarching multinarrator structure, demonstrating Robyn R. Warhol's claim that "theme is always manifest in form. Deviations from formal norms make deviations from dominant ideology visible" ("A Feminist" 12). The privileging of interdependence in the story is matched by collaboration in the structure. The perspective of disability narratology foregrounds how these novels' diegetic representations of disability and formal characteristics mutually inform each other. The interplay of independence and interdependence continues in the next chapter on Emily Brontë's *Wuthering Heights*. The novel's two narrators, Lockwood and Nelly Dean, are both single and proud of their independence; yet, Lockwood's sudden, serious illness makes him dependent on Nelly for information and entertainment. While the two narrators share a horror of Catherine and Heathcliff's deeply codependent relationship, their bond ironically becomes stronger through their storytelling sessions.

~

CHAPTER 5

The Permeable Frame

Gothic Collaboration in *Wuthering Heights*

FROM ITS BEGINNINGS with Horace Walpole's *The Castle of Otranto*,[1] the gothic genre has long used multiple narrators, as Eve Kosofsky Sedgwick and Peter K. Garrett have discussed.[2] In this way, the form of the gothic can appear as winding and labyrinthine as many standard gothic settings. In this chapter and the epilogue that follows, I suggest that the gothic novel often uses multiple narrators to stage the gothicization of the narrative itself. Critics' analyses of the gothic in Emily Brontë's *Wuthering Heights* tend to focus on spaces (the houses or moors), Heathcliff, or Heathcliff and Catherine's relationship.[3] Such readings usually position the novel's two narrators—

---

1. Although most gothic theorists identify *Otranto* as the first gothic novel, A. Williams seeks to puncture the "myth of Walpole" (11) by establishing that "many scenes and episodes in canonical literature belong to a kind of quasi-'Gothic' tradition" even though they were written before *Otranto* (13).

2. To Garrett, the multiple narrators stage "alternative versions" of the story and "raise issues of narrative power and authority" (*Gothic* ix). One of the conventions of the genre, per Sedgwick, is a "discontinuous and involuted" form, "perhaps incorporating tales within tales, changes of narrators, and such framing devices as found manuscripts or interpolated histories" (9). Ridenhour agrees that the "use of multiple narrators is a staple of Gothic novels" (121).

3. Milbank interprets the Heights as a gothic space because it encapsulates oppositions such as "prison and liberation, body and soul, life and death" (162). Heiland considers Heathcliff an "uncanny presence" at the Heights, particularly because he is named for the Earnshaws' dead son (117). Sedgwick uncovers "irreconcilable" gothic doubleness in both Catherine and Heathcliff (107), and DeLamotte discovers the gothic theme of the self being both other and

tenant Lockwood and servant Nelly Dean—outside the novel's gothic core. Generally, scholars have interpreted Lockwood and Nelly as conventional witnesses to—rather than participants in—the novel's gothic elements.[4] I argue, however, that Lockwood and Nelly do not stand outside the gothic, as much as they may want to; rather, in what I call the novel's *permeable frame*, the boundaries between Nelly and Lockwood threaten to dissolve, just as they do between Catherine and Heathcliff. While the boundaries between the two narrators soften and dissipate, Nelly and Lockwood nonetheless attempt to enforce boundaries, resulting in the strange boundary between the two narrators and their narrative productions. These boundaries—violated or surprising—within Nelly and Lockwood's narrative collaboration are a crucial part of the novel's gothicism.

Boundaries—either unnaturally crossed or imposed—are central to many theories of the gothic. Anne Williams highlights how the "Gothic is so pervasively organized around anxieties about boundaries (and boundary transgressions)" (16). Eugenia C. DeLamotte approaches both nineteenth-century gothic broadly and *Wuthering Heights* specifically as "fundamentally concerned with the boundaries of the self" (23); while some "boundaries appear unexpectedly" (22), others "prove unstable, elusive, ineffective, nonexistent." Donna Heiland similarly proposes, "Gothic fiction at its core is about transgressions of all sorts: across national boundaries, social boundaries, sexual boundaries, the boundaries of one's own identity" (3). Although Elizabeth R. Napier doesn't use a gothic framework, she too homes in on "the instability of the boundary" in *Wuthering Heights* (99).[5] I will build on such work by showing how the "instability of the boundary" affects the relationship between, and the narratives of, Lockwood and Nelly. Although the two narrators of *Wuthering Heights* differ in gender, class, and experience, their narrations never factually conflict, and they approach the novel's central story of Catherine and Heathcliff's ill-fated passion similarly; with a mixture of desire and fear, Nelly

---

"inaccessible" in Heathcliff and Catherine's relationship (136). Haggerty, who reads *Wuthering Heights* as "resolving the conflict between Gothic intention and novel form," locates Nelly and Lockwood on the novel's team, where they lack the imagination to grasp the "Gothic meaning" of Catherine and Heathcliff's entanglement (65, 66).

4. To J. Miller (in *Fiction*), Woodring, and Worth, Lockwood is a surrogate for the ordinary reader. To other critics—including W. Anderson, Mathison, McCarthy, and Napier—either one or both narrators serve as negative role models for the reader in their inability to fully appreciate and understand the central story.

5. Kermode, McKibben, and Van Ghent call attention to the novel's proliferation of portals—particularly doorways and windows—that serve as a manifestation of the novel's investment in "movement or passage" (Napier 95).

and Lockwood both attempt to impose an inadequate closure on the love story's terrifying wildness, though such attempts often falter or fail. Rather than interpreting Nelly and Lockwood as stupid or naive "bad readers" who just don't get it, I approach them as understanding the threats to their selfhoods and trying to protect themselves from such threats. Lockwood and Nelly— perpetual bachelor and spinster—safeguard their selves by remaining single and avoiding marriage and romance. And yet, Lockwood and Nelly bond through their storytelling sessions, resulting in a closeness that Lockwood flees from at the close of the novel. Most significantly, the frequent, ambiguous, and subtle narratorial handoffs between Nelly and Lockwood erode the boundaries between the two narrators in a way that resembles Catherine and Heathcliff's boundary-breaking relationship. Lastly, although most critics label Lockwood's narrative a diary, I emphasize the paltry evidence for such a categorization; instead, I show how the ambiguous status of his narrative and the ephemeral nature of Nelly's orally transmitted tale function as another way for the narrators to separate themselves from the stories they tell. The "position of the self" in the gothic, declares Sedgwick, is "to be massively blocked off from something to which it ought normally to have access" (12), and Nelly's and Lockwood's alienation from their productions points to the continued gothicness of their narratives.

NARRATOR TRANSITIONS AND
THE PERMEABLE FRAME

Switches between narrators are, in a sense, border crossings, and *Wuthering Heights* crosses these boundaries unconventionally through untagged, frequent, and oddly placed cuts between Lockwood and Nelly. These transitions differ from those in the other novels I've discussed in *Narrative Bonds*. In most multinarrator Victorian novels, switches are made to be explicit and visible via a specific type of tag: titles (either chapter, section, or book). In all three Wilkie Collins novels addressed in the previous chapter, changes in narrator are usually indicated through titles. The exception is letters embedded in other narratives such as Anne's letter in Walter's narrative in *The Woman in White* and Rosanna's letter in Blake's narrative in *The Moonstone*—these letters do not receive a separate title but are visibly set apart by indentation, quotation marks, or a font change. In Stevenson's *Treasure Island,* all three chapters Dr. Livesey narrates include "Narrative Continued by the Doctor" in the title, and chapter 19's title indicates "Narrative Resumed by Jim Hawkins" (93, 98). Most switches to Esther Summerson's narrative in Charles Dickens's *Bleak House* are heralded with the chapter title "Esther's Narrative."[6] As I will elaborate upon in the epilogue, Bram Stoker's *Dracula* contains an immense number of switches, and yet they are signposted by section headers and, in the original London edition, by running headers at the top of each page. Additionally, in most Victorian multinarrator novels, narrator cuts coincide with chapter breaks—they always do in *Bleak House* and *Treasure Island*. But *Wuthering Heights* includes no chapter, section, or volume titles, let alone ones that announce switches to Nelly's or Lockwood's narratives. Very little beyond context signals the narrator switches in *Wuthering Heights*. Sometimes quotation marks do so, but as I will shortly clarify, quotation mark usage varies by edition and makes for an unreliable signal in this novel. In *Wuthering Heights,* most narrator switches occur within chapters, sometimes within sentences, and in one striking occurrence, within parentheses.

Sometimes quotation marks—their introduction around Nelly's language or their absence around Lockwood's—can indicate a switch between narrators. But quotation marks are a minimal and ambiguous tag since they can signal things other than a narrator switch (quoted dialogue, for example); more importantly, editions of *Wuthering Heights* are not consistently punctuated. No draft, manuscript, or proofs of Emily's novel survive to offer an authoritatively punctuated version of the novel. Charlotte was disappointed in the sloppiness of the first London edition of the novel, published in 1847 by Thomas Newby. After Emily's death, Charlotte edited the novel for an 1850 run, standardizing the punctuation, among other changes.[7] The modern Penguin edition claims that "most modern editions now take the first edition as their starting point" over Charlotte's edited version, and the Penguin edition does the same, "amending only the obvious printing errors" (Nestor xli); however, there are many discrepancies in quotation mark usage between the 1847 edition and the modern Penguin edition. The transitions between Nelly and Lockwood, therefore, play out slightly differently on the page in different editions of the novel. While the 1847 edition tends to use more quotation marks than modern editions do, it still uses them irregularly and sporadically. For

---

6. As I discuss in chapter 2, even though Esther Summerson's first chapter in *Bleak House* jolts and perhaps confuses the reader because of the lack of a tag (the chapter is called "A Progress"), many of Esther's later chapters are labelled "Esther's Narrative."

7. As Nestor explains, Charlotte "was not content simply to correct typographical errors. She also changed the paragraphing to eliminate the prevalence of short paragraphs, altered the punctuation, tending to regularize Emily's rather idiosyncratic style, and modified the rendering of Joseph's dialect in order to make it more comprehensible" (xl).

comparison, the first switch from Nelly to Lockwood proceeds as follows in the original London edition:

> "Before I came to live here," she commenced, waiting no further invitation to her story; "I was almost always at Wuthering Heights . . . (vol. 1, 75)

The quotation marks encircling Nelly's story—marking it as an account framed by Lockwood—continue for three paragraphs but then disappear; however, these particular quotation marks are completely absent in the modern Penguin edition:

> Before I came to live here, she commenced, waiting no further invitation to her story, I was almost always at Wuthering Heights . . . (*Wuthering* 35)

In the modern Penguin edition, this switch proceeds even more smoothly because of the lack of quotation marks. But the original version still features three fluid switches in quick succession (Lockwood to Nelly; Nelly to Lockwood; Lockwood back to Nelly) within a sentence and without titles heralding the changes. The punctuation variations in different editions of *Wuthering Heights,* I suggest, is ultimately a symptom of the novel's odd and distinctive permeable frame rather than merely an effect of individual editors' choices. In short, these fluid, frequent, brief, and sometimes boomerang-like switches are difficult to punctuate conventionally.

In another set of switches late in the novel, the cuts occur unexpectedly, rapidly, and without quotation mark tags; this transitional ease highlights the lack of strong boundaries between the two narrators/narratives. While some switches between Nelly and Lockwood coincide with paragraph breaks, this particular set of switches happens within a parenthetical aside within a longer sentence within a tertiary character's dialogue. Nelly tells Lockwood about a conversation with Zillah, the then-housekeeper at the Heights, in which Nelly learns what is happening at the house in her absence:

> "Joseph and I [Zillah] generally go to chapel on Sundays," (the Kirk, you know, has no minister, now, explained Mrs. Dean, and they call the Methodists' or Baptists' place, I can't say which it is, at Gimmerton, a chapel.) "Joseph had gone," she continued, "but I thought proper to bide at home." (295)

Zillah's speech—"Joseph and I generally go to chapel . . ."—appears in quotation marks within Nelly's narration. A dizzying series of switches proceeds

within the subsequent parenthetical. Nelly directly addresses Lockwood with
"you know." Then, the narrative cuts to Lockwood: "explained Mrs. Dean."
The narrative boomerangs back to Nelly, and she continues her clarification
about the town church. These two cuts appear in quick succession and without quotation marks; additionally, the punctuation within the parenthetical is
the same in the 1847 and modern Penguin editions. Within the parenthetical
space, the narrative moves seamlessly between Nelly and Lockwood.

The fluidity between narrators and the quick and/or untagged transitions
resemble Catherine's mental breakdown—when her mind starts "wandering"
(123). Standing at the open window and staring toward the Heights, which isn't
visible from the Grange, she verbally rambles into the frosty air:

> "Joseph sits up late, doesn't he? He's waiting till I come home that he may
> lock the gate . . . Well, he'll wait a while yet. It's a rough journey, and a sad
> heart to travel it; and we must pass by Gimmerton Kirk, to go that journey!
> We've braved its ghosts often together, and dared each other to stand among
> the graves and ask them to come . . . But Heathcliff, if I dare you now, will
> you venture? If you do, I'll keep you. I'll not lie there by myself; they may
> bury me twelve feet deep, and throw the church down over me; but I won't
> rest till you are with me . . . I never will!"
>
> She paused, and resumed with a strange smile, "He's considering . . .
> he'd rather I'd come to him! Find a way, then! not through that Kirkyard . . .
> You are slow! Be content, you always followed me!" (126, ellipses in original)

The identity of the speaker fluctuates from an "I" (Catherine herself) to a
"we" (Catherine and Heathcliff), and the identity of the addressee fluctuates
from Nelly to Heathcliff. Then, Catherine seems to be repeating or interpreting Heathcliff's response for Nelly's ears ("He's considering . . . he'd rather I'd
come to him!"). Catherine also shifts between the past and present and possible future. Fittingly, she seems obsessed with breached or opened barriers
in this passage: Joseph has not yet locked the gate; she remembers her and
Heathcliff summoning ghosts; she vows her coffin will not constrain her; she
converses with an absent Heathcliff. The narrative itself parallels, rather than
counters, the breakdown of barriers represented by Catherine's mental decline
and by her and Heathcliff's relationship.

Critics have commonly analyzed *Wuthering Heights* as a frame narrative in which the frame is forgettable, but I argue that Lockwood constantly
reminds us of his presence. Presumably, Lockwood transcribes Nelly's oral
story, and Nelly's oral tale is embedded, or framed by, Lockwood's outer nar-

rative.[8] John T. Matthews claims that the "frame portion of *Wuthering Heights* sinks into the background of the monumental passion which it discloses" (27). But the high number of switches between narrators in *Wuthering Heights*—unusual among Victorian frame novels[9]—frequently reminds readers of the novel's frame structure. The simplest frame narrative transitions only twice, once from the frame to the framed and again from the framed to the frame; often, however, this closing transition is omitted as in Henry James's *The Turn of the Screw*. *Wuthering Heights,* on the other hand, switches twenty-one times between the two narrators.[10] Nelly certainly narrates the majority of the novel, but Lockwood persistently pops in, usually narrating briefly, for a few sentences or a paragraph; after his opening narration, his longest interlude lasts eleven pages, which occurs when he decamps from the Grange and unexpectedly returns later and hears Nelly's update about Heathcliff's death. Occasionally, Lockwood emerges as narrator for only two or three words like "explained Mrs Dean" or "continued Mrs Dean" (*Wuthering* 295, 189).[11] These frequent cuts prevent the reader from fully settling into Nelly's story and serve as little reminders of Lockwood's presence, even though, according to Matthews, "frames are meant to be forgotten" (25).

Because of *Wuthering Heights*'s unique transition factors, I propose the term permeable frame to better characterize the novel's frame structure. The frequent, quick, fluid, and subtle handoffs between Nelly and Lockwood foster a hazy separation between the two that creates this permeable frame. The term is separate from—through inspired by—Brian Richardson's concept of the "permeable narrator" that addresses "the uncanny and inexplicable intrusion of the voice of another within the narrator's consciousness" (95). Neither Nelly nor Lockwood are permeable narrators in the sense Richardson means since in *Wuthering Heights* the "intrusion of the voice" is not "without any signal or

---

8. Duyfhuizen addresses the issue of Lockwood's mediation and potential alteration of Nelly's story: "Lockwood's transcription of Nelly's discourse is always double-voiced: a hybrid narrative discourse which is spoken/interpreted/transcribed. This means that we need to be aware of more than one voice speaking (writing) the narrative" (*Narratives* 221).

9. *Dracula* and *Bleak House* contain more switches than *Wuthering Heights* does, but *Dracula* and *Bleak House* are not frame novels; additionally, they are both longer novels and *Dracula* includes more narrators than *Wuthering Heights* does.

10. For contrast, consider Shelley's *Frankenstein*; once the novel switches from Walton's framing narration to Frankenstein's framed narration, Walton's narration does not interrupt Frankenstein's. Frankenstein addresses Walton several times as his narratee (and Frankenstein's narrative frames the creature's narrative), but the novel does not revert to Walton's narrative until Frankenstein's finishes.

11. Boyce graphs *Wuthering Heights*'s frame structure, visualizing points at which "Lockwood's narrative is sometimes reasserted for a moment" (97).

explanation" (95, 104–5); however, Richardson's idea of "distinct figures who merge and blend into one another" helps illuminate the dissipating boundaries between Nelly and Lockwood's selves and narratives (104). Additionally, this term highlights the themes of boundaries and transgressions that apply to Nelly and Lockwood in both the novel's plot and structure. William Nelles asserts that "every embedded narrative must be considered to have strong potential for structural, dramatic, and thematic significance by virtue of the sole fact of its being embedded" ("Stories" 92). Both Mieke Bal and Matthews find meaningful connections between the frame and framed in *Wuthering Heights*. Bal highlights how Lockwood and Heathcliff are both strangers to the area. Matthews argues that the central story's need for the frame, and the frame's need for the central story, emphasize the dynamics of lack that also figure in Catherine and Heathcliff's relationship. I add that the frame and framed both explore the dissolution of boundaries between persons—Catherine and Heathcliff, and Nelly and Lockwood.

BOUNDARIES AND CLOSURE

The novel's central relationship between Catherine and Heathcliff is the ultimate manifestation of the gothic's unstable boundaries and ineffectual constraints. This relationship is many things: a metaphysical oneness ("Nelly, I *am* Heathcliff" [*Wuthering* 82]); a yearning for physical oneness (Heathcliff arranges for their dead bodies to dissolve together); an intense sibling bond (they are raised as brother and sister; Edgar refers to Heathcliff as Catherine's brother); and romantic love (Catherine chooses to marry Edgar over Heathcliff because of Edgar's status and money, but she seems to consider Heathcliff a possible romantic partner otherwise).[12] Their relationship mocks convention and breaks boundaries by invoking incest, necrophilia, and a misalliance; by literalizing the "we are one" language of marriage; and by only being fulfilled in/after death as locals witness their ghosts promenading the moors together. Other critics have also emphasized how the relationship suggests "a radical open-endedness of being" (Bersani 212) and a desire "to escape from separateness and to merge totally with the other" (Wion 372) in a manner that requires "the dissolution of boundaries" (373). Nelly and Lockwood, conversely, attempt to keep the gothic at bay; they try, usually ineffectually, to maintain interpersonal boundaries and impose closure on Heathcliff and Catherine's love story.

---

12. Wion adds that their "love . . . is modeled on the primal bond between child and mother" (367).

Given that romantic entanglement entails death or dissolution of self in the novel—particularly in Catherine and Heathcliff's example but also in many others—it is no surprise that Lockwood and Nelly avoid romance, getting married, and having children. Heathcliff and Catherine repeatedly call the other their "murderer" (*Wuthering* 163); Heathcliff and Isabella continually threaten to kill each other (and he does throw a knife at her head); and Catherine contemplates killing herself if it would also kill her husband Edgar. Nelly overhears or is informed of all these homicidal sentiments. Furthermore, for the novel's women, romantic love leads to marriage, which leads to childbirth, which leads to premature death.[13] A servant girl brings Nelly the news of Hareton's birth and his young mother Frances's certain death in the same breath. Hareton's entrance into the world seems to necessitate Frances's departure: "The finest lad that ever breathed! But the doctor says missis must go" (64). Nelly intimately witnesses this mingling of life and death, as she both cares for the newborn and tends to Frances's sickroom. Later, Nelly recounts Cathy's birth and Catherine's death in the same sentence, syntactically suggesting a cause-and-effect relationship between the two events: "That night, was born the Catherine you saw at Wuthering Heights, a puny, seven months' child; and two hours after the mother died" (166). Although Lisa Sternlieb incorrectly identifies Nelly as "the only woman in the novel who successfully avoids motherhood" (41), as, to our knowledge, neither Zillah nor Cathy has yet had a child, Sternlieb accurately explains that via "spinsterhood, celibacy, and childlessness," Nelly "becomes the only survivor of her generation" (42). Even when mothers survive childbirth, children later instigate parental death. Nelly recalls how Mrs. Linton insists that the ailing Catherine convalesce at the Grange, and Mrs. Linton "and her husband both took the fever [from Catherine], and died within a few days of each other" (*Wuthering* 88). Nelly warns Cathy that continuing her bourgeoning romance with Linton "might kill" her father, perhaps remembering the patricidal effect of Catherine and Edgar's relationship (231). Cathy and Linton's growing closeness parallels Edgar's decline, and their marriage nearly coincides with his death. Nelly would have noticed how mothers prove particularly vulnerable— not one outlives a father.[14] Mrs. Earnshaw dies four years before Mr. Earnshaw; Frances dies four years before Hindley; Catherine dies seventeen years

---

13. S. Gilbert and S. Gubar stress that "female sexuality [is] necessarily deadly" in the novel (286).

14. Wion makes a similar point (368) but excludes Mrs. Linton from the pattern. The novel doesn't indicate if Mr. or Mrs. Linton dies first, only stating that they "died within a few days of each other" (*Wuthering* 88).

before Edgar; and Isabella dies five years before Heathcliff.[15] Lockwood may notice how the left-behind men don't fare much better. Hindley descends into alcoholism, gambling, and tyrannical sorrow; Edgar plateaus into lifeless tranquility; and Heathcliff suffers through a grief-torn existence without his "life" and "soul" (169).

Lockwood associates romantic and maternal love with a dangerous violation of his secure self. One of the few pieces of backstory Lockwood reveals is his failed romance with a girl at the seaside. When the "real goddess" whom he adores finally returns his affection with "the sweetest of all imaginable looks," he "shrunk icily into [him]self, like a snail, at every glance retired colder and farther" until the girl, befuddled, leaves the seaside with her mother (6). Building on Beth Newman's point that the scene reveals "Lockwood's fear of the returning female gaze" (1031),[16] I emphasize that Lockwood responds as if he had been attacked by the girl's loving looks, retreating into his protective shell and ensuring his "self" is not left vulnerable to the woman's repeated assaults. Lockwood's interaction with one of the Heights's demon dogs—the "canine mother"—directly after he recalls the seaside episode again reveals Lockwood's belief that relationships with women carry danger (*Wuthering* 6). Lockwood "attempt[s] to caress the canine mother, who had left her nursery, and was sneaking wolfishly to the back of my legs, her lip curled up, and her white teeth watering for a snatch." As with the seaside belle, Lockwood attempts to communicate his affections to the dog. But while he misconstrues the goddess' glances as attacks, in this case, his effort to "caress" the dog produces actual aggression: "a long, guttural gnarl." The dog soon attacks him: It "broke into a fury, and leapt on [his] knees" (7). Just as Lockwood refuses the girl's glances, he "flung [the dog] back" (7). The dog is specifically a female and a mother. Lockwood describes her as a "canine mother" (6), "bitch" (6), "madam" (7), and "Juno," the mother of the gods (10). Lockwood further stresses her maternity by observing she has just left "her nursery" and has "little ones" (6, 10). The dog is watchful over and combative toward Lockwood, having "guardianship over all [his] movements" and revealing "white teeth" under a "curled up" lip (6). Similarly, Cathy "stare[s]" at Lockwood: "She kept her eyes on me, in a cool, regardless manner" (10). She also "curled her lip" (30). Lockwood interprets the behavior of Cathy, the dog, and the

---

15. To determine these numbers, I have turned to Sanger's chronology of the novel. Boyce, however, revises some of Sanger's dates.

16. Newman links the female gaze in this scene to Freud's "'Medusa's Head,' the direct sight of which evokes the terror of castration in the male spectator, a terror that turns him to stone" (1030–31).

seaside girl as variations on a theme of female menace—they all endanger his safety and personal space.

Because Lockwood associates love with dissolution of self, he distances himself from Cathy even though he is attracted to her and fantasizes about marrying her. His desire "to know [the] history" of "that pretty girl-widow" (33) sparks his request to Nelly "to tell [him] something of [his] neighbours" (35). As Nelly's story continues, Lockwood becomes infatuated, asking Nelly to hang Cathy's portrait above his fireplace and appearing "so lively and interested, when [Nelly] talk[s] about her" (256). But Lockwood also recognizes that Cathy is "not an angel"—he may be "running into temptation" by pursuing her (299, 256). Since he imagines Cathy as a demonic tempter, he treats his last two visits to the Heights as perilous lures; he protects himself from those temptations by framing Cathy by viewing her through doorways and windows whenever possible. When Lockwood visits the Heights to inform Heathcliff he's leaving the Grange, he observes Cathy through a frame-like structure, a doorway. After Lockwood awkwardly chats with a grumpy Cathy, the conversation is hijacked by a spat between Cathy and Hareton over his book thievery. Once Cathy no longer seems interested in conversing with Lockwood, he moves and "took up [his] station in the door-way, surveying the external prospect, as [he] stood" (302). From this position he watches the "external" quarrel and book burning. When Lockwood returns to the Heights for the final time, he spies on Cathy and Hareton's cute reading lesson through a window: "What inmates there were had stationed themselves not far from one of the windows. I could both see them and hear them talk before I entered; and, looked and listened in consequence" (307). To avoid encountering the couple face-to-face at the front door, he rushes around the house to enter by the back door. Later, when he hears them returning from their walk, he "watch[es] their approach through the window" (337). He escapes out the back door while they linger at the front door so he doesn't have to confront them. Lockwood feels more comfortable watching and yearning for Cathy from a safe distance and through the mediation of windows and doorways.[17]

Both Lockwood and Nelly assume that boundaries are necessary and to be respected. Nelly is alternatively mystified and repelled by Heathcliff and Catherine's enduring passion because she believes that boundaries like spatial separation, marriage, and death should constrain their desire. When Catherine confesses to Nelly that she has accepted Edgar's proposal, Nelly logically assumes this will lead to her "separation" from Heathcliff (82), but Catherine

---

17. Matthews adds that Nelly's story serves as a "protective barrier" between Lockwood and Cathy (44).

rails that her relationship with Heathcliff will continue. Nelly considers Catherine's plan to be opposed to the "duties" of her impending marriage (83).
Nonetheless, Catherine and Heathcliff's passion persists despite his absence,
her marriage to Edgar, his marriage to Isabella, her illness, her death, and
(seemingly) his death. Nelly finds this persistence, at turns, annoying, disorienting, dangerous, and outrageous, and she frequently counsels Catherine and
Heathcliff to shut down their relationship. The early calm marriage between
Catherine and Edgar pleases Nelly, but she is upset when Heathcliff's reap-
pearance unsettles the peaceful household. Nelly hopes that "something [will]
happen which might have the effect of freeing both Wuthering Heights and
the Grange of Mr Heathcliff" (107). Once Heathcliff marries Isabella, Nelly
plainly advises him to avoid Catherine—who is recovering from a serious
illness—and perhaps even "move out of this country entirely" (147). When
Heathcliff demands Nelly facilitate a visit to the convalescent Catherine, Nelly
"refuse[s] him fifty times" until he threatens her into reluctant acquiescence
(153). Heathcliff does show up, and he and Catherine violently and intensely
bicker and embrace. Nelly watches, disturbed by the "strange and fearful picture" (160). When Edgar returns to the Grange, Nelly begs Heathcliff to depart
and save Catherine's reputation: "I was horrified" (164). She is "appalled" by
his intense reaction to Catherine's death—slamming his head bloody against
a tree and pleading with Catherine to haunt him (169)—and equally shocked
when he admits to rigging Catherine's coffin so their bodies can decompose
together. Nelly constantly reminds Catherine and Heathcliff of proper boundaries, and yet their relationship consistently breaches or disregards them.

Another way Nelly attempts to shut down and contain Catherine and
Heathcliff's gothic passion is to read death as a peaceful finality. The gothic,
which traffics in ghosts, hauntings, and dead-yet-alive vampires, often hinges
on the prospect that the body continues past death. Nelly briefly admits such
possibilities, wondering if the starving Heathcliff is "a ghoul, or a vampire";
however, she quickly rejects those options as "absurd nonsense" (330). When
Catherine dies, Nelly characterizes her dead body as overwhelmingly peaceful: "*hers* of perfect peace. Her brow smooth, her lids closed, her lips wearing the expression of a smile. No angel in heaven could be more beautiful
than she appeared; and I partook of the infinite calm in which she lay. My
mind was never in a holier frame, than while I gazed on that untroubled
image of Divine rest" (166). Nelly's statement is rife with exaggeration; she
must imaginatively work overtime to force peace onto the body: The "peace"
is alliteratively "perfect," the "calm" is unassailably "infinite," and the "rest"
is nothing less than "Divine." Perfect, infinite, and Divine: these are abso-
lutes, extremes. Nelly overrides, yet tacitly acknowledges, Catherine's turbu-

lent final days and hours by projecting an "untroubled image"—and even a smile!—onto the body. Importantly, Nelly identifies her role as the framer of the scene, highlighting how her perceptions are imbued with her own desires. Her own "mind was never in a holier frame," and so she converts the unangelic Catherine into an "angel." Nelly continues by stating that Catherine's corpse "asserted its own tranquility" (167); however, the very idea of a dead body "asserting" anything undermines Nelly's interpretation of Catherine's body as passively resting. Heathcliff's dead body doesn't conform as easily to Nelly's desire for closure. It refuses to settle into an image of peace and repose. His eyes won't close, his smirk won't dampen, and his face won't look dead; instead, his face wears a "frightful, life-like gaze of exultation" (335). The aliveness of the dead body, in addition to its "sharp, white teeth," echoes Nelly's previous suspicion that Heathcliff is a vampire. Catherine's body—eyes and mouth—are closed. Heathcliff's is open—his eyes "would not shut," and his lips are "parted." In the moment, Nelly cannot construct his body as tranquil, so she quickly labels it "the corpse," linguistically forcing it to be a dead body rather than Heathcliff's body. And although she relays the ghost rumors to Lockwood, she also insists that "the dead are at peace," denying the resistance of Heathcliff's body to her favored discourse of closure, death, and peace (337).

Furthermore, at the points in Nelly's narrative at which she relates Catherine's and Heathcliff's deaths, she and Lockwood enter a quick, digressive debate that unsettles the very closure Nelly proffers. After Nelly goes on at length about the beauty of Catherine's dead body and the joy of the hereafter, she poses a question to Lockwood that reveals she's unconvinced by her own discourse: "Do you believe such people *are* happy in the other world, sir? I'd give a great deal to know" (167). Then, the frame narrative quietly reasserts itself and Lockwood reveals that he considers the question "heterodox," though he "decline[s] answering" Nelly's question aloud. Her earnest question hangs in the air leaving open possibilities: Catherine is not in heaven and/or heaven is not a happy place for all people. The interrogation of Christian precepts and the switch in narrators occur simultaneously. As Nelly is indulging in her heretical wondering, cracking her sense of an ordered and moral universe, the switch in narrators simultaneously opens up a small gap; the narrative whiplash reveals a mobility and openness that ironically points up Nelly's thwarted desire for closure.

At the end of the novel, Nelly explains that most of the Heights will soon be "shut up," and Lockwood jokingly retorts that the Heights will remain open to "such ghosts as choose to inhabit it" (337). Lockwood's comment unsettles the conception of death as ending one's earthly existence and briefly gives credence to the "idle tales" of Heathcliff and Catherine's ghosts wandering the moors together (336). Nelly recounts and discounts those tales in the same breath, but her confession that she's afraid to be on the moors at night or in the Heights alone undermines her disavowal. Nelly answers Lockwood's ghoulish quip with a firm "No, Mr Lockwood" while "shaking her head," verbally and physically trying to board up against such terrifying possibilities (337). She affirms, "the dead are at peace," recalling her attempt to make Catherine's dead body peaceful. But, as Terence McCarthy notes, Nelly's "denial is unconvincing . . . She has an inkling of a visionary world which must be kept at bay—for sanity's sake" (63). Nelly and Lockwood, therefore, take turns questioning the closure they both offer and take turns chiding the other for being "heterodox" (*Wuthering* 167). The narrative imperceptibly switches back to Lockwood during Nelly's report of the "idle tales" (336). Nelly relays that because of these tales, she will be happy when Cathy and Hareton "shift to the Grange"; the next line—"'They are going to the Grange, then?' I said"—is from Lockwood's perspective. The young couple's upcoming domestic "shift" also signals the shift in narrator. The fluid, open storytelling structure of the novel aligns with Catherine and Heathcliff's boundary-defying romance; it is fitting that this final switch in narrators occurs during a discussion of how that romance has transcended death.

In the final paragraphs of the novel, Lockwood visits the graves of Catherine, Edgar, and Heathcliff and attempts to close off the story's gothic possibilities. At the novel's start, Lockwood makes a similar move after experiencing a terrifying visitation by Catherine's ghost. He initially grants that the Heights is "haunted" and "swarming with ghosts and goblins!" (27); however, within a page, he rationalizes the experience as a mere product of his bedtime reading, "which personified itself when I had no longer my imagination under control" (28). On the novel's final page, Lockwood's description of the headstone triumvirate mirrors not only his earlier brush with the gothic but also Nelly's earlier attempts to impose quietness and rest—in short, closure—on the very dead who seem to resist both: "I lingered round them, under that benign sky; watched the moths fluttering among the heath, and hare-bells; listened to the soft wind breathing through the grass; and wondered how any one could ever imagine unquiet slumbers, for the sleepers in that quiet earth" (337). Cemeteries are classic gothic settings, as are ruins, and Lockwood passes the "decay[ing]" and abandoned Kirk—glass missing from the windows, dislodged slates on the roof, no clergyman inside—on his way to the tombstones. And yet, Lockwood's description of the makeshift graveyard drains it of its gothic potential. At every turn of phrase, Lockwood softens, tames, and beautifies the scene: The moths "flutter[ ]," the already "soft wind" "breath[es]" rather than blows, the sky is "benign," and even Lockwood's own actions—"lingered," "listened," "watched," and "wondered"—are calm, stationary, and meditative. As if admitting the hollowness to his sweet description, Lockwood timorously calls out to Heathcliff by evoking "the health"—but no specter answers the partial invitation. J. Hillis Miller writes that Lockwood's "naiveté . . . is imaged in his inability to imagine unquiet slumbers for the sleepers in the quiet earth" (*Fiction* 59). But I interpret Lockwood's idyllic reaction as a willed refusal of the imagination and a willed act of closure rather than as unknowing naiveté. Lockwood's exaggeration bespeaks his conscious attempt to tame the wild energies of scene and story. This effort is particularly manifest in his final line, which is comprised of a striking, loose chiasmus. The sequence of "unquiet" and "slumbers" is reversed into "sleepers" and "quiet" that structurally compels the conventional, restful "quiet" to counter and dissipate the potentiality of "unquiet."

Furthermore, Lockwood attempts to physically distance himself from the story through his early departure from the Grange. As soon as he has sufficiently recovered from his illness, Lockwood leaves for London before his lease ends. But he returns when he "unexpectedly" finds himself near Gimmerton while en route to a friend's house (*Wuthering* 305). Lockwood barely recollects the name of Gimmerton when it's mentioned to him even though his stay in the area was recent and memorable: "'Gimmerton?' I repeated, my residence in that locality had already grown dim and dreamy." Lockwood's location shock recalls Sigmund Freud's identification of the "unintentional return" to a place one is determined to leave as uncanny because one experiences "helplessness" in the face of the "the fateful and the inescapable" (144). Rather than deliberately choosing to return to the area, Lockwood only accidently approaches it. Once he realizes he's near Gimmerton, he does not deliberately decide to visit the Grange and settle his outstanding rent; rather, he feels himself prey to a "sudden impulse" that "seized [him] to visit Thrushcross Grange" (*Wuthering* 305). The land pulls out all of its beautiful summer stops to "tempt[ ]" him to stay again, providing a seasonal inversion of the debilitating snowstorm at the novel's opening that forces him to remain. Lockwood certainly seems fated to return and helpless in resisting the area's pull. But Lockwood eventually musters the energy to run away from Nelly and the Heights after settling his rent and will likely never reappear in the area again; however, the novel concludes with Lockwood at the makeshift cemetery on the moor hill. Since the apparently space-bound narrative doesn't follow Lockwood when he travels to London and doesn't revive until he's near Gimmerton, his narrative can end with only the anticipation of closure-allowing escape.

Although Lockwood is logically aware that the "character[s]" in Nelly's oral tale are real (as he personally meets many of them), he occasionally treats her story like fiction—another effort of control, containment, and closure that inevitably fails (62). Lockwood twice refers to the "sequel" of Nelly's story (90, 309). He worries that Cathy may prove to be "a second edition of the mother" (153), using a publishing metaphor to express his fear that Cathy has inherited her mother's negative qualities. While enduring his prescribed bed rest, Lockwood asks Nelly to "finish her tale": "I can recollect its chief incidents, as far as she had gone. Yes, I remember her hero had run off, and never been heard of for three years: and the heroine was married" (91). Lockwood gives the story a "hero" and a "heroine," transforming the strange history into something conventional and literary.[18] A novel, after all, can always be finished and closed. But Nelly's story cannot be metaphorically closed and put aside, as characters from it knock on Lockwood's own door. Although Lockwood—the extradiegetic narrator—chooses to mingle with characters from Nelly's story whenever he visits the Heights, there's an unsettling feeling of invasion when these characters choose to visit Lockwood at the Grange. Heathcliff, the aforementioned "hero," calls on Lockwood during the latter's illness, and, at another point, the doctor Kenneth's arrival at the house interrupts Nelly's storytelling: "But here is Kenneth—I'll go down" (153). Kenneth appears throughout Nelly's story, including in the previous chapter in which he tends to Catherine in her illness. Lockwood avoids narrating these encounters. He analeptically notes that "Mr Heathcliff has just honoured me with a call" (91) but doesn't narrate the visit itself. He narrates that Nelly "descended to receive the doctor" (153), implying a future meeting with Kenneth, but both the chapter and volume end there, omitting the interaction with the doctor. Lockwood's reluctance to narrate these moments suggests a last-ditch attempt to keep his narrative separate from Nelly's story.

LEVELLING MASTER AND SERVANT

Lockwood and Nelly's divergent social positions—master and servant—function as another barrier to intimacy that crumbles as the novel continues. Nelly often uses the deferential title "sir," and when she puts a question to Lockwood, she "beg[s] pardon for asking" (35). She situates the storytelling, a request from Lockwood, as one of her housekeeping duties alongside sewing

---

18. Berlinger also notices how "Lockwood tries to mitigate the story's impact by casting it as a literary fiction" (190).

and nursing. But their storytelling sessions cause them to become unsuspectingly close. They spend many hours together one-on-one, sometimes late into the night, with Lockwood ill in bed and Nelly familiarly positioned at his bedside. They both admit to liking the other. Lockwood calls Nelly "my good friend" (256) and "unhesitatingly" (300) tells Cathy that Nelly likes him "very well"; however, they both channel Lockwood's romantic feelings to Cathy to drain their own relationship of eroticism. Nelly plays matchmaker, prodding Lockwood to pursue the widowed Cathy, and Lockwood swiftly latches onto that possibility. Nelly's desire for the union seems to fuel his own desire for it: "What a realization of something more romantic than a fairy tale it would have been for Mrs Linton Heathcliff, had she and I struck up an attachment, as her good nurse desired" (304).[19]

Despite Lockwood and Nelly's different backgrounds and statuses, some narrative transitions unite them in moments of mutual looking or shared language. In one set of switches, Nelly sets up the Heathcliff-Edgar-Catherine love triangle and then directs Lockwood's attention to Edgar's portrait on the wall: "He was my late master; that is his portrait over the fireplace. It used to hang on one side, and his wife's on the other; but hers has been removed, or else you might see something of what she was. Can you make that out?" (66–67). Directly after Nelly's question, the narrative switches to Lockwood, who silently describes the painting; to his eyes, Edgar appears "soft-featured," "sweet," "too graceful," and feminine—seemingly incompatible with the wild Catherine (67). Nelly informs Lockwood that the portrait is indeed accurate "but [Edgar] looked better when he was animated; that is his every day countenance; he wanted spirit in general" (67). Nelly then plunges back into her story as the narrative switches back to her; however, this brief interlude shows Lockwood and Nelly literally looking together and sharing a similar interpretation of Edgar's portrait as indicating his lack—of spirit or of masculinity. Interestingly, this fluid transition between times (the interlude examines portraits made at a later point in the story, when the couple is married) and narrators is initiated by a reference to Heathcliff and Catherine's strange bond—despite being courted by the "superior[ ]" Edgar, her attachment to Heathcliff is described as "deep," "constan[t]," and "unalterabl[e]" (66). An exchange about Catherine and Heathcliff's boundary-defying relationship, then, heralds a lack of boundaries in the narrative itself. Another narrator

---

19. Hafley and Sternlieb cite Nelly's matchmaking intentions as evidence of Nelly's scheming, manipulative nature. Hafley transforms Nelly into the "villain of the piece" who "outdoes Iago" in her malicious attempts to vanquish Heathcliff and Catherine and to manipulate Lockwood so she can become mistress of the two houses (199, 209). Sternlieb considers Nelly as "responsible for the destruction of the Earnshaw and Linton families" as Heathcliff is (45).

switch that fuses the narrators occurs at the end of volume one, when the doctor Kenneth arrives at the Grange, and Nelly halts her storytelling, informing Lockwood, "I'll go down, and tell him how much better you are. My history is *dree,* as we say, and will serve to wile away another morning" (153). The narrative then switches to Lockwood: "Dree, and dreary!" London-born Lockwood repeats Nelly's Yorkshire dialect—*dree*—temporarily mimicking her. Though he follows this reiteration with the English translation of the word (dreary), the mirroring of language still marks the cut, pulling together these two narrators of different backgrounds and voices.

Other transitions draw attention to the dismantling of the master/servant boundary through what I term an order-negotiation process. The first narrative switch occurs after Lockwood orders Nelly "to sit and chat an hour" "to tell [him] something of [his] neighbours" (35). Nelly agrees but also takes on a medical authority, insisting on bringing some "gruel" to help alleviate his illness as she speaks; furthermore, even though Lockwood entreats her to gossip about the "neighbours," she promptly starts by enthusiastically talking about herself: "Before I came to live here, she commenced, waiting no further invitation to her story, I was almost always at Wuthering Heights." This order-negotiation process, in which Lockwood makes a demand and Nelly acquiesces with provisos, often unfolds during narrator switches. In the next set of cuts, Nelly notices the late hour and apologizes for "chattering on at such a rate" (61); with a switch to Lockwood, he responds with flattery and orders: "Sit still, Mrs Dean . . . do sit still, another half hour! You've done just right to tell the story leisurely" (62). After chiding him for his sleeping patterns, she gives in to his demand that she "resume [her] chair" but attempts to negotiate, asking "to leap over some three years" in her story, which would presumably allow her to finish faster. Lockwood interrupts her attempt to restart, resisting her intended ellipsis, adding that Nelly, "[his] good friend," is very unlike other servants (63). Nelly consents to a shorter ellipsis of half a year but avows she'll proceed in her own way, "in true gossip's fashion." In this scene, Lockwood asserts his authority, and Nelly counters. But Lockwood also levels himself and Nelly by calling her his "friend," a term that suggests equality; he specifically raises her above the "generality of servants." Later, Lockwood narrates that four weeks of sickness pass; when he feels slightly better, he desires "Mrs Dean to finish her tale" (91). This scene also showcases the order-negotiation process. He rings for her and directs her to sit, take out her knitting, and continue with the story. He also peppers her with four questions about Heathcliff. Nelly agrees to continue, but stresses that she cannot answer how Heathcliff obtained his money or gentlemanly bearing and that she will "proceed in [her] own fashion" (92)—the narrative then switches back to her.

In a subsequent scene that further suggests their equalization, it is Nelly who lobs a series of questions at Lockwood about his feelings for Cathy; in this reversal, it is Lockwood's turn to ask Nelly, "[his] good friend," to cease her questioning and teasing (256).

When Lockwood returns to the Grange and Heights near the novel's close, the protective barriers—Cathy's availability and Nelly's indisputable position as his servant—have disappeared. When Lockwood drops by the Heights to settle with Heathcliff, he recognizes Cathy and Hareton's new intimacy. Nelly and Lockwood have lost their romantic focuser. Nelly is "glad [Lockwood] did not try" "to win Mrs Heathcliff's heart" (316), and Lockwood accepts he has "thrown away the chance [he] might have had" (308). Nelly now lives at the Heights as a pseudo-business partner to Cathy and is effectively Lockwood's landlord. When Lockwood asks to see Nelly's "master," she rejoins that Lockwood "must settle" with her because Heathcliff is dead and Cathy "has not learnt to manage her affairs yet, and [Nelly] act[s] for her" (309). Lockwood and Nelly, therefore, are suddenly equalized. The order-negotiation process continues but is now initiated by Nelly. Nelly precipitates the storytelling and smoothly orders Lockwood about: "But, sit down, and let me take your hat, and I'll tell you all about it. Stop, you have had nothing to eat, have you?" Discomfited, Lockwood evades her offers and counterorders Nelly to sit and start the story: "I want nothing. I have ordered supper at home. You sit down too. . . . Let me hear how it came to pass." Lockwood attempts to retain his comfortable sense of mastery over Nelly by reframing her eagerness to tell as his eagerness to hear.

Appropriate to this situation of parity, Nelly addresses Lockwood more frequently during her last narrative section. In the remaining seventeen pages of her story, which cover Heathcliff's death and Hareton and Cathy's slow-burning romance, Nelly addresses her narratee six times—more consistently than at any other point in the novel. Previously, Nelly would occasionally refer to "you" or "Mr Lockwood," though such addresses usually led to a switch in narrator; here, they are just part of the fabric of her narrative: "*You* see, *Mr Lockwood*, it was easy enough to win Mrs Heathcliff's heart; but now, I'm glad *you* did not try" (316); "*You* know, they both appeared in a measure, my children" (321); "Oh, *Mr Lockwood*, I cannot express what a terrible start I got, by the momentary view" of Heathcliff's dead eyes (329); "Idle tales, *you'll* say, and so say I" (336), and so on (all emphasis added). Nelly proceeds more conversationally as befits two old friends catching up over beers; she no longer acts like a servant obeying orders from her master. Much earlier, Nelly acted self-deprecatingly, worried that Lockwood didn't enjoy her method of storytelling; here, she confidently carries on, gently ribbing Lockwood for not pursuing

Cathy and assuming she and Lockwood share the same viewpoint on the "idle tales" about Catherine and Heathcliff's ghosts.

With the protective barriers gone, Lockwood chooses to hurriedly run away—imposing a boundary of space between himself and Nelly—rather than stay with Nelly further into the night in a potentially romantic situation. When Lockwood unexpectedly arrives, he and Nelly joyously greet one another. He mentally identifies her as "[his] old friend," and she "jumped to her feet" upon noticing him (308). The night is beautiful and dreamy; the moon glows; Cathy and Hareton depart on a lovers' stroll. With this romantic ambiance, Joseph proclaims the impropriety of Lockwood and Nelly's nocturnal rendezvous: "And I heard Joseph asking, whether 'it warn't a crying scandal that [Nelly] should have fellies at her time of life?'" (309). Neither Nelly nor Lockwood denies these suggestions. Nelly "did not stay to retaliate" Joseph's innuendos even though she saucily talks back to him throughout the novel, including earlier in the scene. While Lockwood initially seems unbothered by Joseph's comments, hours later he frets that Joseph judges him as a party in "his fellow-servant's gay indiscretions" (337). To prove his "respectable character," Lockwood throws "a sovereign at [Joseph's] feet" as he flees the Heights (337). "Pressing a remembrance into the hand of Mrs Dean," Lockwood also quickly pays Nelly, whom he describes as Joseph's "fellow-servant" rather than as his own landlord. Eager to escape a potential romantic partner and to disprove Joseph's snide comments, Lockwood, as Philip K. Wion writes, "assert[s] another, more comfortable relationship, that of social superior" by reimbursing Nelly for her information (376). Ironically, the storytelling that brings Nelly and Lockwood together is ultimately what drives them apart, as Lockwood no longer finds Nelly a platonic, and thereby safe, companion. When Nelly's story concludes and the young lovers return, Lockwood "felt irresistibly impelled to escape" (*Wuthering* 337), mirroring his behavior with the girl at the seaside: "retir[ing]" into himself when faced with romantic possibilities (6).

LOCKWOOD'S DIARY?

What exactly *is* Lockwood's narrative? Scholars tend to address this question only in passing by labeling it a "diary" or "journal." I argue, however, that this narrative lacks the common textual and linguistic markings found in other Victorian literary diaries and journals such as Helen's diary in *The Tenant of Wildfell Hall,* Jonathan's and Mina's diaries in *Dracula,* Ezra Jennings's journal in *The Moonstone,* and Marian Halcombe's diary in *The Woman in White.*

Lockwood relays no intention to reread his narrative, shows no evidence of having reread it, and presents the narrative as having been produced without physical exertion or mental reflection—it retains few to no marks of having been written by Lockwood. This strange relationship between Lockwood and his narrative, I argue, evidences Lockwood's attempt to separate himself from his own narrative production, echoing both his attempts to enact closure on the wild story Nelly shares with him and his tendency to shield or extract himself from intimate relationships. In the gothic, Sedgwick writes, the

> self is spatialized in the following way. It is the position of the self to be mas-
> sively blocked off from something to which it ought normally to have access.
> This something can be its own past, the details of its family history; it can
> be the free air. . . . The self and whatever it is that is outside have a proper,
> natural, necessary connection to each other, but one that the self is suddenly
> incapable of making. (12–13)

Lockwood's "incapa[city]" to fully claim and engage with his own narrative production, something that he should "have a proper, natural, necessary connection to," is another aspect of how the gothic pervades the narrative of *Wuthering Heights*.

Though some scholars, including myself, use the neutral term "narrative" to describe Lockwood's account, most scholars explicitly classify it as a journal or diary.[20] Generally, these critics do not provide evidence or justification for such a label beyond Lockwood's use of two dates—1801 and 1802. J. Miller provides two explanations for Lockwood's narrative: Either Ellis Bell is the "editor" of "Lockwood's diary" or Ellis Bell is "the consciousness surrounding Lockwood's consciousness, overhearing what he says to himself, what he thinks, feels, sees, and presenting it again to the reader as though it were entirely the words of Lockwood" (*Fiction* 71). J. Miller's second proposal responds to the impression that Lockwood's narrative is thought, but not written, by him. McCarthy, on the other hand, specifically claims that Lockwood is indeed "writing the book" (48). Matthews concurs, "We may be startled to remember that *Lockwood writes Wuthering Heights*" (41). But diaries within Victorian novels strongly and consistently expose, even revel in, their writtenness—Lockwood's does not. I am not arguing that Lockwood's narrative isn't written. It does include some sparse, tiny inklings of being written,[21] but

---

20. Bersani, Duyfhuizen, and Genette label Lockwood's narrative a journal. Bal, Berlinger, Matthews, J. Miller, Newman, Stewart, and Woodring designate it a diary.

21. For example, at the beginning of chapter 2, Lockwood uses the notation "N. B.," which means "note well" in Latin (*Wuthering* 9). In chapter 3, Heathcliff greets Cathy with an

overall, Lockwood detaches himself from his narrative production by excluding most evidence that it has been created by him.

The first of the diary markings found in most Victorian literary diaries is the use of specific dates to mark each new entry.[22] The first word of *Wuthering Heights* and of Lockwood's narrative is a date (1801), and a second date (1802) is given at the beginning of chapter 18 of volume 2; however, journals include dates much more frequently than Lockwood's narrative does, and the dates stated generally indicate the month, the day of the month, and the year. For example, Helen's diary in *Tenant* starts on and with a specific date: "*June 1st, 1821*" (A. Brontë 130). Two chapters later, the date of August 25th is provided. And then September 1st. And so on. This gives Helen's diary the "staggered composition" common to the diary form (Abbott 24). The excerpt of Ezra Jennings's journal included in *The Moonstone* commences on "1849.—June 15th" (W. Collins 397). The journal contains nine more dates specifying month and day of month since the first date establishes the year; additionally, in the longest entry, written piecemeal as the experiment proceeds, Ezra includes times—five o'clock, seven o'clock, ten o'clock, two o'clock, eleven o'clock—to further demarcate his journal.

The second conventional diary marking is the identification of the narrative as a journal by characters or through titles/headers. Usually, journals are labeled as such in chapter or section titles (such is the case in *Dracula* and *The Woman in White*). Furthermore, in the original British edition of *Dracula*, running headers at the top of most pages name the narrative we are currently reading; therefore, while we are proceeding through Jonathan Harker's journal, the top of every right-hand page says, "Jonathan Harker's Journal." Helen describes her diary as "my diary" (A. Brontë 164). Jennings's "Journal" is labeled as such by Franklin Blake (W. Collins, *Moonstone* 396), and Candy refers to it as a "Diary" and a "Journal" (460, 461), suggesting the two words were used interchangeably. Jennings himself repeatedly calls it a "journal" (410); additionally, the text of the journal is introduced by the following title: "*Extracted from the Journal of* Ezra Jennings" (397). Lockwood's narrative receives no such designation by himself, Nelly, another character, or

---

expletive: "'And you, you worthless—' he broke out as I entered . . . employing an epithet as harmless as duck, or sheep, but generally represented by a dash" (30). Here, Lockwood seemingly calls attention to his use of written punctuation.

22. Prince argues that the diary novel does not require the "superficial journal shape" of "a text divided into a certain number of sections each preceded by a more or less specific date" ("Diary" 477); he specifically categorizes *Wuthering Heights* as a diary novel even though it lacks those dates. And yet, many other Victorian diaries do exhibit this "superficial journal shape."

by Brontë. No one labels Lockwood's narrative a diary in chapter titles, section titles, page headers, or in dialogue.

The third diary marking is a reference, by the diarist, to the physical act of writing. In the diary novel, H. Porter Abbott writes, we often "sit at and read what the diarist describes himself as sitting at, writing, and often, as we are, reading himself" (24). Similarly, Gerald Prince identifies "the theme of writing a diary"—addressing why the narrator writes a diary, the meaning she finds in the action, information about the writing location and diary publication—as the distinctive characteristic of the diary novel ("Diary" 479). In *The Moonstone*, Jennings repeatedly brings up the fact that he is writing; for example, "I turned to my Journal for relief, and wrote in it what is written here" (W. Collins 429). In *The Woman in White*, Marian Halcombe frequently refers to the embodied act of writing the diary, at one point exclaiming, "My very fingers burn as I write it!" (W. Collins 177). Lockwood never mentions the act of writing. He never, as other diarists do, discloses the painful, necessary, exhausting, or calming obligation or desire to write. He does not, as others do, characterize his narrative as a product of his body—his fingers never burn like Marian's, and relief does not flood him as it does Ezra. Nelly never indicates that she has observed Lockwood write despite her frequent presence at his bedside.

The fourth diary marking consists of the diarist imagining an audience, either a specific reader or the diarist themselves at a future time. Abbott writes, "fictive diarists commonly address their remarks to someone—friend, lover, God, the diary itself" (10). Some diarists, such as Helen in *Tenant* and Marian in *The Woman in White*, write about rereading their own diaries. Some diarists read or entrust their diaries to other characters, such as when Helen offers her diary to Gilbert in *Tenant* and when Jonathan gifts his diary to Mina in *Dracula*. Helen often directly addresses other people in her diary, something Lockwood never does in his narrative. Lockwood only once refers to a "you" in the nondialogue parts of his narrative.[23] Helen directs her words to her husband Arthur: "Yes, poor Arthur, I will still hope and pray for you . . . though I write as if you were some abandoned wretch" (A. Brontë 262). Jonathan invokes his fiancée in an entry before undertaking a potentially fatal escape attempt: "Goodbye, all! Mina!" (Stoker 61). Unlike Helen in *Tenant* and the cast of writers in *Dracula*, Lockwood makes no claims about his own truthfulness and shows no investment in convincing a possible reader of his journal's accuracy. In short, Lockwood can't imagine a possible reader of his journal (even himself) and makes no attempt to share his journal with others.

---

23. Even in this one instance, the "you" doesn't materialize a narratee to whom Lockwood is writing or speaking: "Such an individual . . . is to be seen in any circuit of five or six miles among these hills, if you go at the right time" (*Wuthering* 5).

In typical Lockwood fashion, he continues to isolate himself and fear reaching
out, even hypothetically, to others.

Interestingly, when Lockwood first visits Wuthering Heights and sleeps
in the haunted room, he discovers Catherine's "regular diary" written in the
blank spaces of her books (*Wuthering* 20); he immediately labels it a diary and
appraises Catherine's handwriting, neither of which he does with his own supposed writing.[24] In the tradition of other diary-writers, Catherine begins with
the date—"An awful Sunday!" She also reflects on the physical act of writing
and refers to her writing materials: "I reached this book, and a pot of ink from
a shelf, and pushed the house-door ajar to give me light, and I have got the
time on with writing for twenty minutes" (22). Catherine, therefore, engages
with "the theme of writing a diary" (Prince, "Diary" 479). Lockwood identifies
Catherine's diary as a diary but offers no classification for his own narrative,
deepening the ambiguous status of his text.

Nelly too separates herself from her story by accepting its ephemeral
nature. Nelly is literate; she writes letters; she brags about reading books to
Lockwood. And yet, she doesn't write down the story in a more permanent
medium, such as a diary; instead, she relates it orally to an itinerant and short-
term visitor. Lockwood only signed a twelve-month lease for the Grange, but
Nelly knows that the London gentleman won't stay long once he recuperates
from his illness. When she pushes the possibility of Lockwood staying and
marrying Cathy, he replies, "I'm of the busy world, and to its arms I must
return" (*Wuthering* 256). When he unexpectedly reappears in the area, he
informs Nelly—before she resumes her story—that he's only staying overnight:
"I depart again to-morrow" (309). Nelly gives no indication that she has told
the story to anyone else previously. Her indecision at points in how exactly to
tell it—how much time to skip on one occasion—suggests the novelty of the
project. In telling the story—for the first time—to Lockwood, she shows no
concern over whether he is writing it down (something neither one of them
mentions), and, if he is, whether he is doing so accurately. Conversely, when
Frankenstein speaks his story to Walton, Frankenstein demands to review
Walton's dictation and then revises it himself: "Frankenstein discovered that
I made notes concerning his history: he asked to see them, and then himself corrected and augmented them in many places" (Shelley 146). Neither
Nelly nor Lockwood exhibits the investment that Franklin Blake shows in

---

24. Capuano argues that, in the nineteenth-century novel, hands and handwriting become
newly visible and significant; the shift from eighteenth-century literature's emphasis on faces
occurs because "an unlikely convergence of scientific, industrial, and religious discourse
coalesced around 1830 to make the human hand the most generative but also the most heavily
contested site in the British cultural imaginary" (5).

the durability and utility of a specifically written document even though legal questions of inheritance, property, crime, and guilt are just as much at play in *Wuthering Heights* as they are in *The Moonstone*: "The whole story ought, in the interests of truth, to be placed on record in writing—and the sooner the better" (W. Collins 21). As DeLamotte says of the boundary-obsessed gothic, some boundaries are terrifyingly crossed and "other boundaries appear unexpectedly" (22). In their fear of "the boundaries of the self" (23) being breached and compromised, as indeed they are in and through the collaborative narrative, Nelly and Lockwood erect this final barrier, a barrier between each of them and their narrative productions. Perhaps the story, they imagine, now out of them, can cease to haunt them.

In conclusion, the gothic and the frame structure often go hand in hand considering titles such as Walpole's *The Castle of Otranto,* Mary Shelley's *Frankenstein,* James's *The Turn of the Screw,* Sheridan Le Fanu's "Green Tea" and "Carmilla," Elizabeth Gaskell's "Old Nurse's Tale" and "The Grey Woman," and many others. The frame, often more conventional in tone and setting, introduces and gently leads us into the strange, terrifying gothic world that follows, while tantalizingly asking us to make connections between the frame and framed—between, say, the maritime adventures of the explorer Walton and the outré experiments of Frankenstein. These structures often leave us unsettled, trapped even, when they fail to return to the frame or do so only briefly. This sensation highlights how the frame narrative creates and then crosses boundaries through its very structure—boundaries of time, place, perspective, and even fictionality when the frame introduces the subsequent narrative as an authentic case or real manuscript. *Wuthering Heights* is unique among all the above examples for how frequently and subtly it crosses the boundary between the two narrators and narratives—a *permeable* frame. The epilogue that follows continues to explore the multinarrator gothic novel by considering how Bram Stoker's *Dracula* and Richard Marsh's *The Beetle* also use multiple narrators to extend the gothic from the plot into the structure.

〜

Returning and Nonreturning Multinarration in *Dracula* and *The Beetle*

C RITICS OFTEN COMPARE Bram Stoker's *Dracula* and Richard Marsh's *The Beetle*. Both gothic novels were published to success in 1897.[1] They both feature a reverse colonization plot[2] in which the foreign monster—who is an amalgamation of various "othered" qualities[3]—invades the metropole and threatens the lives, ideals, and identities of the British characters. Scholars have analyzed how both novels engage with fin-de-siècle anxieties, particularly related to gender, sexuality, and imperialism.[4] Of relevance

---

1. Vuohelainen's careful work on *The Beetle* in "Richard Marsh's *The Beetle* (1897): A Late-Victorian Popular Novel" reveals that the novel was originally serialized in *Answers* starting in March 1897 as *The Peril of Paul Lessingham: The Story of a Haunted Man* and then published in book form (in either September of October of the same year) under the new title of *The Beetle: A Mystery*. *Dracula* came out in June 1897 while *The Beetle*'s serialization was nearing completion.

2. Arata coins this term for narratives, including *Dracula*, in which "problematic or disruptive figures come from the periphery of the empire to threaten a troubled metropole" (107).

3. Halberstam asserts, "Dracula is otherness itself" ("Technologies" 249), and Garnett similarly reads the Beetle as "a composite symbol, primarily of a dominant European constitution of the Oriental" (35).

4. Hurley argues that the Beetle manifests the Victorian fear of female sexuality by "unman[ning]" the male characters (Hurley 143). To Halberstam, the Beetle's indeterminate gender and Marjorie's donning of male clothing reveal the novel's "fear of female masculinity" ("Gothic" 110). Harris and Vernooy highlight the queerness of *The Beetle*, and Craft exposes the "postponed and never directly enacted" homosexual desire in *Dracula* (110). Garnett situates both *Dracula* and *The Beetle* in their imperial contexts and examines how each novel expresses

to this epilogue, both novels utilize a multinarrator structure in which the monster—Dracula and the Beetle—doesn't narrate. In response, critics such as Rhys Garnett, J. Halberstam (in "Gothic"), and Anna Maria Jones have explicitly lumped together the two novels' structures; however, a close narratological analysis reveals many differences between these two similar-at-first-glance structures. I propose two new terms—*returning* and *nonreturning*—to anatomize the multinarrator structures of *Dracula* and *The Beetle*. I conclude *Narrative Bonds* with an examination of these two novels written at the end of the Victorian period to reaffirm how looking closely at a novel's multinarrator structure—including the number of narrators, the pace of narrator transitions, and the length of individual narratives—can yield a new understanding of the connection between the novel's structure and the novel's meaning as well as a new understanding of the bonds between the narrators. *Dracula*'s returning structure provides the collaborative glue for the triumphant vampire-hunting group, while *The Beetle*'s nonreturning structure alienates its narrators from one another, highlighting the inefficacy of its monster-fighting team. Both the story and structure of *Dracula* focus on an effectual monster-slaying group, while the story and structure of *The Beetle* center on characters' horrifying one-on-one encounters with the monster.

The Beetle contains four sections, each narrated by a different character; the final narrator, Augustus Champnell, compiles and edits the narratives years after the Beetle's disastrous London sojourn. In the novel, the titular character, an Egyptian human-insect shapeshifter, travels to London to revenge herself upon her escaped prisoner, Paul Lessingham, who is now a liberal M. P. and affianced to Marjorie Lindon. The Beetle mesmerizes an unemployed London man, Robert Holt, to aim her in her schemes. At the end of the novel, the Beetle leaves Holt to die and abducts Marjorie; meanwhile, a team of men—Paul; the scientist-inventor Sydney Atherton, childhood friend of Marjorie; and the detective Augustus Champnell—track the Beetle and eventually discover the traumatized Marjorie in a crashed train carriage. Champnell "rapidly sketche[s]" his narrative "several years" after the strange events (Marsh 319); he also obtains the other three narratives that precede his: Holt's, Sydney's, and Marjorie's. Because Holt dies before putting his experience to paper, Champnell explains that his narrative is "compiled from the statements" he made to other characters (321). Critics' relatively meager attention to *The Beetle*'s structure largely focuses on the secondhand nature

---

"imperial and sexual fear and guilt" (31). Bulfin categorizes *The Beetle* within "the subgenre of Gothic Egyptian fiction" in which an Egyptian figure—usually a mummy—enacts revenge in England (128); this plot "obliquely raises questions of British imperial guilt and Egyptian retaliation" (132).

of Holt's narrative.[5] Marjorie, institutionalized after her traumatic abduction, repeatedly writes (seemingly unconsciously) of the incident; according to Champnell, the one existent copy of that manuscript "is herein placed before the reader" (322). Champnell offers no explanation for the genesis of Sydney's narrative; like Champnell's, it was likely written years after the events occurred because it doesn't take a dated form like a diary or letter. In the final chapter, Champnell also confesses to changing names (specifically Paul's, although that change implies alterations for those in Paul's circle) throughout all four narratives, implying his editorial control of the final product.

In *Dracula,* the creation of the impressive collaborative narrative is central not only to the novel's plot but also to the group's successful vanquishing of the vampire. Mina Harker (née Murray) initiates the creation of the master narrative by typing up her convalescing husband Jonathan Harker's journal and her own for vampire-expert Van Helsing's perusal; more than midway through the novel in chapter 17 (out of twenty-seven total), she asks Dr. Seward if she can type his phonographic diary.[6] This transcription inspires her and her husband Jonathan to "chronological[ly] order" and "collat[e]" the materials gathered up until that point (Stoker 239, 240)—the above journals, relevant letters, telegrams, memos, and newspaper articles—into "a whole connected narrative" (240). This process fulfills the promise of the unsigned opening note to the novel: "How these papers have been placed in sequence will be made manifest in the reading of them" (6). The creation of this "connected narrative," which Mina continues to supplement, takes time, energy, and substantial narrative space—it is crucial to the plot of the novel. It is arguably the turning point of the novel since the initial ordering of the texts makes the group's "guiding purpose" clear to them: They must pursue and destroy Dracula (336).

Critical consensus on *Dracula*'s structure—as argued by David Seed, Thomas Richards, Friedrich Kittler, and Leah Richards—is that the master narrative serves as a potent offensive *and* defensive weapon against the Count. Individually, the narrators' knowledge is limited and their senses untrusted; together, their knowledge is expanded and their senses verified. Every main character reads the newly collated manuscript before a meeting at which they will "arrange [their] plan of battle with this terrible and mysterious enemy" (Stoker 251), positioning the manuscript as battle prep. Mina's later rereading of the whole manuscript inspires her stunningly accurate "discovery" about how to track Dracula, which again suggests that the document is a piece of war

---

5. The uniquely second-hand nature of Holt's narrative makes it "unreliable" to Wolfreys (Introduction 31) and "extremely unstable" to Allin (120).

6. Mina's secretarial role and ease with technological apparatuses such as the typewriter and phonograph have received attention from Case, Fleissner, Kittler, and Wicke.

technology and intel (373). Dracula accurately views the group's writing as a threat to his victory; therefore, when he can, he prevents writing by removing writing materials (which he does to Jonathan in the castle), destroying writing (razing Seward's phonograph records and one copy of the manuscript in the asylum), and thwarting the desire to write (both Mina and Lucy, when under his thrall, write less or struggle to write). Because of the master-narrative's weapon-like function, the characters view writing as a duty—to each other and to humanity—that they must fulfill despite exhaustion or annoyance.

The differences, then, between the two similar-at-first-glance structures are many. *The Beetle* has four narrators; *Dracula* has at least fourteen, not counting the uncredited writers of the four included newspaper articles. *Dracula* switches narrators ninety-two times, while *The Beetle* switches narrators three times. Each narrator in *The Beetle* narrates only once, a one-and-done structure I'm calling nonreturning. The nonreturning structure is rare amongst Victorian multinarrator novels. Six of *Dracula's* narrators return to narrate again—a structure I'm calling returning. *Dracula* switches to Seward twenty-nine times, to Mina twenty-two times, to Jonathan Harker twelve times (he narrates thirteen times since the novel opens with him), to Van Helsing eight times, to Lucy seven times, and to Arthur twice. Since, in *Dracula,* the narrator may switch after as little as a sentence, paragraph, or page, *Dracula* has an overall pace of fast cutting; at one point in the novel, there are three narrators on one page. The lengthy—though of unequal lengths—narratives in *The Beetle* give the novel a slow cutting pace. In both novels, all switches are tagged (labeled) by titles. In *The Beetle,* narrator switches only occur at the beginning of new books, and the book titles indicate the narrator. In *Dracula,* the narrator often switches within chapters, but section headers name the narrator and the medium (diary, letter, telegram, and so on). In addition, the original British version of *Dracula* includes running page headers; the top right-hand side of every page identifies the narrative on that page: "Jonathan's Harker's Journal" or "Letter, Lucy to Mina." These headers help potentially whiplashed readers keep track of who is narrating. No other Victorian multinarrator novel that I am familiar with contains so many narrators, so many switches in narrator, or so many returns of individual narrators as *Dracula* includes. *Dracula* highlights this excess by giving almost every text—every telegram and letter—its own distinguishing header, thereby raising Quincey Morris and Arthur Godalming to the status of narrators even though the former only narrates one short letter early in the novel and the latter authors two brief telegrams and one succinct letter. *The Beetle,* on the other hand, downplays the number of voices and texts integrated into the novel. For example, Champnell's narrative includes a letter written by the Beetle, a policeman's "report" (Marsh 290), several telegrams, and a note—all authored by characters other than Champnell—but they are all appropriated by Champnell's narrative and not given individual, separating headers listing the author, date, and medium. Furthermore, while the characters join forces to assemble and update the master-narrative in *Dracula,* Champnell in *The Beetle* seems to be solely responsible for obtaining and editing the documents. These differences in structure, I argue, are integral to how *Dracula* centers on an effective monster-slaying group while *The Beetle* centers on solitary horror and the inability of a group to truly come together to fight the monster.

Dracula makes an implicit connection between the way a narrative is presented and the situation a narrator is in—a connection between plot and structure; consequently, Jonathan's castle diary is presented as an uninterrupted whole to mirror his solitary imprisonment in Castle Dracula. After the opening note to readers, the novel begins with the longest unbroken narrative in the novel: the fifty-four pages of Jonathan's journal detailing his harrowing trip to, and increasingly horrifying stay at, Castle Dracula. The castle diary provides approximately half of Harker's total words and about 14 percent of the novel. This part of the novel is the major and most drastic exception to Mina's plan to "have every item put in chronological order" (Stoker 239).[7] Jonathan's journal spans from May 3 to June 30. After his journal ends on June 30 with his intention to escape the castle, the novel presents several narratives dated before then: three letters between Mina and Lucy dated May 9, "Wednesday" (63), and May 24; the first entry from Seward's phonographic diary recorded on May 25; a letter from Morris to Arthur Godalming dated May 25; and a telegram from Arthur to Morris dated May 26. These six documents do *not* interrupt the presentation of Jonathan's castle diary even though they occur within its timespan; in the rest of the novel, individual entries from journals are interwoven with other materials according to dates. This unbroken presentation of Jonathan's diary echoes Jonathan's stated "dread loneliness" and utter solitude (43). He confides to his diary, "I fear I am myself the only living soul within the place (32). Because Jonathan has no helper, no group, no free communication with other humans (Dracula burns his secret shorthand letter to Mina and dictates the letters sent to Jonathan's friends), his journal must be

---

7. In most other examples of the nonchronological ordering of documents, materials are only slightly out of order. Mina's journal from August 18–19 is followed by Sister Agatha's letter dated August 12 (Mina mentions receiving the letter in her August 19 entry). Seward's diary entry from September 18 is followed by Lucy's dying memorandum written the evening of September 17 (Seward does not find the document until the next day). Mina's journal entry dated July 24 is followed by a section of Seward's diary spanning June 5 to July 20 (the entries are all focused on Renfield, perhaps explaining why they are presented as a group); Mina's journal entry from July 26 follows Seward's entries.

structurally presented alone. Five of the six narratives that directly follow the diary are letters or telegrams, further stressing the exchange and communication Jonathan is denied while imprisoned at the castle.

After Jonathan's lengthy, lonely, uninterrupted castle diary, the novel's structure—fast cutting between narrators and the returning structure of narratorial returns—helps create, rather than just reflect, the tightly bonded group that Christopher Craft christens the "Crew of Light" that is necessary to defeat Dracula (109).[8] I agree with Peter K. Garrett's assessment that "the process of narrative integration thus both represents and enacts the integration of the group, incorporating their fragmentary accounts in a unified sequence" (*Gothic* 129); however, Garrett does not observe the change from Jonathan's solitary account to the fast cutting that follows. Opposed to the uninterrupted fifty-four pages of Jonathan's journal, narratives now last a couple pages at most or a sentence or paragraph at the least, creating a fast-paced rhythm of narratorial switches. Seward reports that Mina and Jonathan "are knitting together in chronological order every scrap of evidence they have" (Stoker 240), but this project also "knit[s] together" the characters by physically and visibly weaving together their private narratives.[9] As both Halberstam and Garrett note, sharing and reading each other's "secrets" creates intimacy in *Dracula* (Stoker 251).[10] After Van Helsing reads Mina's diary, he insists he is now her "friend," even though Mina suspiciously counters "you do not know me" since they have just met (Stoker 196). But later, Mina seems to agree with Van Helsing's process of friend-making since she tells Seward "you will know me better" after he reads her proffered journal (236). After he reads it, he concurs with her prediction, telling her "I know you now," before reciprocally allowing her access to his journal. Her experience of listening to his phonographic journal convinces her that she now understands his "heart" and "soul" (237). When everyone has read the collated manuscript, they assemble as a "board or committee" (251), Van Helsing addresses them all as "[his] friends" (252), and they "all took [each others'] hands" around the table (253). The group hand-holding mimics the connected narratives. Similarly, the men— Godalming, Morris, Seward, and Van Helsing—bond through having their blood blend in Lucy's beloved and continually drained body (though Godalm-

8. Given that Seward, Harker, and Van Helsing are lawyers and/or doctors, Daly highlights that "this new social group [is] composed largely of professional men" (189).

9. Pope zeroes in on Mina's use of the word "knitting" that "cast[s] . . . her textual work as textile work" and evinces her effort to "revis[e] the terms of feminine activity and wifely duty to accommodate her wider aspirations" (212).

10. Halberstam finds "a marked sexual energy to the reading and writing of all the contributions to the narrative" ("Technologies" 250). Garrett likens "the collective production of the narrative" to "group sex" (*Gothic* 132).

ing is ignorant of the other men's donations). In Jonathan's concluding note to the novel, he shares that his and Mina's son's "bundle of names links all our little band of men together" (402). Mina's two creations—the baby and the master narrative—resemble each other in the way they both symbolize and enact group bonding through a "bundle of names": the son's extensive name and the master narrative's crowded bylines.

While the writing and collating of the master narrative bond the group, the contributions to that master narrative are unequal. For all the critical focus on Mina as "the-woman-who-writes" (G. Wall 16), Seward and Harker narrate substantially more than she does. Seward narrates a surprising 39 percent of the novel, Harker 27 percent, Mina 21 percent, Van Helsing 3 percent, and Lucy 3 percent; the remaining 7 percent is made up from contributions from Godalming, Quincey, onetime writers of letters and telegrams, and the authors of the newspaper articles.[11] Rebecca A. Pope writes, "Even the form and structure of [Mina's] compilation is subtly anti-patriarchal because it is not hierarchical" (213); however, Seward, Harker, and Mina—all middle-class British professionals—narrate nearly 90 percent of the novel, while the American Quincey, the Dutch Van Helsing, the leisured Lucy (who doesn't work like Mina), and the aristocratic Lord Godalming narrate very little. Rather than contributing writing to the group, Godalming donates money, Morris sacrifices his robust body, and Van Helsing doles out his folkloric and medical wisdom. L. Richards's point about *Dracula* also applies to *The Beetle*: "English professionals" write the most (444). In *The Beetle,* Holt narrates 18 percent of the novel, Sydney 33 percent, Marjorie 17 percent, and Champnell 32 percent.[12] Victoria Margree notes that *The Beetle* "undermin[es]" the narratives by the unemployed man—Holt—and the New Woman—Marjorie—by "decentr[ing]" them: Neither Marjorie nor Holt is directly or consciously the author of their narratives (77). Marjorie's and Holt's narratives are further undermined, I would add, by their relative brevity; Sydney and Champnell, middle- to upper-class professional men, each narrate for nearly twice as long as Marjorie or Holt does.

Dracula's Seward and *The Beetle*'s Sydney—two men who are quite alike— narrate the most in their respective novels. Both men also form the center of their novels' various interpersonal circles. Seward is a former student of Van

---

11. In the presentation of these percentages, I have rounded to the nearest whole number; these numbers, therefore, are approximate and serve to give a general sense of how much each narrator narrates. While I indicate that Van Helsing and Lucy both narrate for 3 percent of the novel, Van Helsing narrates several hundred words more than Lucy does.

12. Like with my *Dracula* calculations, I have rounded these percentages to the nearest whole number.

Helsing; he is "old pal[s]" with Morris and Arthur (Stoker 69); he proposes
to Lucy, whom he was introduced to by Arthur; Renfield is a patient in his
asylum; and the asylum he operates sits next door to Dracula's newly pur-
chased estate. Sydney has been close with Marjorie since childhood, is familiar
enough with Paul Lessingham to know his servant by name, and is "friends
of a good many years standing" with the detective Champnell (Marsh 250);
even the Beetle claims Sydney as a "friend" and "kin" (105, 143). No wonder
Sydney's eventual wife Dora quips of his friend count, "I never knew a man
who had so many!" (122). In *Dracula*, when Lucy first meets Seward, she finds
him impressively accomplished for a young man; she gleefully wonders "what
a wonderful power he must have over his patients" (Stoker 63). He yearns to
"advance [his] own branch of science" and ponders "invent[ing] a new classification for" his insect-and-animal-eating patient Renfield (80). In *The Beetle*,
Sydney is also recognized for his scientific knowledge, inventions, and "hypnotic power" over others (Marsh 194). This "power" over others enables the
two men to resist victimization by their novels' monsters, which is one reason
they narrate more than other, more attacked and more affected, narrators.
Sydney and Seward's similar characteristics, as well as their similar positions
in the plot and the narrative, highlight the extent to which these "power[ful]"
and professional male characters remain central, even in novels with multiple narrators that include New Woman narrators like Mina and Marjorie.
As I noted in the introduction to *Narrative Bonds*, the Victorian multinarrator
novel may be more inclusive but does not usually unseat the primacy of the
middle-class, English, male narrator.

   Since the "power of combination" is so important to the crew of light,
they erroneously imagine that power is unique to them and lacking in vampires (Stoker 254). After enumerating Dracula's staggering capabilities and
strengths, Van Helsing encourages his merely human team by listing their own
compensatory qualities: "We, too, are not without strength. We have on our
side power of combination—a power denied to the vampire kind." But Van
Helsing is incorrect: Vampires aren't denied the "power of combination." The
nameless female vampires who also inhabit Castle Dracula are an inseparable,
cackling threesome who never break ranks; together they gleefully seduce Jonathan, bit-by-bit appear in the moonbeams coming through the window, and
taunt the almost-vampire Mina to join their sisterhood. Dracula also proves
quite able to hire people to do his bidding. The "gipsy party" (this term for the
Romani people is now considered derogatory) safeguards Dracula's earth-box
from the attacking crew of light, killing Morris in the fight (399). In Victorian
parlance, "combination" was a word applied to working-class unionization
and demonstrations; as Nicholas Daly points out, Van Helsing's invocation of
"combination" implies that the middle- and upper-class crew of light is "not

above learning a lesson from the working class" (191). Van Helsing's usage of "combination" takes on an additional meaning in relation to the "whole connected narrative" that he has just read when he deploys that term (Stoker 240). Although Dracula can read and write—Jonathan sees him doing both—he is denied a proper place in the group's collaborative narrative. There is one letter from Dracula within the text, appearing early in Jonathan's castle diary—it is a short epistle welcoming Jonathan to the Carpathians and giving instructions for the final leg of his journey; however, this narrative is denied a separate section and header as other letters in the novel are given. Dracula's letter may be included in the novel, embedded within Jonathan's diary, but Dracula is refused the position of narrator. He is refused the "power of" narrative "combination."

Dracula's effective, intimate group (partially created by the returning narrative structure that weaves their stories together) successfully destroys Dracula, while *The Beetle*'s feeble, short-lived group flails and flunks its similar task, a failure reflected in its nonreturning structure.[13] The group fares very well at the end of *Dracula*: The communally made decisions of the group over five weeks lead them to the climactic, sun-dropping snowstorm race through the mountains at which every group member is present. The killing of Dracula is a collectively performed and witnessed event. Everyone, including Mina, aims their guns at Dracula's drivers; the men except for Van Helsing fight the drivers; and Dracula is physically decapitated by Jonathan, staked by Morris, and turns to dust "before our very eyes" (Stoker 400). Mina's phrasing—"our very eyes"—highlights the group's shared vision. After Dracula's definitive destruction, the Eucharist burn that marked Mina as a vamp-to-be vanishes from her forehead. Toward the end of *The Beetle*, a makeshift monster-fighting group does emerge, comprising Paul, the detective Champnell, and the scientist-inventor Sydney. The group seeks to track Marjorie, who has been kidnapped by the Beetle. This group, however, is tentative, weak, full of bickering, and only exists for a few hours (as opposed to weeks in *Dracula*). The group does eventually locate Marjorie in a smashed train car, but the "accident[al]" event of a train crash is what seemingly destroys the Beetle and frees Marjorie, not the actions of the bungling group (Marsh 317). Unlike the end of *Dracula*, at the end of *The Beetle*, no one sees what happens to the Beetle, and Champnell admits they will likely never know what happened. Champnell can only relay that some strange, possibly nonhuman stains on the carriage floor may beto-

---

13. Garnett initially equates how characters in *Dracula* and *The Beetle* "bond[ ] themselves into a cohesive, aggressive class unit" but quickly admits the quality of the bonding is different in the two novels: "extensively and uniformly in *Dracula*, belatedly and less coherently in *The Beetle*" (44).

ken the Beetle's annihilation.[14] Unlike Mina's instant purification at the end of
Dracula, Marjorie can't even speak when found and then spends "three years
under medical supervision as a lunatic" (Marsh 319). There is no sense in *The
Beetle* that the group is forever bonded by their experience. Unlike the ending of *Dracula, The Beetle* doesn't close with the group rhapsodizing over old
times while they play with the child named after all of them.

While *Dracula* quickly becomes a novel about the human group versus
Dracula, which is reflected in its returning structure, *The Beetle* unfolds as
a series of one-on-one, horrifying face-to-faces with the Beetle, which is
reflected in its nonreturning structure in which narrators narrate only once.
The Beetle is separated into four books, each narrated by a different character: Holt, Sydney, Marjorie, and Champnell. All the characters emphasize
how alone they are when they encounter the Beetle. Holt meets the Beetle
when he enters a seemingly "empty" house (48); Sydney, while alone in his
laboratory and, later, practically alone, as his friend Percy lies unconscious
outside in the yard; Marjorie, first while alone in her bed and later "alone"
in a seemingly empty house (231); and Paul (as shared in Champnell's narrative), when he wanders "unaccompanied" into an "empty" café in Cairo (238,
239). Just as these characters from *The Beetle* experience this solitary horror,
their narratives stand, like silos, aloof from one another. Because of the slow
pace of narratorial switches, the reader lingers with each narrative, experiencing the horror and dread alongside the isolated narrator. The structure presents four sequestered narrators lost in their own encounters, not an emerging,
united group. By comparison, Dracula sometimes attacks victims while they
are alone—such as Renfield in his cell and Lucy in the graveyard—but also
comes for Lucy while her mom is in the room and feeds from Mina while her
husband is present; furthermore, narratively, *Dracula* focuses less on detailing vampire attacks from the victims' perspectives and more on showing the
group's unified response to such attacks: the men's blood donations to drained
Lucy, the men's sexualized staking of vampire Lucy, and the crowd crashing of
Mina and Dracula's bizarre feeding scene.

The generic diversity of *The Beetle*'s four narratives also enforces this
silo-like separation between them. Holt's gruesomely detailed section reads
most like horror. Sydney's narrative, often set in his laboratory and featuring
his experiments, evokes science fiction. In that vein, Jones finds that Sydney
resembles "other mad scientists" (78). Marjorie's account launches with the
declaration that she is the "happiest woman in the world" because of Paul's

---

14. Allin, Vuohelainen (in "You Know Not"), and Wolfreys (in "Hieroglyphic") emphasize
the uncertainty and ambiguity at the end of Champnell's narrative.

love (Marsh 187), immediately positioning her narrative as a romance. Even Champnell reads it this way, calling it "the story of her love" (322). Champnell is a "confidential agent" and his narrative, which concludes the novel, is "extracted from [his] case-book" (235). Paul becomes Champnell's client and asks for his help in "unravel[ing] the tangled thread" of the mystery of the Beetle (247); this section's discovery of clues, interviewing of witnesses, and tracking of the villain resemble detective fiction.[15] In opposition to the separation of narratives and isolation of characters in *The Beetle,* the narratives and characters of *Dracula* are intercut, woven together, and thereby bonded.

Another difference between the novels' structures is while the writing and compiling of the narratives in *Dracula* are done "exactly contemporary" with events (Stoker 6), in *The Beetle,* the writing and compiling are done "several years" later (Marsh 319). In *Dracula,* Van Helsing tells his former student Seward "that knowledge is stronger than memory, and we should not trust the weaker" (Stoker 130), so the characters frequently comment that they have brought their records "up to the moment" (285). For the manuscript to continue being an effective weapon and defense against Dracula, they know it must be constantly sharpened, so to speak, with new entries. In *The Beetle,* however, the characters are not keeping contemporaneous records; most of the narratives are written after the fact and compiled years later by Champnell in an attempt to master their group's enduring trauma and confusion resulting from the Beetle's assaults. At the point of compilation, the Beetle no longer exists as an active threat, as the Beetle vanishes after the railway crash and strange stains on the carriage floor seemingly indicate her destruction. Champnell claims that Marjorie's healing was "entirely satisfactory" and Paul "has ceased to be a haunted man" (Marsh 319, 320); yet, both Paul and Marjorie leave the room whenever beetles are mentioned, Paul suffers from flashbacks, and Marjorie never regains her conscious memory of her kidnapping by the Beetle. Champnell and Sydney "have talked it [the Beetle] over many and many a time, and at the end [they] have got no 'forrarder'" (322). This repetitive yet ultimately ineffective confab—"many and many a time"—resembles Marjorie's repetitive writing—"She told, and re-told, and re-told again the story of her love." Just as the men's conversation doesn't go "forrarder," Marjorie also cannot get any "forrarder," as her "MSS. invariably began and ended at the same point" (322): realizing she is "alone" with the Beetle in the house (231). Even years later, Marjorie, Sydney, Champnell, and Paul are all stuck, unable to go forward; even worse, Paul is pulled back "to that awful nightmare

---

15. Wolfreys identifies the novel's "mixing of genres . . . from parody of New Woman fiction to pastiche of detective genre" as one aspect of its "deformed and disfigured" shape ("Hieroglyphic" 182, 181).

of the past" through his flashbacks (320). The purpose, then, for the collaborative narrative differs in the two novels: It is forward-looking in *Dracula* (a
tool for the future destruction of the vampire) and backward-looking in *The
Beetle* (an attempt to make sense of their traumatic experiences of the past).

As I argued in the previous chapter on *Wuthering Heights,* narratives
themselves can become gothic, and narrative collaboration in *Dracula* and
The Beetle subtly resembles the gothic monster's tactics. Critics of both novels
have already pointed out how some of the crew of light's actions mirror Dracula's and how Sydney resembles the Beetle.[16] There are also similarities, furthermore, between the narrative collaborations and the monsters. Something
monstrous underlies and potentially undermines the collaboration in these
gothic novels. Mina's modern act of typewriting, so crucial to the group's success, also "partakes of the vampiric" (Wicke 476).[17] Jennifer Wicke calls attention to how Mina's "typewriter has a function called 'Manifold' that allows it
to make multiple copies in threes. This function is positively vampiric, even to
the name it has been given, reverberating with the multiplicity of men Dracula
is, the manifold guises of the vampire, and the copying procedure which itself
produces vampires" (476). Building on Wicke's argument, I add that Jonathan
hints at his awareness of this connection when he disparages Mina's typewritten masterpiece years later in his final note: "We were struck with the fact,
that in all the mass of material of which the record is composed, there is
hardly one authentic document: nothing but a mass of type-writing" (Stoker
402). The documents are an inauthentic pile—"nothing but a mass"—that can
no longer function as "proofs of so wild a story." Mina's typewritten version
of Seward's phonographic journal corresponds to a vampire in ways other
than the use of manifold paper that Wicke mentions. Vamped Lucy is no longer Lucy but a "foul Thing which had taken Lucy's shape without her soul"
(Stoker 228).[18] Similarly, when Mina types up Seward's phonographic records,
she indicates that her typed version eradicates Seward's "soul crying out" that

---

16. Craft compares the vampire's toothy biting and the draining of Lucy with the men's
constant needling of Lucy's body to give her blood transfusions. Given that Sydney specializes
in destructive weapons, Jones reads the Beetle as Sydney's "double" (75). Allin, as well as Harris
and Vernooy, connect the Beetle and Sydney.

17. Stewart also associates Mina's typewriting and vampirism ("'Count Me In'"). Garrett
likewise connects the "narrative collaboration" with "the obscene intimacies of vampirism"
(*Gothic* 130). Kittler, conversely, concludes that "women have two options: typewriter or vampirism" after comparing Mina's and Lucy's differing fates (161).

18. Alternatively, L. Richards interprets Jonathan's comment as expressing "anxieties about
the age, specifically the technological spread of information, none of which is authentic when it
reaches its audience" (442). Armstrong reads this moment as a movement away from vampiric
repetition (Mina's typed iterations of documents) to the "celebration of reproduction" represented by her child (*How* 132).

she heard in the records: "I have copied out the words on my typewriter, and none other need now hear your heart beat, as I did" (237). The copy may have the same shape—words—as the original, but it does not have the original's "soul" or "heart beat," two things vampire Lucy also lacks.

In *The Beetle*, not only does Marjorie produce her narrative in a sort of trance that resembles the mesmerized state the Beetle puts characters in, but Champnell also improperly publicizes Marjorie's narrative, thereby treating her as the Beetle did. Champnell hypothesizes that the Beetle "hypnotised" Marjorie into a "trance" and led her through London (Marsh 286, 285). Margree points out, "Marjorie's narration is revealed to have been produced under the conditions of something that uncannily resembles the very condition of being in a mesmerised trance" (76).[19] Additionally, Marjorie "*confided* to pen and paper" her story, to use Champnell's words (Marsh 322; emphasis added). She shared this secret with the paper. She wrote it privately, while "under medical supervision as a lunatic" (319). And yet, Champnell now gives her manuscript "publicity" (319). Champnell does not mention obtaining Marjorie's permission to include her manuscript nor does it seem likely she would give it as "she would never speak of what she had written" (321); furthermore, once her mental treatment concludes, the incident "passed from her memory as wholly as if it had never been," making her unable to grant any true consent to the manuscript's publicity at a later point (320). Under the Beetle's sway, Marjorie was "paraded through London in the tattered masculine habiliments of a vagabond" (319). Sydney is particularly horrified that Marjorie was taken through "the streets of London" in such disreputable clothing (286). But now Champnell has publicly paraded her narrative through London readership under a name that is not her own. Just as those "tattered masculine habiliments" cover her true identity, the changed names in the narratives prevent her from being "recognised" (319). In short, Marjorie did not "contribut[e]" her narrative as Champnell claims (321); rather, Champnell takes it, just as the Beetle presumably forces her to don Holt's clothes and walk through London.

Additionally, Sydney exerts a power over Holt's storytelling that resembles the Beetle's control of Holt. Marjorie observes that when Holt repeats his story to both her and Sydney, Sydney's presence affects the shape of that story: "Mr. Holt repeated the tale which he had told me, only in more connected fashion than before. I fancy that Sydney's glances exercised on him a sort of hypnotic effect, and this kept him to the point,—he scarcely needed a

---

19. Luckhurst categorizes *The Beetle* and *Dracula* as "*trance texts*" and contextualizes the "somnambulic, mesmeric and hypnotic states" in the novels with the discussion of such issues in fin-de-siècle England (159).

word of prompting from the first syllable to the last" (210). Just like the Beetle mesmerizes Holt with eyes that "held [him] enchained, helpless, spell-bound" (54), Sydney's "glances" have a "hypnotic effect" on Holt's storytelling, binding him "to the point," resulting in a "more connected" tale (210). As previously mentioned, other critics have recognized the parallels between Sydney and the Beetle—their hypnotic power and their destructive potential; however, critics haven't noticed how Sydney plays a Beetle-like role specifically in relation to Holt. Sydney culls a tighter, quicker, more seamless story from Holt just by looking at him.

The very creation of Holt's narrative does to Holt what the monstrous Beetle already does to him—puts words into his mouth. When the Beetle instructs Holt how to steal from Paul, she programs him to pronounce "THE BEETLE!" if he encounters Paul in person. When Paul interrupts Holt mid-robbery, the Beetle's dictum binds Holt:

> something entered into me, and forced itself from between my lips, so that I said, in a low, hissing voice, which I vow was never mine,
> "THE BEETLE!" (76)

The Beetle, even at a distance from Holt, manages to "enter[ ] into" Holt and manipulate his voice and language. A few pages later, Holt again experiences this takeover of his voice, yelling "THE BEETLE" "in tones which I should not have recognized as mine" (82). When the dying Holt is found in the back of a brothel, only Sydney—not the inspector or doctor—elicits meaningful words from him because Sydney "had reached a chord in the man's consciousness" (306). The notion of Sydney awakening Holt, reaching into his mind, and striking a chord therein sounds much like the Beetle's mental invasion of Holt. Holt soon undergoes a "paroxysm" that kills him; interestingly, this fit occurs in Sydney's presence, not the Beetle's. Sydney quips, "there'll be no conjuring him back again," suggesting that he magically brought Holt from the brink a few minutes prior. The Beetle, too, brings the "as good as dead" Holt back to life with a "kiss" in an earlier scene (57). Even though Champnell claims that Holt's narrative "was compiled from the statements which Holt made to Atherton, and to Miss Lindon" (321), Marjorie is clearly not in a state to offer anything beyond her own trance-produced narrative. It must be Sydney that reconstructs and writes down Holt's story from memory. The Beetle's words appear in Holt's brain and force themselves out of Holt's mouth, transforming Holt into a ventriloquist doll; similarly, Sydney puts his account of Holt's story into Holt's mouth and pen, hiding the fact that Holt isn't the literal origin of the narrative.

Even as the gothic infects these narrative structures, narrators in *The Bee-tle* and *Dracula* remain reliable on the axis of reporting. Narrators agree on the facts in all of the Victorian multinarrator novels I've discussed in *Narra-tive Bonds*. Julian Wolfreys writes of *The Beetle*: "That there *are* four narrators rather than simply one is, I would contend, indicative of the late Victorian anxious comprehension that there is no consistent or stable language with which to address any matter or concern" (Introduction 29). But such an argu-ment doesn't hold. To give one example, multiple characters describe the Beetle's neighborhood using very similar language (a tactic I reference in chapter 2 as well). Holt wanders into what he calls the "unfinished . . . land of desolation" (Marsh 45). Marjorie observes an "unfinished" road, "wilder-ness," and "large spaces of waste land" (217). Champnell sees "an unfinished cheap neighbourhood" in a "wilderness of waste land" (258, 259). *The Beetle* is a *"repeating* narrative" in which "the same event can be told several times" (Genette, *Narrative* 116, 115), but the different narrators give strikingly similar accounts of the same events. Holt and Sydney give matching versions of their unexpected meeting outside Paul's house. Sydney and Marjorie speak simi-larly about his proposal of marriage to her, about Paul's speech in Parliament and the events immediately following, and about her visit to his lab to confide in him. The end of Marjorie's account, which tells of her and Sydney's meet-ing with Holt and exploration of the Beetle's house, is verified by Champnell's narrative, in which Sydney summarizes those prior events. Although Marjo-rie's and Sydney's differing feelings about his proposal understandably color their portrayals of that episode, none of the narratives blatantly contradicts another one. Carol A. Senf argues that all of *Dracula*'s narrators are unreliable and their accounts subjective ("*Dracula*"). But while *Dracula*'s narrators are neither perfectly self-aware nor perfectly objective—no homodiegetic narra-tor is—Van Helsing's triumphant speech that follows his studying of the "con-nected narrative" indirectly highlights how much the individual narratives corroborate one another (Stoker 240). He addresses the assembled team and begins to delineate Dracula, power by power, tendency by tendency, weakness by weakness; all of his evidence is based on their own experiences as recorded in their narratives: "as again Jonathan observe. . . . as Madam Mina saw him . . . and as friend John saw him . . . and as my friend Quincey saw him. . . . as again Jonathan saw. . . . we ourselves saw Miss Lucy . . ." (255). Van Hels-ing powerfully and persuasively concludes, "We have seen it with our eyes" (256).[20] Their narratives align, and they see with a communal vision. Overall,

---

20. In Moretti's view, "it is more accurate to speak of a 'collective' narrator than of differ-ent narrators" in the second half of the book (*Signs* 98); this passage is one of the few places in which I see such a narrator materialize.

the Victorian multinarrator novel evinces optimism that different narrators can see the world in similar ways and agree on the facts. Even in the presence of the monsters and ghosts of gothic literature, reality remains firm, verified from multiple perspectives.

Narrative Bonds demonstrates that the Victorians employed setups besides the omniscient narrator and first-person narrator throughout the Victorian period, including in the fin-de-siècle. The Victorians did not create the multinarrator form, and it also has outlasted the period. It continues to thrive in today's literary landscape, particularly in thrillers and young adult literature.[21] Briefly examining Gillian Flynn's massively popular *Gone Girl,* published in 2012 and followed by a successful movie in 2014, highlights both what is distinctive to the Victorian multinarrator novel and how the multinarrator subtypes I present in *Narrative Bonds* can be used to interpret contemporary works. For its first half, *Gone Girl* alternates between Nick Dunne's chapters chronicling the aftermath of his wife Amy's disappearance in 2012 and entries from Amy's diary from 2005 to 2012, documenting her increasing terror of her casually cruel husband. After Amy's final diary entry, presented halfway through *Gone Girl,* we learn that the diary was a ruse—faked and planted to frame Nick for Amy's murder in revenge for Nick's adultery with his student Andie. For the second half of the novel, chapters alternate between Nick and Amy, detailing how they decide to remain married and settle into a hostile familiarity. Amy's diary is marked as such via a "diary entry" header; Nick's narrative and Amy's post-diary narratives aren't explicitly written or spoken, though they both occasionally address and attempt to persuade a "you."

Most startlingly, *Gone Girl*'s narrators can and do lie. These narrators don't just misinterpret or misevaluate as Victorian narrators could, they willfully and extensively misreport—they are unreliable on the axis of facts. Even Fosco—articulate and charming villain par excellence—doesn't outright lie in his masterful narrative in *The Woman in White. Gone Girl*'s midway twist shocks readers *because* they have believed the diary entries, falling for the conception of the diary as a more private, and hence more truthful, outlet and account. But "Diary Amy," "Actual Amy" tells us, was "a work of fiction" (Flynn 220), authored specifically to make Amy "likeable" (237) and Nick detestable to its readers. The reader may feel silly and gullible at this moment for having been so easily manipulated. And we should have seen it coming, given the amount Nick lies in his narrative. Early in the novel, he casually admits, "It was my fifth lie to the police," and the stunned reader wonders

---

21. In "'Mind to Mind': The Gothic Loss of Privacy in the Twilight Saga and Chaos Walking Trilogy," I consider how the introduction of multiple narrators into the later books of these two young adult series "mirrors the increasing openness of the protagonists" (170).

what the other four lies were (37). He proudly owns being "a big fan of the lie of omission" (133), paving the way for the later confession about his mistress, whom he excluded from the narrative until that point. Although it may be comfortable to view Amy's post-diary narratives as reliable and truthful because they come from "Actual Amy," who claims they are "a *true* story" (220), Amy also undercuts any notion of a core identity when she admits to frequently "chang[ing] personalities" (222).

Gone Girl, like Charles Dickens's *Bleak House* and Dinah Mulock Craik's *A Life for a Life*, features a *back-and-forth* multinarrator structure. Its rhythm of switches is extremely regular: Every chapter the narrative switches between Nick and Amy. They each narrate for thirty-two chapters. Nick opens the book, and Amy closes it. In chapter 2 of *Narrative Bonds*, I argued that this particular structure strongly bonds narrators by steadily interweaving them, encouraging us to see the similarities between the two narrators and their accounts. While this effect may seem incongruous with *Gone Girl*, Nick and Amy are uniquely and even disturbingly bonded and intertwined by the end of the novel—parasitically and poisonously so. Early on, both characters desire to be free of the other (as well as free from the other person's expectations of them), and yet, the novel tracks their paths back to each other rather than to a permanent separation. Late in the novel, Amy and Nick have twin realizations: "Nick and I fit together" and "We complete each other in the nastiest, ugliest possible way" (Flynn 353, 393). Several days after returning to Nick, Amy plans on "hold[ing] [her]self to him like a climbing, coiling vine until [she has] invaded every part of him" (400). This image of them physically and mentally entwined mirrors their braided narratives.

The uncanny awareness Nick and Amy have of each other, as well as the subtle echoes between their narratives, emphasize their bizarre convergence. Nick and Amy constantly recall what the other said and imagine what the other would say; their physical absence from each other ironically fosters an obsessiveness that conjures presence. Nick muses, "She was gone, and yet she was more present than anyone else" (214). Amy similarly acknowledges, "I have shed myself of Nick, and yet I think about him more than ever" (244). Eerie echoes dot their narratives. At the end of one chapter, Nick narrates, "Something bad was about to happen" (338), and, soon after, Amy narrates, "I feel like something very bad is going to happen" (362). When Amy realizes she shouldn't have trusted her ex-boyfriend Desi, she "wonder[s] then if [she has] made a very big mistake" (341); the next sentence, on the next page, belongs to Nick: "I made a mistake" (342). In both cases, the narrators' arrogance causes the "mistake." These repetitions posit a deep, if unconscious, link between the two characters, a connection Nick senses: "All this time I'd thought we were strangers, and it turned out we knew each other intuitively, in our bones, in our blood" (385). Scenes late in the novel where she seems to read his mind and he seems to read hers feel like an extension and culmination of that "intuitive[ ]" interpersonal knowledge. How else does Amy know that she's getting the "last word" at the end of the novel (415)?

What does the multinarrator form do, or *afford*, to use Caroline Levine's useful term? In *Forms: Whole, Rhythm, Hierarchy, Network,* Levine considers forms in terms of their affordances: "the potential uses or actions latent in materials and designs" (6). To return to the title of this book, the multinarrator form affords *bonding*. Pulling together that which is different—unexpected connections. A child and adult narrate in *Treasure Island*; a servant and master narrate in *Wuthering Heights*; an unnamed heterodiegetic narrator and orphaned homodiegetic narrator narrate in *Bleak House*; a cross-selection of a town narrates in *A Beleaguered City*; nondisabled and disabled characters narrate in W. Collins's novels. Boundaries of age, class, (dis)ability, gender, race, and narrator type are traversed as narrators, joined, agree on the facts and create a stable reality. But a bond can also be a yoke. Livesey attempts to dominate Jim, and Jim squirms to escape oppression in *Treasure Island*. In the gothic novels I've discussed, bonds can be both boons and burdens; collaboration can be both effectual and monstrous. While I'm not as ready as Levine is to tout the inevitable permanence of all forms throughout different historical and geographic contexts, *Gone Girl* exhibits the same affordances as witnessed in earlier examples of the back-and-forth structure. The multinarrator structure itself umbrellas various subtypes that, because of their designs, enable various valiances of bonding: back-and-forth, quick switch, permeable frame, patchworks, returning and nonreturning.

In Virginia Woolf's *To the Lighthouse,* Mrs. Ramsay contemplates the beauty of her daughter's fruit centerpiece and notices dinner guest Augustus Carmichael doing the same. Mrs. Ramsay then ponders, "That was his way of looking, different from hers. But looking together united them" (Woolf, *Lighthouse* 97). The multinarrator structure unites various lookers, binding their stories into the collaborative, interdependent narrative. Those lookers—narrators—are often brought closer despite their divides and differences. The multinarrator form structurally embodies interpersonal relations between characters. Structure, after all, always connects to the story, facilitating, highlighting, and mirroring certain aspects of the plot, bonding, so to speak, not just the narrators, but also content and form.

WORKS CITED

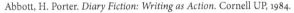

Abbott, H. Porter. *Diary Fiction: Writing as Action.* Cornell UP, 1984.

Ablow, Rachel. "Hypochondria and the Failure of Relationship." *Nineteenth-Century Gender Studies,* issue 11.3, Winter 2015, http://ncgsjournal.com/issue113/ablow.htm.

Akutagawa, Ryūnosuke. *Rashōmon and Seventeen Other Stories.* Translated by Jay Rubin, Penguin, 2006.

Allin, Leslie. "Leaky Bodies: Masculinity, Narrative and Imperial Decay in Richard Marsh's *The Beetle.*" *Victorian Network,* vol. 6, no. 1, Summer 2015, pp. 113–35.

Altick, Richard D. *The English Common Reader.* 2nd ed., The Ohio State UP, 1998.

Altman, Janet Gurkin. *Epistolarity: Approaches to a Form.* The Ohio State UP, 1982.

Anderson, Robert. "What Is the Rashomon Effect?" *Rashomon Effects: Kurosawa,* Rashomon *and Their Legacies,* edited by Blair Davis et al., Routledge, 2016, pp. 66–85.

Anderson, Walter E. "The Lyrical Form of *Wuthering Heights.*" *University of Toronto Quarterly,* vol. 47, no. 2, Winter 1977–78, pp. 112–34.

Arac, Jonathan. *Commissioned Spirits: The Shaping of Social Motion in Dickens, Carlyle, Melville, and Hawthorne.* Columbia UP, 1989.

Arata, Stephen. *Fictions of Loss in the Victorian Fin de Siècle.* Cambridge UP, 1996.

Armstrong, Nancy. *Desire and Domestic Fiction: A Political History of the Novel.* Oxford UP, 1987.

———. *How Novels Think: The Limits of British Individualism from 1719–1900.* Columbia UP, 2005.

Auerbach, Erich. *Mimesis: The Representation of Reality in Western Literature.* 50th anniversary ed., Princeton UP, 2003.

Axton, William. "The Trouble With Esther." *Modern Language Quarterly,* vol. 26, no. 4, Dec. 1965, pp. 545–57.

Baker, William, and William M. Clarke, editors. *The Letters of Wilkie Collins, Volume 2: 1866–1889.* Macmillan/St. Martin, 1999.

Bakhtin, Mikhail. "Discourse in the Novel." *The Dialogic Imagination: Four Essays*, translated by Caryl Emerson and Michael Holquist, U of Texas P, 1981, pp. 259–422.

———. *Problems of Dostoevsky's Poetics*. Translated by Caryl Emerson, U of Minnesota P, 1984.

Bal, Mieke. "Notes on Narrative Embedding." Translated by Eve Tavor. *Poetics Today*, vol. 2, no. 2, Winter 1981, pp. 41–59.

Ballantyne, R. M. *The Coral Island*. Penguin, 1995.

Bassett, John, editor. *William Faulkner: The Critical Heritage*. Routledge, 1975.

Berlinger, Manette. "'I am Heathcliff': Lockwood's Role in *Wuthering Heights*." *Brontë Studies*, vol. 35, no. 3, 2010, pp. 185–93. *Taylor and Francis Online*, https://doi.org/10.1179/1474893 10X12798868307806.

Bersani, Leo. *A Future for Astyanax: Character and Desire in Literature*. Little, Brown, 1976.

Bleikasten, André. *Faulkner's As I Lay Dying*. Translated by Roger Little, Indiana UP, 1973.

Bloom, Edward. Introduction. *Evelina*, by Fanny Burney, Oxford UP, 1982, pp. vii–xxxi.

Bock, Carol A. "Miss Wade and George Silverman: The Forms of Fictional Monologue." *Dickens Studies Annual*, vol. 16, 1987, pp. 113–26.

Bogdan, Robert. *Freak Show: Presenting Human Oddities for Amusement and Profit*. U of Chicago P, 1990.

Boone, Troy. *Youth of Darkest England: Working-Class Children at the Heart of Victorian Empire*. Routledge, 2005.

Booth, Bradford A., and Ernest Mehew, editors. *The Letters of Robert Louis Stevenson, Volume One*. Yale UP, 1994.

Booth, Wayne C. *The Rhetoric of Fiction*. 2nd ed., U of Chicago P, 1983.

Bourrier, Karen, and Jennifer Esmail. "Disability." *The Encyclopedia of Victorian Literature*, general editor, Dino Franco Felluga, Wiley-Blackwell, 2015, pp. 443–49.

Boyce, Conal. "A Map: Plotting 300 Pages of 'Longitude' Against 300 Years of 'Latitude' to Elucidate the Nested Narratives of Emily Brontë's *Wuthering Heights*." *Brontë Studies*, vol. 38, no. 2, Apr. 2013, pp. 93–110. *Taylor and Francis Online*, https://doi.org/10.1179/14748932 13Z.00000000056.

Bradbury, Malcolm. *Possibilities: Essays on the State of the Novel*. Oxford UP, 1973.

Brantlinger, Patrick. "What Is 'Sensational' About the 'Sensation Novel'?" *Nineteenth-Century Fiction*, vol. 37, no. 1, June 1982, pp. 1–28. *JSTOR*, https://ncl.ucpress.edu/content/37/1/1.

Bristow, Joseph. *Empire Boys: Adventures in a Man's World*. HarperCollins, 1991.

Broderick, James H., and John E. Grant. "The Identity of Esther Summerson." *Modern Philology*, vol. 55, no. 4, May 1958, pp. 252–58. *JSTOR*, https://www.jstor.org/stable/434948.

Brontë, Anne. *The Tenant of Wildfell Hall*. Penguin, 1996.

Brontë, Charlotte. *Jane Eyre*. Penguin, 2006.

Brontë, Emily. *Wuthering Heights*. Penguin, 2003.

———. *Wuthering Heights*. London, Newby, 1847.

Bulfin, Ailise. "'In that Egyptian den': Situating *The Beetle* within the Fin-de-siècle Fiction of Gothic Egypt." *Richard Marsh, Popular Fiction and Literary Culture, 1890–1915*, edited by Victoria Margree et al., Manchester UP, 2018, pp. 127–47.

Burgan, Mary. "Mapping Contagion in Victorian London: Disease in the East End." *Victorian Urban Settings: Essays on the Nineteenth-Century City and Its Contexts*, edited by Debra N. Mancoff and D. J. Trela, Routledge, 1996, pp. 43–56.

Burney, Fanny. *Evelina*. Oxford UP, 1982.

Butler, Arthur John. Review of *Treasure Island,* by Robert Louis Stevenson. *Athenaeum,* 1 Dec. 1883. *Robert Louis Stevenson: The Critical Heritage,* edited by Paul Maixner, Routledge, 1981, pp. 130–31.

Buzard, James. *Disorienting Fiction: The Autoethnographic Work of Nineteenth-Century British Novels.* Princeton UP, 2005.

Caleb, Amanda Mordavsky. "Questioning Moral Inheritance in *The Legacy of Cain.*" *Wilkie Collins: Interdisciplinary Essays,* edited by Andrew Mangham, Cambridge Scholars Publishing, 2007, pp. 122–35. *ProQuest ebrary.*

Capuano, Peter J. *Changing Hands: Industry, Evolution, and the Reconfiguration of the Victorian Body.* U of Michigan P, 2015.

Carens, Timothy L. "Outlandish English Subjects in *The Moonstone.*" *Reality's Dark Light: The Sensational Wilkie Collins,* edited by Maria K. Bachman and Don Richard Cox, U of Tennessee P, 2003, pp. 239–65.

Case, Alison A. *Plotting Women: Gender and Narration in the Eighteenth- and Nineteenth- Century British Novel.* UP of Virginia, 1999.

Chase, Karen. *The Victorians and Old Age.* Oxford UP, 2009.

Choi, Tina Young. *Anonymous Connections: The Body and Narratives of the Social in Victorian Britain.* U of Michigan Press, 2016.

Christensen, Allan Conrad. *Nineteenth-Century Narratives of Contagion: 'Our Feverish Contact.'* Routledge, 2005.

Clayton, Jay. "Inherited Behavior in Wilkie Collins's *The Legacy of Cain*: Victorian Studies and Twenty-First-Century Science Policy." *19: Interdisciplinary Studies in the Long Nineteenth Century,* vol. 7, 2008, https://doi.org/10.16995/ntn.484.

Cohen, Jane R. *Charles Dickens and His Original Illustrators.* The Ohio State UP, 1980.

Cohn, Dorrit. *Transparent Minds: Narrative Modes for Presenting Consciousness in Fiction.* Princeton UP, 1978.

Colby, Robert, and Vineta Colby. "*A Beleaguered City:* A Fable the Victorian Age." *Nineteenth-Century Fiction,* vol. 16, no. 4, March 1962, pp. 283–301. *JSTOR,* https://www.jstor.org/stable/2932406.

Collins, Philip, editor. *Dickens: The Critical Heritage.* Routledge, 1995.

——. "Some Narrative Devices in *Bleak House.*" *Dickens Studies Annual,* vol. 19, 1990, pp. 125–46.

Collins, Wilkie. The case of Roxalana Druse. 1887, Harry Ransom Center, U of Texas, Austin, MS-0881.

——. *The Legacy of Cain.* Wildside.

——. *The Moonstone.* Penguin, 1998.

——. *The Woman in White.* Penguin, 2003.

Cooke, Stewart J., editor. Reviews. *Evelina,* by Fanny Burney, Norton, 1998, pp. 358–61.

Cothran, Casey A. "Mysterious Bodies: Deception and Detection in Wilkie Collins's *The Law and the Lady* and *The Moonstone.*" *Victorians Institute Journal,* vol. 34, 2006, pp. 193–214.

Craft, Christopher. "'Kiss Me with Those Red Lips': Gender and Inversion in Bram Stoker's *Dracula.*" *Representations,* no. 8, Autumn 1984, pp.107–33. *JSTOR,* https://www.jstor.org/stable/2928560.

Craik, Dinah Mulock. *A Life for a Life.* British Library, Historical Print Editions.

Craton, Lillian. *The Victorian Freak Show: The Significance of Disability and Physical Differences in 19th-Century Fiction.* Cambria P, 2009.

Daly, Nicholas. "Incorporated Bodies: *Dracula* and the Rise of Professionalism." *Texas Studies in Literature and Language*, vol. 39, no. 2, Summer 1997, pp. 181–203.

Daugherty, Tracy Edgar. *Narrative Techniques in the Novels of Fanny Burney.* Peter Lang, 1989.

Dawson, Paul. *The Return of the Omniscient Narrator: Authorship and Authority in Twenty-First Century Fiction.* The Ohio State UP, 2013.

Deane, Bradley. "Imperial Boyhood: Piracy and the Play Ethic." *Victorian Studies,* vol. 53, no. 4, 2011, pp. 689–714. *Project Muse,* https://muse.jhu.edu/article/458229.

Deen, Leonard W. "Style and Unity in *Bleak House.*" *Criticism,* vol. 3, no. 3, Summer 1961, pp. 206–18.

Delafield, Catherine. *Women's Diaries as Narrative in the Nineteenth-Century Novel.* Ashgate, 2009.

DeLamotte, Eugenia C. *Perils of the Night: A Feminist Study of Nineteenth-Century Gothic.* Oxford UP, 1990.

Delespinasse, Doris Stringham. "The Significance of Dual Point of View in *Bleak House.*" *Nineteenth-Century Fiction,* vol. 23, no. 3, 1968, pp. 253–64. *JSTOR,* https://doi.org/10.2307/2932554.

Dickens, Charles. *Bleak House.* Penguin, 2003.

——. *Hard Times.* Oxford UP, 2008.

——. *Little Dorrit.* Penguin, 2003.

"duck and drake, n." *Oxford English Dictionary Online.* Oxford UP, 2019.

Duyfhuizen, Bernard. "Framed Narrative." *Routledge Encyclopedia of Narrative Theory,* edited by David Herman et al., Routledge, 2008, pp. 186–88.

——. *Narratives of Transmission.* Fairleigh Dickinson UP, 1992.

Eldredge, Patricia R. "The Lost Self of Esther Summerson: A Horneyan Interpretation of *Bleak House.*" *The Literary Review,* vol. 24, no. 2, Winter 1981, pp. 252–78.

Eldridge, C. C. *Victorian Imperialism.* Hodder & Stoughton, 1978.

Emrys, A. B. *Wilkie Collins, Vera Caspary and the Evolution of the Casebook Novel.* McFarland, 2011.

Epstein, Julia L. "Evelina's Deceptions: The Letter and the Spirit." *Fanny Burney's* Evelina, edited by Harold Bloom, Chelsea House Publishers, 1988, pp. 111–29.

Esty, Jed. *Unseasonable Youth: Modernism, Colonialism, and the Fiction of Development.* Oxford UP, 2012.

Ewing, Juliana Horatia. *A Great Emergency, and Other Tales.* London, 1877. *Google Books.*

Faulkner, William. *As I Lay Dying.* Vintage, 1990.

——. *The Sound and the Fury.* Vintage, 1990.

Felber, Lynette. "'Delightfully Irregular': Esther's Nascent *écriture féminine* in *Bleak House.*" *The Victorian Newsletter,* vol. 85, Spring 1994, pp. 13–20.

Fleissner, Jennifer L. "Dictation Anxiety: The Stenographer's Stake in *Dracula.*" *Nineteenth-Century Contexts,* vol. 22, no. 3, 2000, pp. 417–55.

Flint, Kate. "Disability and Difference." *The Cambridge Companion to Wilkie Collins,* edited by Jenny Bourne Taylor, Cambridge UP, 2006, pp. 153–67.

Fludernik, Monika. "Letters as Narrative." *Routledge Encyclopedia of Narrative Theory,* edited by David Herman et al., Routledge, 2008, p. 277.

Flynn, Gillian. *Gone Girl.* Crown, 2012.

Foucault, Michel. *Discipline and Punish: The Birth of the Prison.* Translated by Alan Sheridan, Vintage-Random, 1995.

Frank, Lawrence. "'Through A Glass Darkly': Esther Summerson and *Bleak House*." *Dickens Studies Annual*, vol. 4, 1975, pp. 91–112.

Frawley, Maria H. *Invalidism and Identity in Nineteenth-Century Britain*. U of Chicago P, 2004.

Free, Melissa. "'Dirty Linen': Legacies of Empire in Wilkie Collins's *The Moonstone*." *Texas Studies in Literature and Language*, vol. 48, no. 4, Winter 2006, pp. 340–71. *Project Muse*, https://doi.org/10.1353/tsl.2007.0000.

Freud, Sigmund. *The Uncanny*. Translated by David McLintock, Penguin, 2003.

Garland-Thomson, Rosemarie. "Integrating Disability, Transforming Feminist Theory." *The Disability Studies Reader*, 3rd ed., edited by Lennard J. Davis, Routledge, 2010, pp. 353–73.

Garnett, Rhys. "*Dracula* and *The Beetle*: Imperial and Sexual Guilt and Fear in Late Victorian Fantasy." *Science Fiction Roots and Branches: Contemporary Critical Approaches*, edited by Rhys Garnett and R. J. Ellis, St. Martin's, 1990, pp. 30–54.

Garrett, Peter K. "Double Plots and Dialogical Form in Victorian Fiction." *Nineteenth-Century Fiction*, vol. 32, no. 1, 1977, pp. 1–17. JSTOR, https://doi.org/10.2307/2933448.

———. *Gothic Reflections: Narrative Force in Nineteenth-Century Fiction*. Cornell UP, 2003.

Gaughan, Richard T. "'Their Places Are a Blank': The Two Narrators in *Bleak House*." *Dickens Studies Annual*, vol. 21, 1992, pp. 79–96.

Gaylin, Ann. "The Madwoman Outside the Attic: Eavesdropping and Narrative Agency in *The Woman in White*." *Texas Studies in Literature and Language*, vol. 43, no. 4, Fall 2001, pp. 303–33.

Genette, Gérard. *Narrative Discourse: An Essay in Method*. Translated by Jane E. Lewin, Cornell UP, 1980.

———. *Paratexts: Thresholds of Interpretation*. Translated by Jane E. Lewin, Cambridge UP, 1997.

Gilbert, Sandra M., and Susan Gubar. *The Madwoman in the Attic*. 2nd ed., Yale UP, 2000.

Gillooly, Eileen. *Smile of Discontent: Humor, Gender, and Nineteenth-Century British Fiction*. U of Chicago P, 1999.

Gladstone, David. "The Changing Dynamic of Institutional Care: The Western Counties Idiot Asylum, 1864–1914." *From Idiocy to Mental Deficiency: Historical Perspectives on People with Learning Disabilities*, edited by Anne Digby and David Wright, Routledge, 2002, pp. 134–60.

Gladstone, William. "England's Mission." *The Nineteenth Century*, vol. 4, London, 1878, pp. 560–84.

———. *Political Speeches in Scotland, November and December 1879*. Revised ed., Edinburgh, 1879. *Google Books*.

Grass, Sean C. "*The Moonstone*, Narrative Failure, and the Pathology of the Stare." *Dickens Studies Annual*, vol. 37, 2006, pp. 95–116.

Graver, Suzanne. "Writing in a 'Womanly' Way and the Double Vision of *Bleak House*." *Dickens Quarterly*, vol. 4, no. 1, 1987, pp. 3–15.

Gubar, Marah. *Artful Dodgers: Reconceiving the Golden Age of Children's Literature*. Oxford UP, 2009.

Guerard, Albert J. "*Bleak House*: Structure and Style." *Southern Review*, vol. 5, 1969, pp. 332–49.

Hafley, James. "The Villain in *Wuthering Heights*." *Nineteenth-Century Fiction*, vol. 13, no. 3, 1958, pp. 199–215.

Haggerty, George E. *Gothic Fiction/Gothic Form*. Pennsylvania State UP, 1989.

Halberstam, Judith. "Gothic Nation: *The Beetle* by Richard Marsh." *Fictions of Unease: The Gothic from* Otranto *to* The X-Files, edited by Andrew Smith et al., Sulis P, 2002, pp. 100–118.

———. "Technologies of Monstrosity: Bram Stoker's *Dracula*." *Cultural Poetics at the Fin de Siècle*, edited by Sally Ledger and Scott McCracken, Cambridge UP, 1995, pp. 248–266.

Hall, Jasmine Yong. "What's Troubling About Esther? Narrating, Policing, and Resisting Arrest in *Bleak House.*" *Dickens Studies Annual,* vol. 22, 1993, pp. 171–94.

Hardesty, Patricia Whaley, William H. Hardesty III, and David Mann. "Doctoring the Doctor: How Stevenson Altered the Second Narrator of *Treasure Island.*" *Studies in Scottish Literature,* vol. 21, 1986, pp. 1–22.

Hardesty, William H. III, and David D. Mann. "Historical Reality and Fictional Daydream in *Treasure Island.*" *The Journal of Narrative Technique,* vol. 7, no. 2, Spring 1977, pp. 94–103. *JSTOR,* https://www.jstor.org/stable/30225608.

Harris, W. C., and Dawn Vernooy. "'Orgies of Nameless Horrors': Gender, Orientalism, and the Queering of Violence in Richard Marsh's *The Beetle.*" *Papers of Language and Literature,* vol. 48, no. 4, Fall 2012, pp. 339–81.

Harvey, W. J. *Character and the Novel.* Cornell UP, 1965.

Heiland, Donna. *Gothic and Gender: An Introduction.* Wiley-Blackwell, 2004.

Heller, Tamar. *Dead Secrets: Wilkie Collins and the Female Gothic.* Yale UP, 1992.

Hennessy, James Pope. *Robert Louis Stevenson.* Simon and Schuster, 1974.

Hirsch, Gordon. "The Stevenson-Osbourne Collaboration." *Approaches to Teaching the Works of Robert Louis Stevenson,* edited by Caroline McCracken-Flesher, MLA, 2013, pp. 162–67.

Hite, Molly. Introduction. *The Waves,* by Virginia Woolf, Harvest/Harcourt, 2006, pp. xxxv–lxvii.

Hogan, Patrick Colm. *Narrative Discourse: Authors and Narrators in Literature, Film, and Art.* The Ohio State UP, 2013.

Hornback, Bert G. "The Narrator of *Bleak House.*" *Dickens Quarterly,* vol. 16, no. 1, 1999, pp. 3–12.

House, Humphry. *The Dickens World.* 2nd ed., Oxford UP, 1942.

Hurley, Kelly. *The Gothic Body: Sexuality, Materialism, and Degeneration at the Fin de Siècle.* Cambridge UP, 1996.

Hutchinson, Jonathan. *Archives of Surgery.* Vol. 10, London, 1899. *Google Books.*

Hutter, Albert D. "Dreams, Transformations, and Literature: The Implications of Detective Fiction." *Victorian Studies,* vol. 19, no. 2, 1975, pp. 181–209.

Jacobs, N. M. "Gender and Layered Narrative in *Wuthering Heights* and *The Tenant of Wildfell Hall.*" *The Journal of Narrative Technique,* vol. 16, no. 3, Fall 1986, pp. 204–19. *JSTOR,* https://www.jstor.org/stable/30225153.

Jadwin, Lisa. "'Caricatured, Not Faithfully Rendered': *Bleak House* as a Revision of *Jane Eyre.*" *Modern Language Studies,* vol. 26, no. 2–3, Spring-Summer 1996, pp. 111–33. *JSTOR,* https://www.jstor.org/stable/3195452.

Jaffe, Audrey. *Vanishing Points: Dickens, Narrative, and the Subject of Omniscience.* U of California P, 1991.

James, Henry. "Mary Elizabeth Braddon." *Henry James: Literary Criticism,* The Library of America, 1984, pp. 741–46.

Jay, Elisabeth. *Mrs. Oliphant: 'A Fiction to Herself': A Literary Life.* Clarendon P, 1995.

Jones, Anna Maria. "Conservation of Energy, Individual Agency, and Gothic Terror in Richard Marsh's *The Beetle,* or, What's Scarier Than an Ancient, Evil, Shape-Shifting Bug?" *Victorian Literature and Culture,* vol. 39, no. 1, 2011, pp. 65–85.

Jordan, John O. *Supposing Bleak House.* U of Virginia P, 2011.

Katz, Wendy R. Introduction. *Treasure Island,* by Robert Louis Stevenson, edited by Wendy R. Katz, Edinburgh UP, 1998, pp. xix–xli.

Kearns, Michael S. "'But I Cried Very Much': Esther Summerson as Narrator." *Dickens Quarterly,* vol. 1, no. 4, 1984, pp. 121–29.

Kennedy, Valerie. "*Bleak House:* More Trouble with Esther?" *Journal of Women's Studies in Literature,* vol. 1, no. 4, 1979, pp. 330–47.

Kermode, Frank. *The Classic.* Faber & Faber, 1973.

Kiely, Robert. *Robert Louis Stevenson and the Fiction of Adventure.* Harvard UP, 1964.

Kinkead-Weekes, M. "*Clarissa* Restored?" *The Review of English Studies,* vol. 10, no. 38, May 1959, pp. 156–71. *JSTOR,* https://www.jstor.org/stable/511806.

Kittler, Friedrich. "Dracula's Legacy." Translated by William Stephen Davis. *Stanford Humanities Review,* vol. 1, no. 1, Spring 1989, pp. 143–73.

Lams, Victor J. *Clarissa's Narrators.* Peter Lang, 2001.

Le Bon, Gustave. "The Mind of Crowds." *The Fin de Siècle: A Reader in Cultural History, c. 1880–1900,* edited by Sally Ledger and Roger Luckhurst, Oxford UP, 2000, pp. 55–61.

Letley, Emma. Notes. *Treasure Island,* by Robert Louis Stevenson, Oxford UP, 1985, pp. 201–10.

Levine, Caroline. *Forms: Whole, Rhythm, Hierarchy, Network.* Princeton UP, 2015.

Linder, Lynn M. "Dual-ing Diaries, Intersecting Identities: Victorian Subjectivity and Dinah Mulock Craik's *A Life for a Life.*" *VIJ: Victorians Institute Journal,* vol. 39, 2011, pp. 203–26. *EBSCOhost,* http://search.ebscohost.com.lynx.lib.usm.edu/login.aspx?direct=true&db=lfh&AN=82513263&site=ehost-live.

Linehan, Katherine Bailey. "Taking Up With Kanakas: Stevenson's Complex Social Criticism in 'The Beach of Falesá.'" *English Literature in Transition, 1880–1920,* vol. 33, no. 4, 1990, pp. 407–22. *Project Muse,* https://muse.jhu.edu/article/373540.

Lodge, David. *Consciousness and the Novel: Connected Essays.* Harvard UP, 2002.

Loman, Andrew. "The Sea Cook's Wife: Evocations of Slavery in *Treasure Island.*" *Children's Literature,* vol. 38, 2010, pp. 1–26. *Project Muse,* https://muse.jhu.edu/article/380758.

Lonoff, Sue. "Multiple Narratives & Relative Truths: A Study of *The Ring and The Book, The Woman in White,* and *The Moonstone.*" *Browning Institute Studies,* vol. 10, 1982, pp. 143–61.

Loxley, Diana. *Problematic Shores: The Literature of Islands.* St. Martin's, 1990.

Luckhurst, Roger. "Trance-Gothic, 1882–97." *Victorian Gothic: Literary and Cultural Manifestations in the Nineteenth Century,* edited by Ruth Robbins and Julian Wolfreys, Palgrave, 2000, pp. 148–67.

Majumdar, Robin, and Allen McLauren, editors. *Virginia Woolf: The Critical Heritage.* Routledge, 1975.

Mangum, Teresa. "Wilkie Collins, Detection, and Deformity." *Dickens Studies Annual,* vol. 26, 1998, pp. 285–310.

Mann, David D., and William H. Hardesty, III. "Stevenson's Revisions of *Treasure Island:* 'Writing down the Whole Particulars.'" *Text,* vol. 3, 1987, pp. 377–92.

Margree, Victoria. "'Both in Men's Clothing': Gender, Sovereignty and Insecurity in Richard Marsh's *The Beetle.*" *Critical Survey,* vol. 19, no. 2, 2007, pp. 63–81.

Marsh, Richard. *The Beetle: A Mystery.* Broadview, 2004.

Mathison, John K. "Nelly Dean and the Power of *Wuthering Heights.*" *Nineteenth-Century Fiction,* vol. 11, no. 2, 1956, pp. 106–29.

Matthew, H. C. G. *Gladstone, 1875–1898.* Clarendon, 1995.

Matthews, John T. "Framing in *Wuthering Heights.*" *Texas Studies in Literature and Language,* vol. 27, no. 1, Spring 1985, pp. 25–61. *JSTOR,* https://www.jstor.org/stable/40754765.

Maudsley, Henry. *Responsibility in Mental Disease.* New York, 1875. *Google Books.*

Mayhew, Henry. *London Labour and the London Poor.* Penguin, 1985.

McCarthy, Terence. "The Incompetent Narrator of *Wuthering Heights.*" *Modern Language Quarterly,* vol. 42, 1981, pp. 48–64.

McCulloch, Fiona. "'Playing Double': Performing Childhood in *Treasure Island.*" *Scottish Studies Review,* vol. 4, no. 2, 2003, pp. 66–81. *EBSCOhost,* http://search.ebscohost.com/login.aspx?direct=true&db=aph&AN=12083750&site=ehost-live.

McIntire, Gabrielle. "Heteroglossia, Monologism, and Fascism: Bernard Reads *The Waves.*" *Narrative,* vol. 13, no. 1, 2005, pp. 29–45. *JSTOR,* https://www.jstor.org/stable/20107361.

McKibben, Robert C. "The Image of the Book in *Wuthering Heights.*" *Nineteenth-Century Fiction,* vol. 15, no. 2, 1960, pp. 159–69.

Michie, Helena. "'Who Is This in Pain?': Scarring, Disfigurement, and Female Identity in *Bleak House* and *Our Mutual Friend.*" *NOVEL: A Forum on Fiction,* vol. 22, no. 2, Winter 1989, pp. 199–212. *JSTOR,* https://www.jstor.org/stable/1345803.

Milbank, Alison. "The Victorian Gothic in English Novels and Stories, 1830–1880." *The Cambridge Companion to Gothic Fiction,* edited by Jerrold E. Hogle, Cambridge UP, 2002, pp. 145–65.

Miller, D. A. *The Novel and the Police.* U of California P, 1988.

Miller, J. Hillis. *Charles Dickens: The World of His Novels.* Harvard UP, 1958.

———. *Fiction and Repetition: Seven English Novels.* Harvard UP, 1982.

———. *The Form of Victorian Fiction.* U of Notre Dame P, 1968.

Mitchell, David, and Sharon Snyder. "Narrative." *Keywords for Disability Studies,* edited by Rachel Adams et al., NYU P, 2015, pp. 126–30.

———. *Narrative Prosthesis: Disability and the Dependencies of Discourse.* U of Michigan P, 2000.

Moretti, Franco. *Signs Taken for Wonders: Essays in the Sociology of Literary Forms.* Translated by Susan Fischer et al., Verso, 1988.

———. *The Way of the World: The* Bildungsroman *in European Culture.* Translated by Albert Sbragia, new ed., Verso, 2000. *Google Books.*

Moseley, Merritt. "The Ontology of Esther's Narrative in *Bleak House.*" *South Atlantic Review,* vol. 50, no. 2, May 1985, pp. 35–46. *JSTOR,* https://www.jstor.org/stable/3199233.

Mossman, Mark. "Representations of the Abnormal Body in *The Moonstone.*" *Victorian Literature and Culture,* vol. 37, no. 2, 2009, pp. 483–500. *JSTOR,* https://www.jstor.org/stable/40347242.

Napier, Elizabeth R. "The Problem of Boundaries in *Wuthering Heights.*" *Philological Quarterly,* vol. 63, no. 1, Winter 1984, pp. 95–107.

Nayder, Lillian. *Unequal Partners: Charles Dickens, Wilkie Collins, and Victorian Authorship.* Cornell UP, 2002.

Nelles, William. "Embedding." *Routledge Encyclopedia of Narrative Theory,* edited by David Herman et al., Routledge, 2008, pp. 134–35.

———. "Omniscience for Atheists: Or, Jane Austen's Infallible Narrator." *Narrative,* vol. 14, no. 2, May 2006, pp. 118–31.

———. "Stories within Stories: Narrative Levels and Embedded Narrative." *Studies in the Literary Imagination,* vol. 25, no. 1, 1992, pp. 79–96.

Nestor, Pauline. A Note on the Text. *Wuthering Heights,* by Emily Brontë, Penguin, 2003, pp. xl–xli.

Newman, Beth. "'The Situation of the Looker-On': Gender, Narration, and Gaze in *Wuthering Heights.*" *PMLA,* vol. 105, no. 5, Oct. 1990, pp. 1029–41. *JSTOR,* https://www.jstor.org/stable/462732.

Oliphant, Margaret. *A Beleaguered City and Other Stories.* Oxford UP, 1988.

Oost, Regina B. "'More Like Than Life': Painting, Photography, and Dickens's *Bleak House.*" *Dickens Studies Annual,* vol. 30, 2001, pp. 141–58.

Page, Norman, editor. *Wilkie Collins: The Critical Heritage.* Routledge/Kegan Paul, 1974.

Parkes, Christopher. "*Treasure Island* and the Romance of the British Civil Service." *Children's Literature Association Quarterly,* vol. 31, no. 4, Winter 2006, pp. 332–45. *Project Muse,* https://muse.jhu.edu/article/209099.

Patten, Robert L. "Serial Illustration and Storytelling in *David Copperfield.*" *The Victorian Illustrated Book,* edited by Richard Maxwell, U of Virginia P, 2002, pp. 91–128.

Perkins, Pamela, and Mary Donaghy. "A Man's Resolution: Narrative Strategies in Wilkie Collins' *The Woman in White.*" *Studies in the Novel,* vol. 22, no. 4, Winter 1990, pp. 392–402.

Peters, Catherine. *The King of Inventors: A Life of Wilkie Collins.* Princeton UP, 1993.

Peters, Joan Douglas. *Feminist Metafiction and the Evolution of the British Novel.* UP of Florida, 2002.

Phelan, James. *Living to Tell about It: A Rhetoric and Ethics of Character Narration.* Cornell UP, 2005.

Poore, G. V. "Clinical Lecture on A Case of Tailor's Cramp, and Other Troubles Affecting the Functions of the Hand." *The Lancet,* 16 Aug. 1890, pp. 327–29.

Pope, Rebecca A. "Writing and Biting in *Dracula.*" *Lit: Literature Interpretation Theory,* vol. 1, no. 3, 1990, pp. 199–216.

Porter, Dennis. *The Pursuit of Crime: Art and Ideology in Detective Fiction.* Yale UP, 1981.

Prince, Gerald. "The Diary Novel: Notes for the Definition of a Sub-Genre." *Neophilologus,* vol. 59, 1975, pp. 477–81.

———. *Dictionary of Narratology.* Revised ed., U of Nebraska P, 2003.

"Pulling the Ears." *Herald of Health,* vol. 25, New York, Jan. 1875, pp. 30–31. *Google Books.*

Reed, John R. "English Imperialism and the Unacknowledged Crime of *The Moonstone.*" *Clio,* vol. 2, no. 3, 1973, pp. 281–90.

Reid, Julia. "Robert Louis Stevenson and the 'Romance of Anthropology.'" *Journal of Victorian Culture,* vol. 10, no. 1, Spring 2005, pp. 46–71. *Academic Search Premier.*

Richards, Leah. "Mass Production and the Spread of Information in *Dracula*: 'Proofs of So Wild a Story.'" *English Literature in Transition, 1880–1920,* vol. 52, no. 4, 2009, pp. 440–57. *Project Muse,* https://muse.jhu.edu/article/271189.

Richards, Thomas. *The Imperial Archive: Knowledge and the Fantasy of Empire.* Verso, 1993.

Richardson, Brian. *Unnatural Voices: Extreme Narration in Modern and Contemporary Fiction.* The Ohio State UP, 2006.

Richardson, Robert O. "Point of View in Virginia Woolf's *The Waves.*" *Texas Studies in Literature and Language,* vol. 14, no. 4, Winter 1973, pp. 691–709. *JSTOR,* https://www.jstor.org/stable/40754236.

Richardson, Samuel. *Clarissa.* Everyman's Library, 1962. 4 vols.

Ridenhour, Jamieson. *In Darkest London: The Gothic Cityscape in Victorian London.* Scarecrow, 2013.

Robson, W. W. *The Definition of Literature and Other Essays.* Cambridge UP, 1982.

Rodas, Julia Miele. "'On the Spectrum': Rereading Contact and Affect in *Jane Eyre.*" *The Madwoman and the Blindman: Jane Eyre, Discourse, Disability,* edited by David Bolt et al., The Ohio State UP, 2012, pp. 51–70.

———. "Tiny Tim, Blind Bertha, and the Resistance of Miss Mowcher: Charles Dickens and the Uses of Disability." *Dickens Studies Annual,* vol. 34, 2004, pp. 51–97.

Rose, Jacqueline. *The Case of Peter Pan, or The Impossibility of Children's Fiction.* Macmillan, 1984.

Ross, Angus. Introduction. *Clarissa,* by Samuel Richardson, Penguin, 2004, pp. 15–26.

Rosso, Martha. "Dickens and Esther." *The Dickensian,* vol. 65, 1969, pp. 90–94.

Rubik, Margarete. *The Novels of Mrs. Oliphant: A Subversive View of Traditional Themes.* Peter Lang, 1994.

Ryan, Marie-Laure. "Stacks, Frames, and Boundaries." *Narrative Dynamics: Essays on Time, Plot, Closure, and Frames,* edited by Brian Richardson, The Ohio State UP, 2002, pp. 366–86.

Sadrin, Anny. "Charlotte Dickens: The Female Narrator of *Bleak House.*" *Dickens Quarterly,* vol. 9, no. 2, 1992, pp. 47–57.

Sandison, Alan. *Robert Louis Stevenson and the Appearance of Modernism: A Future Feeling.* Macmillan, 1996.

Sanger, C. P. "The Structure of *Wuthering Heights.*" *Critical Essays on Emily Brontë,* edited by Thomas John Winnifrith, G. K. Hall, 1997, pp. 132–43.

Sawicki, Joseph. "'The Mere Truth Won't Do': Esther as Narrator in *Bleak House.*" *The Journal of Narrative Technique,* vol. 17, no. 2, Spring 1987, pp. 209–24.

Scholes, Robert, James Phelan, and Robert Kellogg. *The Nature of Narrative.* 40th anniversary ed., Oxford UP, 2006.

Schor, Esther H. "The Haunted Interpreter in Oliphant's Supernatural Fiction." *Margaret Oliphant: Critical Essays on a Gentle Subversive,* edited by D. J. Trela, Susquehanna UP, 1995, pp. 90–110.

Sedgwick, Eve Kosofsky. *The Coherence of Gothic Conventions.* Methuen, 1986.

Seed, David. "The Narrative Method of *Dracula.*" *Dracula: The Vampire and the Critics,* edited by Margaret L. Carter, UMI Research P, 1988, pp. 195–206.

Senf, Carol A. "*Bleak House:* Dickens, Esther, and the Androgynous Mind." *The Victorian Newsletter,* vol. 64, Fall 1983, pp. 21–27.

———. "*Dracula:* The Unseen Face in the Mirror." *The Journal of Narrative Technique,* vol. 9, no. 3, Fall 1979, pp. 160–70.

Serlen, Ellen. "The Two Worlds of *Bleak House.*" *ELH,* vol. 43, no. 4, Winter 1976, pp. 551–66. JSTOR, https://www.jstor.org/stable/2872737.

Shelley, Mary. *Frankenstein.* Norton, 1996.

Showalter, Elaine. *The Female Malady: Women, Madness, and English Culture, 1830–1980.* Pantheon, 1985.

Shuttleworth, Sally. "'Preaching to the Nerves': Psychological Disorder in Sensation Fiction." *A Question of Identity: Women, Science, and Literature,* edited by Marina Benjamin, Rutgers UP, 1993, pp. 192–222.

Siebers, Tobin. *Disability Aesthetics.* U of Michigan P, 2010.

Smith, Margaret, editor. *The Letters of Charlotte Brontë, Volume Two: 1848–1851.* Clarendon, 2000.

Smith, Victoria Ford. *Between Generations: Collaborative Authorship in the Golden Age of Children's Literature.* UP of Mississippi, 2017.

Sotirova, Violeta. *Consciousness in Modernist Fiction: A Stylistic Study.* Palgrave, 2013.

Stanback, Emily B. *The Wordsworth-Coleridge Circle and the Aesthetics of Disability.* Palgrave, 2016.

Stanzel, F. K. *A Theory of Narrative.* Translated by Charlotte Goedsche, Cambridge UP, 1984.

Steig, Michael. *Dickens and Phiz.* Indiana UP, 1978.

Sternlieb, Lisa. *The Female Narrator in the British Novel: Hidden Agendas.* Palgrave, 2002.

Stevenson, Robert Louis. *The Master of Ballantrae.* Penguin, 1996.

———. "My First Book." *Treasure Island,* by Robert Louis Stevenson, Oxford, 1998, pp. 192–200.

———. "Note to *The Master of Ballantrae.*" *The Master of Ballantrae,* by Robert Louis Stevenson, Penguin, 1996, pp. 221–28.

———. *Strange Case of Dr. Jekyll and Mr. Hyde.* Norton, 2003.

———. *Treasure Island.* Oxford UP, 1998.

Stewart, Garrett. "'Count Me In': *Dracula,* Hypnotic Participation, and the Late-Victorian Gothic of Reading." *Lit: Literature Interpretation Theory,* vol. 5, no. 1, 1994, pp. 1–18.

———. *Novel Violence: A Narratography of Victorian Fiction.* U of Chicago P, 2009.

Stillinger, Jack. *Multiple Authorship and the Myth of Solitary Genius.* Oxford UP, 1991.

Stoddard Holmes, Martha. "'Bolder with Her Lover in the Dark': Collins and Disabled Women's Sexuality." *Reality's Dark Light: The Sensational Wilkie Collins,* edited by Maria K. Bachman and Don Richard Cox, U of Tennessee P, 2003, pp. 59–93.

———. *Fictions of Affliction: Physical Disability in Victorian Culture.* U of Michigan P, 2004.

———. "The Twin Structure: Disabled Women in Victorian Courtship Plots." *Disability Studies: Enabling the Humanities,* edited by Sharon L. Snyder et al., MLA, 2002, pp. 222–33.

Stoker, Bram. *Dracula.* Penguin, 2003.

Talairach-Vielmas, Laurence. *Wilkie Collins, Medicine, and the Gothic.* U of Wales P, 2009.

Taylor, Anne Robinson. *Male Novelists and Their Female Voices: Literary Masquerades.* Whitston, 1981.

Taylor, Jenny Bourne. *In the Secret Theatre of Home: Wilkie Collins, Sensation Narrative, and Nineteenth-Century Psychology.* Routledge, 1988.

Taylor, Jenny Bourne, and John Kucich. "Multiple Narrators and Multiple Plots." *The Nineteenth-Century Novel, 1820–1880,* edited by John Kucich and Jenny Bourne Taylor, Oxford UP, 2012, pp. 256–73.

Thoms, Peter. *The Windings of the Labyrinth: Quest and Structure in the Major Novels of Wilkie Collins.* Ohio UP, 1992.

Thon, Jan-Noël. "Toward a Transmedial Narratology: On Narrators in Contemporary Graphic Novels, Feature Films, and Computer Games." *Beyond Classical Narration: Transmedial and Unnatural Challenges,* edited by Jan Alber and Per Krogh Hansen, De Gruyter, 2014, pp. 25–56. *ProQuest Ebook Central.*

Toker, Leona. *Eloquent Reticence: Withholding Information in Fictional Narrative.* UP of Kentucky, 1993.

Trela, D. J. "Introduction: Discovering the Gentle Subversive." *Margaret Oliphant: Critical Essays on a Gentle Subversive,* edited by D. J. Trela, Susquehanna UP, 1995, pp. 11–27.

Trench, Mrs. Richard. *Thoughts of a Parent on Education.* New ed., London, 1837. *Google Books.*

Trilling, Lionel. *The Liberal Imagination: Essays on Literature and Society.* Doubleday, 1953.

Valint, Alexandra. "'Mind to Mind': The Gothic Loss of Privacy in the Twilight Saga and Chaos Walking Trilogy." *New Directions in Children's Gothic: Debatable Lands,* edited by Anna Jackson, Routledge, 2017, pp. 160–75.

Van Ghent, Dorothy. *The English Novel: Form and Function.* Rinehart, 1953.

van Marter, Shirley. "Richardson's Revisions of *Clarissa* in the Second Edition." *Studies in Bibliography,* vol. 26, 1973, pp. 107–32. *JSTOR,* https://www.jstor.org/stable/40371572.

Visser, Nicholas. "Roaring Beasts and Raging Floods: The Representation of Political Crowds in the Nineteenth-Century British Novel." *The Modern Language Review,* vol. 89, no. 2, April 1994, pp. 289–317. *JSTOR,* https://www.jstor.org/stable/3735234.

Vrettos, Athena. *Somatic Fictions: Imagining Illness in Victorian Culture.* Stanford UP, 1995.

Vuohelainen, Minna. "Richard Marsh's *The Beetle* (1897): A Late-Victorian Popular Novel." *Working with English: Medieval and Modern Language, Literature and Drama*, vol. 2, no. 1, 2006, pp. 89–100.

———. "'You Know Not of What You Speak': Language, Identity, and Xenophobia in Richard Marsh's *The Beetle: A Mystery* (1897)." *Fear, Loathing, and Victorian Xenophobia*, edited by Marlene Tromp et al., The Ohio State UP, pp. 312–30.

Wagner, Tamara S. "Ominous Signs or False Clues? Difference and Deformity in Wilkie Collins's Sensation Novels." *Demons of the Body and Mind: Essays on Disability in Gothic Literature*, edited by Ruth Bienstock Anolik, McFarland, 2010, pp. 47–60.

Wall, Barbara. *The Narrator's Voice: The Dilemma of Children's Fiction.* St. Martin's, 1991.

Wall, Geoffrey. "'Different from Writing': *Dracula* in 1897." *Literature and History*, vol. 10, no. 1, 1984, pp. 15–23.

Ward, Hayden W. "'The Pleasure of Your Heart': *Treasure Island* and the Appeal of Boys' Adventure Fiction." *Studies in the Novel*, vol. 6, no. 3, Fall 1974, pp. 304–17.

Warhol, Robyn R. "Describing the Unseen: The Visceral and Virtual Construction of Spaces in *Bleak House*." *Style*, vol. 48, no. 4, Winter 2014, pp. 612–28.

———. "A Feminist Approach to Narrative." *Narrative Theory: Core Concepts and Critical Debates*, by David Herman et al., The Ohio State UP, 2012, pp. 9–13.

———. *Gendered Interventions: Narrative Discourse in the Victorian Novel.* Rutgers UP, 1989.

West, Gillian. "The 'Glaring Fault' in the Structure of *Bleak House*." *The Dickensian*, vol. 89, no. 1, 1993, pp. 36–38.

"What Stevenson Read—His Personal Library." *The RLS Website*, http://robert-louis-stevenson.org/robert-louis-stevensons-library/. Accessed 30 Apr. 2019.

Wicke, Jennifer. "Vampiric Typewriting: *Dracula* and Its Media." *ELH*, vol. 59, no. 2, Summer 1992, pp. 467–93. *JSTOR*, https://www.jstor.org/stable/2873351.

Williams, Anne. *Art of Darkness: A Poetics of Gothic.* U of Chicago P, 2009.

Williams, Merryn. Introduction. *A Beleaguered City and Other Stories*, by Margaret Oliphant, Oxford UP, 1988, pp. vii–xix.

Wilt, Judith. "Confusion and Consciousness in Dickens's Esther." *Nineteenth-Century Fiction*, vol. 32, no. 3, Dec. 1977, pp. 285–309. *JSTOR*, https://doi.org/10.2307/2933386.

Wion, Philip K. "The Absent Mother in *Wuthering Heights*." *Wuthering Heights*, edited by Linda H. Peterson, Case Studies in Contemporary Criticism, 2nd ed., Bedford/St. Martin's, 2003, pp. 364–78.

Wolfreys, Julian. "The Hieroglyphic Other: *The Beetle*, London, and the Abyssal Subject." *A Mighty Mass of Brick and Smoke: Victorian and Edwardian Representations of London*, edited by Lawrence Phillips, Brill/Rodopi, 2007, pp. 169–92.

———. Introduction. *The Beetle*, by Richard Marsh, Broadview, 2004, pp. 9–34.

Wood, Naomi J. "Gold Standards and Silver Subversions: *Treasure Island* and the Romance of Money." *Children's Literature*, vol. 26, 1998, pp. 61–85.

Woodring, Carl R. "The Narrators of *Wuthering Heights*." *Nineteenth-Century Fiction*, vol. 11, no. 4, March 1957, pp. 298–305. *JSTOR*, https://doi.org/10.2307/3044458.

Woolf, Virginia. *To the Lighthouse.* Harvest/Harcourt, 1981.

———. *The Waves.* Annotated ed., Harvest/Harcourt, 2006.

Worth, George J. "Emily Brontë's Mr. Lockwood." *Nineteenth-Century Fiction*, vol. 12, no. 4, March 1958, pp. 315–20. *JSTOR*, https://www.jstor.org/stable/3044427.

Wright, David. "'Childlike in His Innocence': Lay Attitudes to 'Idiots' and 'Imbeciles' in Victorian England." *From Idiocy to Mental Deficiency: Historical Perspectives on People with Learning Disabilities,* edited by Anne Digby and David Wright, Routledge, 2002, pp. 118–33. *ProQuest ebrary.*

———. *Mental Disability in Victorian England: The Earlswood Asylum, 1847–1901.* Clarendon P, 2001.

Zwerdling, Alex. "Esther Summerson Rehabilitated." *PMLA,* vol. 88, no. 3, May 1973, pp. 429–39. *JSTOR,* https://www.jstor.org/stable/461523.

INDEX

THEORY AND INTERPRETATION OF NARRATIVE

James Phelan, Katra Byram, and Faye Halpern, Series Editors
Robyn Warhol and Peter Rabinowitz, Founding Editors Emeriti

Because the series editors believe that the most significant work in narrative studies today contributes both to our knowledge of specific narratives and to our understanding of narrative in general, studies in the series typically offer interpretations of individual narratives and address significant theoretical issues underlying those interpretations. The series does not privilege one critical perspective but is open to work from any strong theoretical position.